MW01493693

SILENCE
AND
RESISTANCE

Memoir of a Girlhood in Haiti

SILENCE
AND
RESISTANCE

Memoir of a Girlhood in Haiti

MONIQUE CLESCA

This is a work of Nonfiction.
Silence and Resistance
Memoir of a Girlhood in Haiti

ISBN
978-1-959811-91-6 (Hardcover)
978-1-959811-92-3 (e-Book)

Library of Congress Control Number: 2025905994

Book Cover Design: Christina Plampridis
Cover Art: Author potrait by Hatian painter Luce Turnier
Interior Design: Amit Dey
Editor: Winsome Hudson
Author Photo Credit: Mike Charles@MikoMike257

1ˢᵗ Edition

Website: www.wordeee.com
Twitter.com/wordeeeupdates
Facebook: facebook.com/Wordeee/
e-mail: contact@wordeee.com
Published by Wordeee in the United States, New York, New York
Printed in the USA

"Remembering is a noble and necessary act...
It is incumbent upon us to remember the good we have received
and the evil we have suffered."

—Elie Wiesel

"At times of great crisis, all peoples go back instinctively to the past
in order to search in their history for lessons of collective patriotism,
for new rules of conduct, whether it be for the purpose of being able to
better defend their threatened existence, or for recovering more rapidly
from their fall."

—H. Pauleus Sanon

For Viola, who shared the joy, the dreams and nightmares, and held my hand through it all.

ADVANCE PRAISE

Silence and Resistance: Memoir of a Girlhood in Haiti by Monique Clesca delves into the author's reckoning with her country's history and a devastating family secret. Clesca delicately knits together the beauty and violence of her childhood in a fascinating narrative encapsulating not just the geography of her own life but the socio-political landscape of Haiti. Through her reflective and evocative storytelling, Clesca invites readers on a transformative journey through memory, trauma, and the quest for meaning in the wake of multiple tragedies. This intimate and well-crafted memoir illustrates how breaking one's silence can become a tool of resistance and survival.

—Edwidge Danticat,
author of *Brother, I'm Dying*.

Monique Clesca's *Silence and Resistance* is an intimate, evocative, and unforgettable account of governmental failure, family secrets, and generational trauma. Clesca's life beyond her troubled Haitian childhood is an inspiration; her personal journey is filled with stories of pride, fearlessness, defiance, and grace.

—Dinty W. Moore,
author of *The Mindful Writer*.

In the aftermath of the 2010 earthquake in Haiti, Monique Clesca delves into captivating memories of her atypical childhood, family structure, and values in a skillfully crafted, unputdownable memoir. *Silence and Resistance: Memoir of a Girlhood in Haiti* offers glimpses of the intriguing history of Haiti, its complex culture and society, in an earnest, spellbinding voice.

—Elsie Augustave,
author *The Roving Tree*.

Monique Clesca's memoir recalls with searing honesty the class and color prejudices that marked her childhood in Haiti, the jarring changes in her adolescence as an immigrant to the United States and her transformation into a courageous advocate for women and children, all contributing to her current role as a persuasive proponent of the democracy that eludes her native land.

—Joel Dreyfuss,
Pioneering Haitian-American journalist.

CONTENT

THE GEOGRAPHY OF MY LIFE

A telephone rang in my jacket pocket. My sister Viola, said, "I just heard that a massive earthquake hit Haiti; are you OK?" thereby giving a name to the reality I was living. She was calling from Miami, which seemed so very far away at that moment. Yet her voice brought it so joyfully close.

"I'm alive," I murmured as if I were whispering in the ear of a feverish child.

I had just stepped away from my blue forget-me-not hedges because my legs were shaking wildly from the trembling ground. "It's an earthquake," I immediately told my thirty-year-old godson, Daniel, who was installing a light fixture when the ground started shaking beneath our feet. "Quick, get off the stepladder." He flew down, miraculously landing on his feet. Then I yelled to the gardener, "*Calixte, vit, vit, vinn jwen nou*," as he ran down the front steps of the house. I heard a rumbling like thunder coming from the earth's belly as it violently shook the plants, the car, the walls, and the pavement on which I stood that late afternoon. I heard the howls of neighbors; they sounded like an omen of collective human folly.

Then, the ground stilled, and, for a few seconds, it was eerily quiet.

The sudden cut-off of Viola's call made my isolation even worse. I reached for the hand-size transistor radio—which by habit I always carried with me—and heard the soothing voice of the Radio France International journalist informing listeners that at 4:52 p.m. the fault lines of the underbelly of Haiti had ruptured over the course of forty seconds.

It was an extremely violent seismic shift of 7.0 on the Richter scale, and it was merciless. The capital, Port-au-Prince, was leveled. The national palace and most public, commercial, and industrial buildings were likely destroyed, and hundreds were feared dead under the debris of the city's tragically ill-prepared neighborhoods.

Minutes later, the voice from France updated the number of dead to thousands. I was horrified. I thought of my friends, hoping they had been spared this tragedy. I ached for the thousands who had reportedly died. The scale of the destruction the journalist described was incomprehensible.

That day, January 12, 2010, when Haiti's most devastating earthquake in a hundred and fifty years struck, I was in the middle of my vacation in my home country, standing in the garden of my residence in a semi-rural area above Port-au-Prince.

From my vantage point high up in the mountains above the city, I could see several neighborhoods in the vast metropolitan area. Clouds of concrete dust rose above them—the residue of buildings toppled down like decks of cards, some packed with people. Still, it all seemed somewhat distant.

Had I been driving two hours north towards my beach house with its potential buyer as planned, or shopping for vacation souvenirs for my colleagues as I had started to do before abruptly leaving the city, I would most likely have died. Fortunately, I had decided to exile myself at home, thus remaining in the serenity of the hills in my garden of blooming lilies, irises, and orchids.

Amidst the turmoil of the earthquake, I knew one thing for sure: I had survived nature's fury. But I was lost.

After the roar of the seismic shift came a haunting stillness.

I, with Daniel and Calixte, sat on children's chairs in the street during most of the evening. I held on tightly to the radio and the cell phone with no signal—they represented the world outside, and they grounded me. I knew the basic facts: my name, that I was the daughter of Odette and Max, and mother of Aïssatou and Karim-Daniel. Yet, I was truly lost. Could it really be that all of the landmarks of my life were destroyed? Something lodged in my body and clutched at my heart.

Aftershocks are the loyal companions of earthquakes, and each one tore away at my body. The first one I felt came about thirty minutes after the initial shock. My feet first, then my whole body shook, along with the chair I was sitting on. By the time I realized it was another earthquake, it was over. I looked around, but Daniel and Calixte said nothing, so I kept my anxiety to myself.

The sun started to hide and tinted the sky with shades of orange that reflected on the side of the mountain I faced. My unpaved street was uncannily empty, but every now and then, someone walked by my front gate. I saw each person as a testimony of life, and I greeted each one with a Bonsoir. I asked where they were when the fault lines broke and whether they had suffered any damage. One woman answered in Haitian Creole with the vivid imagery so characteristic of that language: "God is *the* most powerful bull. Every once in a while, he commands in a manner designed to show man how small he really is." I reflected on her way of thinking of God as a strong, brutish figure with a "let's show them" attitude. I smiled to myself.

My feet trembled again as we sat talking in hushed voices. My stomach turned. Then, the chair shook. I held my breath and the chair, hoping they could still me, but it was the earth shaking again. This time, there was no rumbling noise from below. Later I would learn that there were about eight aftershocks in the two hours after the main earthquake.

Eventually, a car passed. A miracle, I thought, and felt some measure of hope that all was not lost.

Finally, at around 10:00 p.m. I went timidly up the steps into the house and looked around to inspect the damage. Only three wine glasses had broken. Daniel toured the grounds with a flashlight and reported the outside walls were intact and had no obvious fissures. Standing in the cool tropical night, I could not help but ask, "Why was my house spared? Why was I alive?"

A few days before I had traveled from New York where I worked in international development at the United Nations, focusing on youth and women's sexual health and rights issues affecting sub-Saharan Africa. I've spent much of my life helping victims of domestic and sexual violence survive, building the capacity of civil servants to carry on advocacy and communication, training journalists on reporting on children's and women's rights, and convincing traditional chiefs to abolish child marriage in their communities. I spent most of my time in the field, to use the language of development workers, meaning in the trenches throughout Haiti and in close to forty countries in Africa. But at the time of the earthquake, I was based at my agency's headquarters in New York, helping develop policy papers and engaging with diplomats and other high-level decision-makers to advocate for their governments' massive investments in social justice. In a way, at fifty-eight and six years away from retirement, I had a good life in the best of several worlds. I was living in one of the world's most vibrant cultural centers; I accomplished short work missions in fascinating exotic places like Senegal, Chad, Madagascar, Ethiopia, and Rwanda; and I traveled often to Miami to spend time with my tribe of women— my mother, my daughter, and my sister Viola, as well as with the rest of the family.

Then came my trip to Haiti and the seismic shift.

At 6:30 the morning after the quake, the dead phone miraculously rang. I was thrilled to hear my daughter, Aïssatou, who lived with my mother in Miami; "Mommy, thank God you're alive! How are you?"

Viola had joined them as the sun rose and each shared news seen on TV. We all cried. Aïssatou promised to call her brother, Karim-Daniel to tell him I was alive; he was a university student in Paris. Viola asked when I was coming back, just before the telephone went dead again.

I picked up my tiny radio and cradled it preciously as I searched the dial for news while I sleepwalked to my home office. The French station was still the only one broadcasting. Every half-hour, as I heard the headline news, tears streamed down my face as the names of the dead were called out. Among them, the parents of a childhood friend, now a government minister. My scream silenced the radio and brought Daniel and Calixte to where I sat. It was too much to bear.

After a couple of hours of nothingness, I felt horribly useless and terribly isolated. I needed to see my city and help somehow. I asked Daniel, a tall, muscular, dark chocolate young man who looked and walked like a middle-weight boxer, "Would you go with me to the city?"

"Yes, Godmother," he replied, using the affectionate name that described our special relationship. With him at my side, I drove my fire-engine red 4x4 Montero down the mountain road. I kept my eyes on the road but constantly looked at both sides of the street. I was glad that this part of town didn't suffer any visible physical damage. Along the way, I picked up my best friend, Florence, who hopped in the backseat. Her house was standing, but she said her sister's crumbled into small pieces.

"So sorry to hear this. How did you get home from work yesterday?" I asked Florence, who worked in Petion-Ville, a suburb of Port-au-Prince situated half an hour down the hill from my residence.

"I got a ride from a colleague," she told us. "It was a total panic, with cars abandoned in the middle of the street and people screaming and running in all directions."

The horror became real a few minutes later when we reached downtown Petion-Ville. The first bodies I saw were strewn here and there in the streets, some covered with plastic bags, others with a piece of clothing or a sheet. Cars were crushed by concrete. Buildings were lying on the ground as fallen construction blocks, and men and women were pulling away at debris with their bare hands, trying to free people trapped beneath. I could see feet sticking out of the rubble. I drove a few miles down to try to go to Port-au-Prince through Bourdon Road, but this major passageway to the capital was closed. With my window down, I overheard that the Montana Hotel down the street had collapsed, and efforts were underway to rescue the hundreds unaccounted for. I turned back, aiming for the Canape Vert Road to downtown, but it was also shut off with scenes of death and desolation nearby.

It was apocalyptic. Nothing I had ever seen matched the doom signaled by bright white sheets covering ballooning black bodies strewn in the middle of sun-drenched city streets; the acrid pestilence of neighborhoods frozen in the moment and the haunting nothingness in the eyes of some survivors walking in the street covered in dust in a trance-like march to nowhere.

No one said anything. There was nothing to say.

We went to see Florence's ninety-five-year-old mother at a nursing home on the east edge of Petion-Ville; mercifully the building was undamaged. When we reached her she was sitting on her bed and was visibly energized by our visit.

I tried my phone: it was dead. Daniel and Florence did the same with the same result. I looked at their somber faces and said, "Let's go home."

On the way, I stopped by a side street to check on a friend. Her house was split in two—miraculously both sides stayed up, arrogantly defying the earth. With her Blackberry I sent a message to my office: "Ashby, I am alive." My assistant responded immediately as if she had been waiting for that signal. How fortunate that data could travel via satellite, I thought.

When I reached home, the neighborhood was eerily quiet. I stared into space and felt useless. Why am I alive? I kept wondering.

On the second morning after the quake, while sitting at my desk, I found a Haitian radio station. Death entered when I heard the familiar voice of journalist Yves-Marie Chanel giving the roll call of friends: Myriam Merlet, Anne-Marie Coriolan, and Magalie Marcelin. Citing their names honors them as all three were committed feminist leaders of women's rights organizations. I had had lunch with Myriam the day before the earthquake to plan how I could contribute to her feminist documentation center. When she arrived on the restaurant balcony, she had her usual disobedient stance, and everyone stared at her tall, large frame adorned with an African-print dress. My friend had a beautiful smile, eyes the color of amber, long black dreadlocks, and a brilliant mind. Her strong baritone voice was so convincing that no military dictatorship managed to silence it, nor the others for that matter. Now they were silenced by the earthquake as each was stuck under the remains of a house somewhere in the crumbling city. As this news registered, my body rebelled with a primal scream from deep in my stomach. I fell to my knees.

Hours later, my sense of uselessness pushed me back into town to check on family and friends. Again, Daniel came with me, and again we picked up Florence. This time I was able to go into Port-au-Prince via the Canape Vert Road. I first went to Bas-Peu-de-Chose, an old middle-class neighborhood that I knew well from having lived on several of its streets during my childhood. I struggled, seeing several concrete houses in pieces, but fortunately, the wooden ones resisted. I passed through rubble on my way to Rue Waag to check on my cousin Leslie, an orthopedic surgeon. The sun was out, but the street was empty as was his medical clinic located steps away from my first home; both stood intact. I came out of my stupor when I heard, "*Madame, Madame.*" It was his receptionist on the sidewalk who announced: "He is alive and has been on duty at the main public hospital since the quake." I mustered a thank you.

Then I pulled in front of my dead grandmother's and my former home on Rue Oswald Durand. I saw no destruction, but rather a body in the middle of the street. I wondered if the neighbors were afraid of the man—or was it a woman? I couldn't tell—who was now transformed into a big black balloon? Pain overwhelmed me. I found it impossible to stop. I drove home.

On the third day after the seism, I was filled with sadness at the news that numerous United Nations colleagues were presumed dead. I decided to go to the U.N. headquarters to pay my respects but also to request help to travel back to New York. I had run out of water and the stores were closed. I had run out of money and the banks were closed, and all I had left were two cans of soup. Daniel came along, and so did Florence. I drove to my agency's local office in the upper-middle-class Bourdon area where most of the houses were hidden behind high walls and tall gates. Upon our arrival, I was surprised that the metal gate to the compound was not only wide open but was protected by a lone security guard when it was usually manned by three to five heavily armed men and women.

"*Bonjour Monsieur*," I said. The uniformed man waved me in nonchalantly. My surprise turned into shocking horror when I didn't see any of the grand buildings that had graced the vast courtyard. Instead, I saw an enormous pile of rubble. And no one. The air changed, and I couldn't breathe well, so I rapidly turned the car around and headed for the exit.

"*Kote moun yo?* Where are the people?" I asked the guard who was holding his machine gun.

"The ones still alive are working near the airport," he responded, graciously explaining the location of the temporary operational base set up by the U.N.

I left immediately, turning right into the dead-end street just behind the guard and the fallen U.N. buildings. I was aghast as one out of two houses I passed had collapsed. The smell of death was everywhere. I wore a mask, but the smell permeated my clothes, my body, my heart, and my psyche. Death smelled so wretched. I wanted to pray for the souls of the parents of my childhood friend, whose probable deaths were announced the morning after. I limped out of the car in front of the concrete and twisted iron remnants of the large house I knew well, the home and art gallery of Auntie Carmele and Uncle Cavour. I stood in the sun, bowed my head respectfully to them, still under the wreckage like many of their neighbors. I learned later that the Mexican rescue team who found Uncle's body sixty hours after the earthquake said he didn't suffer, having died instantly in front of his TV, whereas Auntie lived some long hours under the beams and concrete before taking her last breath. As my gaze scanned the demolished houses emptied of life, my eyes filled with water. My mind went blank.

When, a few minutes later I got my senses back, Daniel took the wheel and drove across the city toward Toussaint Louverture International Airport. I sat next to him. My transistor radio was at full volume in the car as we headed towards the airport, and I heard that the geographer, the writer, the economist, the artist, the mason, the electrician, the juice vendor, the shoemaker...had all died. And thousands more: Delmas, Nerette, Morne-a-Turf, Sainte-Marie, Morne Lazare, Boutilliers; the list of shattered neighborhoods that now characterized my crumbling country was growing.

Passing through the city offered such an astounding view of crumbled buildings with people helplessly standing around them, and others picking rocks, blocks, and concrete trying to unearth their family members; cars that stood immobilized in the middle of the street, covered with debris; haggard men and women; and bodies covered with white sheets. I felt numb as I was catapulted into a world of dust, wreckage, corpses, zombies…nothingness.

About half an hour later, I reached the shipping containers they'd quickly set up to serve as the UN office, where everyone was running, speaking on a phone or crying, some in visible distress because about one hundred of the headquarters staff of MINUSTHA, as the U.N. Haiti Mission was called, were still under the debris of their collapsed building a few blocks from where I had gone; hope was fading of finding them alive. I also saw staffers with handwritten "peer counselor" tags on their chests huddling around individuals or groups providing comfort. Among the chaos and desolation, I found the head of my agency; she assured me the staff was OK. We hugged for a very long time as if each was transmitting a lifeline to the other. Reluctantly, I registered for a flight out of Haiti, feeling shamefully privileged and dreadfully guilty at the luxurious option I had, when so many others did not.

On the way back to Petion Ville, we stopped at the Canadian Embassy and Florence registered herself and her mother for evacuation to Canada.

To feel a bit useful, I decided to visit the 94-year-old mother of a New York friend whose house was damaged. Lily had suffered a broken leg, but she stood up with her widest smile to greet me. We fell into each other's arms, and she thanked me for coming. She held on tightly to her book of crossword puzzles, telling me that the puzzles helped keep her mind focused and her memory intact. Quite excitedly, she said, "Monique, Albert Camus was right about the absurdity of life." Breathlessly, she explained how during over fifty years she didn't trust anyone to dust off her treasured paintings by Haitian masters—and yet, in less than two minutes, the earth shook, flooring all the paintings and giving reason to Camus. We hugged again as I said goodbye.

On the way home, I detoured by a soccer stadium that had become a refuge for many people since the earthquake. I seethed that after three days the children, women, and men there were stripped of all dignity in an open space with no water, no food, no electricity, and no security. This particularly when they could have been moved to another area, such as the high school across the street, to access bathrooms and running water. I prayed to hold the rain in the sky. They huddled together quietly, perhaps to protect themselves from hunger, thirst, desolation, or even from life. But they were together, and it was that solidarity that characterized my people and the moment, I told myself.

Still, life was beyond cruel.

Death lurked at every corner, but somehow life chose to tame me into zombie mode, disassembling me into a series of mechanical parts, all numbly on autopilot, save for my volatile heartbeat.

On the fourth day, the radio announced that the city of Leogane was destroyed, and that 80 percent of its citizens had no shelter. The journalist added that the town of Petit-Gôave was decimated, and the road that connected Port-au-Prince to the seaside city of Jacmel, where I spent the previous weekend, and my childhood vacations was severed. Somehow I didn't cry, frozen in an anxious silence.

I was traveling to New York at midday, but to get to the airport, the car needed petrol in short supply since most gas stations were either closed or destroyed. Fortunately, my cousin Harry's station, located deep into Port-au-Prince, had some. To get there, we went through the Bas-peu-de-Chose neighborhood again. We drove into rue de l'Enterrement—literally "Funeral Street." Through my window I glanced at more bodies, groups of eight, of ten; stiff huge balls of flesh, uncovered. We closed all the car windows and masked our noses and mouths with our T-shirts, but the stench of death knew no boundaries. I was suffocating. We were all crying, for it was a hecatomb.

In Haiti, when we bury our dead, we say that they go back to Guinea, our metaphor for the African ancestral land. That return journey is a way to appease the gods for the searing, transatlantic voyage from which free men and women trafficked from Africa emerged as captives enslaved in Haiti. I resisted thinking that this earthquake would shatter this centuries-old cultural ritual because of the impossibility of burying the nearly 200,000 dead, let alone with any semblance of dignity. This only partly explained the ramifications of not carrying out this cultural ritual. The other explanation lies probably in the belief of many of us Haitians that the dead don't really die; they are simply invisible. They watch over and protect us, the living. But they can only do so if they are properly buried and at peace, and it's our responsibility as the living to ensure this. But if their return journey was neither completed nor peaceful, they might be unable to watch over and protect us—a case of us being doubly orphaned. I was desperately sad, for like many, I struggled against part of this immense collective grief that was the possibility of this double agony.

Utterly grief-stricken, I traveled to a small private terminal a few feet away from the large international one already overwhelmed with private, military, and commercial airplanes unloading rescuers, aid workers, supplies, and materials. After saying goodbye to Daniel, I flew out of Haiti as rapidly as the birds of prey flew in. As I left Port-au-Prince with eleven foreigners on the tiny UN plane to Santo Domingo, I looked down at the devastated city that had birthed me and wondered how it had come to this. The question of why I was alive continued to haunt me. My sobs did not provide either answers or comfort for what I left behind. After a brief overlay long enough to change my ticket but not erase my stupor; I remained in a fog as I flew to New York.

Unbeknownst to me, as is often the case with survivors of disasters, I was suffering from shock and Post-Traumatic Stress Syndrome (PTSD). Trauma had enveloped me. Pitilessly, the earthquake replayed itself over and over again through monstrous nightmares and calamitous visions. I experienced inertia, hyperventilation, sleeplessness, uncontrolled tears, and a dissociation from reality as I continued to see the dying on everybody's face. Time seemed endless as I descended into nothingness and profound isolation. I simply could not explain what I was feeling. I didn't understand whether there was another way to feel. I didn't know how to think about the earthquake, despite sensing that thinking was not a viable option, considering my state of mind. The problem was not simply the *tabula rasa* that was Haiti—for close to a quarter of a million people had perished, thousands were disabled, and hundreds of thousands had been rendered homeless as entire neighborhoods had been destroyed. It was also about the souls of the rest of us mortals, hoping to escape the cataclysm we had lived and were still living, and how to face our new reality.

Amidst the collective turmoil of such magnitude and my debilitating PTSD, I realized that all my visual cues and symbols, all my vistas, all my reference points had collapsed. I was lost. The geography, as much as the politics of my girlhood had shaped my life, and now it had been seismically and irrevocably upended. The Haiti I knew had been annihilated. It was a perverse reality that my birthplace, Port-au-Prince, was the city most destroyed—as if my childhood lived on rue Waag, rue 3, rue Oswald Durand, and rue Baussan had been obliterated along with the vibrant city and the landscape I so loved. My past and everything that anchored me were all gone. Would I ever recapture it, I wondered? Who was I if everything I thought I was and had were gone? I had become a wandering soul. Anguish rushed in, then receded, then rushed back.

To survive; no, to live, I felt compelled to journey back to my origin story, to revisit it all: not only the joys, loves, fears, and tragedies, but also the secrets, mysteries, untruths, and above all, the "beski"—the ghastly and unexplained silences of my life on the four streets that constituted my world as a Haitian child. Mine was a girlhood full of both the beauty and the brutality of Haiti. As these long-buried childhood memories struggled to the surface, I felt as if I were in the hospital awaiting the birth of my daughter and later my son, with so many powerful and unprecedented emotions welling up in anticipation.

Only now I was a metaphor for that child being born, and all of the bloody pain was, I hoped, part of the birth of a new life and identity.

RUE WAAG

TOGETHER

Mandedette stands out in every frame of my childhood, even when she was absent, as my ethereal, strong, and elegant mother.

But when life first began for me in 1952, there were four of us: Mandedette, Papa, my older sister Viola and me. Odette was my mother's name, but by the time I was born, Viola had combined *maman* with *Odette* to shorten it into Mandedette.

Snapshots of my first years occasionally pop into my consciousness: names of streets like Chemin-des-Dalles; a very narrow river, Ravine Bois-de-Chene, crossing down the middle of the city, a few feet from our front door. Its big story of utter devastation leaps into my mind; the time its flooded waters washed away men, women, children, pigs, goats, chickens, and a multitude of objects into the drowning sea while I hid under the sheets, terrorized by the thunder and lightning of the monstrous Hurricane Hazel in 1954.

My first precise recollections started in 1956 when I was four years old, Viola six, and all my illusions were still intact, one of which was hibiscus paste. I chased hibiscus flowers to pull the stamens out of them. Just for fun. It was to make a reddish but aromatic soggy mess out of the petals of the perpetually flowering red hibiscus that lined the short pathway to our veranda. It had a balustrade made of wood of different colors laced together Victorian style. Our brown wooden house was partially hidden behind a doctor's clinic on rue Dr. Waag and it was my all-encompassing world.

The sun was always steaming hot during the day, but still, I ran around after Viola, in front of Viola, or looking for Viola. I was always with her as we played games like hide and seek, bone—played with five dried-up goat knee bones—or hopscotch, or skipped rope. When I was very lucky, Viola asked our maid Marlene to move the baby piano from the parlor to the tiny garden in the front. There, surrounded by the hibiscus hedges, she played harmonious notes on the piano while I watched adoringly. Viola was always exuberant, and I was mostly quiet, so she let me walk, laugh, and cry in her shadow.

I sometimes had the happy illusion that I was one person with Viola. Part of this is because Mandedette often called us "Viola *et* Monique," as if my sister and I were really one person. We weren't twins, but we were as close as two people born two years apart could be. Viola was taller, lighter, more peach-colored like Mandedette, and I was the color of a mahogany tree like Papa, but when we wore the same multicolored dresses, mostly picked by Viola or Mandedette, we looked more alike.

The highlight of my week was Sunday morning when our half-brother Serge came to spend the day with us; on the other days, I had only his photograph on the living-room credenza to smile at. I rushed into Serge's arms for him to lift me to the sky and twirl me until I couldn't laugh anymore. Then I kissed him hello as Viola and Mandedette, who assumed the role of affectionate stepmother, greeted him. He lived with his own mother, with whom Papa had had a long liaison, years prior to meeting Mandedette. Serge was really simply my brother because there was no half in the relationship or in the love we had for each other. Seven years older than I, he was Papa's eldest and had his last name, bushy eyebrows, and tall, lanky frame. He sometimes gazed straight at me with a faraway look on his face while he tickled me senseless. His games of hide and seek captivated me and laughter consumed my time with him. I was so happy to be the constant center of his attention. I missed my brother all week.

Then there were Mandedette and Papa.

In our living room, and sitting on the immense sideboard as if it were a trophy was a picture, one of the things I most admired in our house. I couldn't resist lingering in front of my parents' black-and-white wedding photograph, framed in a gold-toned, sculpted metal. My curiosity was intense, so every morning I spent a few minutes studying everyone's face. I tried to decipher an expression or a detail that would tell me something about my parents' marriage, at the very least at the moment of the wedding. Frozen in time was the stamped date of September 18, 1948. The photograph showed four people posing next to a giant five-tier wedding cake and several baskets filled with flowers. I adored the magnificent image of Mandedette's face and head adorned with a crown of flowers around her bouffant hairstyle and a flowing, white lace veil that extended several feet on the floor. I didn't notice even a hint of a smile, which implied her modesty or perhaps her unhappiness. Her demeanor was regal as if she were a princess from a timeless place in her long, white lace V-neck dress. Papa, in his impeccable white suit and contrasting skinny black tie, looked down shyly, although everyone else faced the camera.

A towering woman with large, half-moon eyes in an ebony face, topped with a hat tilted to the side stood to Mandedette's left. She exemplified elegance and self-possession. The matron of honor, she was Mandedette's older cousin, Tante Yolande, with her corpulent body, ample bosom, and disconcerting beauty. Then there was Papa's best man, a tall, very dark man at the other end of the photograph. With his imposing erect posture and faint smile, he looked diecast in his crisply pressed, beige bomber-jacket army uniform. He was Colonel Paul Eugene Magloire, who became president of Haiti a couple of years after the wedding. Papa told me once, with a very proud smile, that the president of Haiti at the time, Dumarsais Estimé, was to have been his best man; however, being otherwise engaged the day of the wedding, he asked Colonel Magloire to be his substitute.

I didn't see any emotion on the four faces in the photograph. But what a "power couple" Papa and Mandedette must have been to assemble such a cast of characters for their wedding party. Even as a child, I wondered if behind the façade or in the faint shadows of the posed image of this sacred union, there weren't secret things little children like me should not know.

At the time, children weren't allowed to ask questions. But I, as a most adventurous one, dared the forbidden every once in a while, although not without consequences. I asked, "Why didn't you smile in the picture?" and "Were you happy?"

Mandedette didn't react often, and I usually stood looking at her as I waited for an answer until I got tired and walked away angry. But

16

when she did respond, it was often to say "*Beski*," a meaningless word she had invented to silence Viola and me.

The first time she told me that, I was so surprised that I asked the question again: "Were you happy the day of your wedding?"

She repeated, "*Beski,*" and there was a sly smile on her face.

That was my cue: it meant nothing. In reality, she was telling me, "I will not respond to your question." Not bad in terms of imagination, but how utterly strange. It was similar to giving us a placebo to calm our curiosity. When I heard "*Beski*," I felt shame, as if I had been caught doing something terribly wrong. In truth, almost all the time, I was enquiring about something quite ordinary. It was just that our house was a silent one. Mandedette was never much for noise and company; she thrived in the quiet. We children were simply expected to accept the silent treatment, respond only when talked to, and also thrive in the quiet.

Sometimes I got lucky, or my perseverance was rewarded. Once, when I asked about the wedding picture, I got a few tiny pearls of information.

"How come Papa knew a president?" I queried.

In 1946, around the time Papa met Mandedette, he worked in the security detail of President Dumarsais Estimé. A former school teacher, senator, and three-time government minister, Estimé, born in the very proud Black bourgeoisie of Haiti's provincial cities, ran under the slogan "A Black Man in Power." He was known as a *noiriste*, someone who espoused the cultural and political philosophy that sought the empowerment of Black-skinned Haitians and their integration into government bureaucracy after decades of preferential placement of mulattoes or Haitians with light skin. In 1946, this became public policy when he was elected president by a huge margin in what was called the "Revolution of 1946." The *noiriste* political philosophy extended to a popular literary and artistic movement called "*indigenous*," later named "*noirisme*" or "*negritude*." It advocated for the affirmation of black-skinned Haitians in the arts and the need for artists to source inspiration in Africa rather than copy Europeans for their creations.

At a certain point in his twenties, Papa had started cultivating men of power. It was a choice not totally motivated by dogma or ideology, even though in the 40s, Papa was sympathetic to the *noiriste* political philosophy put in practice by his boss. In the Port-au-Prince of the era, with its population of about 200,000 people, Papa's power connections were mostly black-skinned Haitians from his Bas-Peu-de-Chose working-class neighborhood, those he had met at social encounters or playing games of chance like poker, or at the Masonic lodge since he was also a Freemason.

"Ask Papa," Mandedette whispered.

"Why was Tante Yolande your matron of honor?" I wondered.

Tante Yolande's lively, take-charge personality and her eyes that stared like a bulldog assessing its prey made her an imposing presence in our lives. When I was little she lived in Brooklyn and visited Haiti often, having left behind her mother and her cheating, government minister husband. She wore suits tailored immaculately to her body, with gloves and a hat decorated with multicolored feathers. Whenever she spoke, and it was often, everybody listened attentively. Viola and I were usually asked to leave since she peppered her language with expressions not meant for our virgin ears. I liked her controlled flamboyance, her personification of refinement and power, so much so that I hovered close to her, hoping part of her flair would wear off on me. Her heart was as large as her bosom and she gave us extravagant gifts, like Viola's baby piano. I would learn that her generosity was so exceptional that friends called her a one-woman immigration office. As it turned out, she helped several hundred Haitians—later including Mandedette and my godmother Tyanne—get visas to travel to New York by providing them the much-revered affidavits guaranteeing them support once they arrived.

"Tante Yolande is the one who arranged my marriage," Mandedette responded.

"How is a marriage arranged?" I asked.

"You find two people who aren't married and marry them. No more questions, please," she said and returned to her book, meaning "I am busy." I stayed by her side, hoping she would tell me more, but instead, the silence grew uncomfortable, and I walked away.

One of the Haitian variations of arranged marriages was to mate a promising older public servant with little education, lots of street smarts, powerful connections, and potentially money, with a younger and better-educated woman. Happiness was not a primary consideration in these arrangements. My parents fit the profile. Still, Mandedette and Papa's church marriage was not the norm because among most Haitians in rural areas and in provincial cities, common-law marriage was more prevalent. This match, made by the much richer and politically powerful Tante Yolande, ensured that her baby cousin would not be an old maid or go to a nunnery, which at the time were viable alternatives for smart, independent women or unlucky ones. Tante Yolande's plan was that Mandedette would marry and have children who would be well-bred and properly schooled and who could break the glass ceilings of class—that was the social project.

For Papa at forty-one, Mandedette at twenty-four years old was the perfect choice. He had most likely never met a woman like her, with the bearing of Fulani royalty of West Africa, the graceful silhouette of a gazelle, the piercing eyes of a tiger, and a tested intellect. He must have been enticed by Mandedette's poise and elegance. She had peach-colored, satin-smooth skin, a round face, and hair neatly coiffed in bobs or twists that highlighted her strong bone structure and plump lips. Her fingers were very long, like a piano player's, and her manicured nails were always lacquered with pale pink polish. Her tall frame carried the strong, alluring amber scent of Shalimar. She wore her starchy-pressed dresses, skirts, and richly embroidered, white cotton voile tops, typical of the day and indicative of status, close to her svelte body. They felt so good when I rubbed against her; years later, I collected similar ones at flea markets.

Mandedette may have had many suitors, but she was most interested in reading and listening to music, both solitary pleasures. Racine, Lamartine, Marcel Proust, Mozart, and Chopin were her favorite men, her delight in them inherited from the Renaissance man who was her father, Julien, a civil engineer and lawyer very active in fighting for

Haitians' political and social rights in the late 30s. Yet, Mandedette's childhood had been a series of mostly lows, going back and forth with her mother between two aunts' houses, except for the joyous vacations on the family homestead in Maseillan with her grandmother Elisiane and blind great-grandmother Asi.

Education defined Mandedette, and she embraced it. Her mother and father instilled in her the belief that education was the assured road to success in life. It became her value system. She had a diploma from the prestigious Women's Teachers' College and held a highly respected position for intelligent middle-class or bourgeois women as an elementary school teacher. She worked in the public school system, so the pursuit of money was most definitely not her objective. "You can never, ever miss a day of school," she told us at the beginning of each school year, instituting her simple rule for Viola and me: school attendance was non-negotiable. She even taught us to question whether headaches or tiredness—or other minor physical ailments—could be excuses to miss classes, but then I so loved school that missing one day would have felt like torture.

In Port-au-Prince, single and unattached, Mandedette often participated in several organizations and went to cultural events and political meetings in her spare time, where she met poets, novelists, and other intellectuals who would become her friends, some for life. This was a choice.

After her introduction to Papa, she curtailed most of her cultural and political activities. That was not quite what she had set her sights on, but then Tante Yolande took over some of her rights with the setup of this rushed transaction with a man seventeen years her senior. This was not a choice.

They had different backgrounds, his urban and hers provincial—and very different interests. The marriage sealed their union and clearly showed their decision to put their differences aside as they strove to create a family life for themselves. But Papa had an all-consuming poker addiction. At night, he went to the poker rooms, his own and other people's, where the stakes were the highest and the company dubious. He already had one son that Mandedette was aware of, and everyone knew he had a passion for the conquest of women. Many of the men in his security and political power circle reveled in a society that heavily favored men. Often, while married, they had one main mistress—*la maîtresse*, kind of like a second wife who sometimes had children. Papa had the temperament for all of that, but domestic life was a different thing altogether, and his faithfulness had not yet been tested in a marriage.

Viola was born two years after their wedding; it was my turn two years later. In the Port-au-Prince of the early 1950s, with connections to the highest echelons of power, my parents' lives could have been full of promise.

Rue Dr. Waag, where we lived, lay in the center of Port-au-Prince, a city that opened its arms wide to Gonave Bay and had its back propped up by the highest mountain peaks in the country. The street was named after an older German doctor who lived down the road from us. Back in those days, as the city grew, it was customary to name roads such as rue Dr. Aubry, rue Dr. Roy, and Impasse Clesca after the prominent personalities who lived or worked on them. Even though we were a fifteen-minute walk to the Champ-de-Mars Park, Papa sometimes drove us there to play. I galloped back and forth past the larger-than-life statues of Toussaint, Dessalines, Christophe, and Petion, national heroes so prominent that one name sufficed to identify them—for they had led the movement that freed all captives, declared Haiti free of slavery, started the revolution that defeated Napoleon's French imperial troops and led Haiti onto the world stage to its independence as the First Black Republic on January 1, 1804.

In one ear, I heard the legends, the allegories, the stories about them from Papa, and mostly from Mandedette, but what penetrated my little mind was the word *liberté*… freedom. Mandedette made each outing a pretext for teaching us something and the two streets that bordered rue Dr. Waag formed the starting point for my first history lessons. They were named for strong, determined, heroic military officers, Mandedette said. To the west of us, rue Capois honored Francois Capois, a general of the Revolutionary Army who, with his soldiers, won the decisive Battle of Vertieres over Napoleon's troops in November 1803, paving the way for Haiti's independence two months later. Avenue Christophe, to the east, bore the name of Henry Christophe, the freed slave who fought in the Battle of Savannah with the Americans prior to arriving in Haiti where he became a general in the Revolutionary Army and later our first monarch: King Henry I. Much as kids are proud of their mythic superheroes, I was proud of the courage of these men.

Most of my early memories of rue Waag centered on the porch and the yard. Mandedette had moved several large pots of huge dracaenas and palms with the help of a gardener to transform the veranda into a lush living area bathed with diffused sunlight. It was her favorite place in the house and where she spent endless hours sitting on one of the patio chairs. Her daily ritual was reading. Sometimes I saw her caressing the book she was holding as if it were a sacred object. I don't recall ever seeing Papa with a book in hand, much less reading one, but at the time, I didn't recognize any disconnect between their lifestyles. Mandedette and Papa shared the bedroom closest to the front of the house. A thick mahogany bedroom set decorated the space, each piece with the rounded edges of the Art Deco style in vogue. Viola and I shared a tiny bedroom next to theirs. It held our two small beds, a wooden dresser, and two chairs used when someone combed our hair, one a low child's chair and the other of normal height for the adult.

There was something else about living on rue Waag that brought me simple joy. Sometimes I glimpsed Dr. Waag tending his stunning rose garden. With his shoulders bent, his wild tuft of white hair facing the sun, he walked baby steps from one bush to the other and smelled each flower. I always savored the moment.

DAMIEN

Suddenly, one day, we left home for Damien. Mandedette said we were going on a short trip, and our bags were already packed. I jolted from joy at the idea of a journey.

But why Damien, a vast flatland full of vegetation located north of the capital? Perhaps because August 1956 was unusually hot, and Mandedette thought a few weeks on a secluded farm near a river would do us good. Perhaps it was something more sinister.

I remember she was not smiling that day. She didn't tell us anything more, but then that was her nature. I remember we got into a large car and Mandedette sat in the front next to a driver we didn't know. I thought maybe Papa was busy because he was usually the one who drove us to places. Viola and I sat in the back as the car rode silently for what seemed like a very long time through the expansive Cul-de-Sac flatlands. Colossal trees dotted the countryside. About an hour after we left home, the driver turned left down a very long and narrow driveway before dropping us off in front of an isolated house.

I remember well the very tall, very pale, very skinny man who came out of the main door of the house to greet us. He looked like a long twig with wire glasses. He took Mandedette in his arms and told her, "Bienvenue, ma fille." I was so intrigued by his calling her *ma fille* that I asked her about it. Her explanation: Toyo had been her father's best friend and after his death, acted as her surrogate father. Then, he bent down almost to the floor, as if he were an acrobat, to kiss Viola and me. Toyo smiled broadly as if he wanted to giggle with us. His wife, almost as tall as he was, and their two teenage daughters came to kiss us, followed quietly by an older brother. They made me feel welcomed. Then they all disappeared inside the house.

I remember perfectly the enormous veranda of their home that faced a dense wooded area. Gigantic lianas hung from tree tops. We were in the government house Toyo and his family occupied on the grounds of the agriculture ministry. Toyo, an agronomist, was the ministry's director general.

I remember well that when his shoes hit the multicolored mosaic floor of the house, they made a strange music. We followed him inside while a servant took our bags to a large bedroom with two beds draped with mosquito nets hanging from the ceiling. I shared the bigger bed with Viola, and Mandedette slept on the other. That was my new home. For how long, Mandedette didn't say.

I remember that in the mornings, Viola and I roamed the trails of the farm, which seemed as large as the city. I saw grass as tall as I was and multitudes of mangoes, avocados, sapotes, and guavas hanging from their trees. I discovered different varieties of palms, infinite rows of corn stalks and Musaceae, banana and plantain trees, and fields of pots full of plants and seedlings by the base of larger trees. I saw zig-zagging white clouds in the vast sky, the bluest ones I had ever seen. I played hide-and-seek with Viola under the unforgiving sun until I was dizzy. I pretended to be a fish when I dipped under the water in the nearby river. We played splash war, and even when I splattered the water uncontrollably, Viola always won.

I remember the morose look on Mandedette's face, usually late in the afternoon when we came back for snacks. Then, I ran into her wide skirt to get a timid smile that carried so much love in it before she walled herself in again. She never laughed. This didn't sadden me. I saw that nothing seemed to please her except whispering to Toyo while sweetly rocking her chair and reading her book.

Drunk from fatigue, I struggled to keep my eyes open until dusk, but failed miserably. I remember that each night I had the impression that mosquitoes and other insects invaded the space to create their own symphony orchestra. Fortunately, when I laid my head down to sleep the nights away I was protected by the wide, white net.

I remember my tears when four or so weeks after our arrival, Mandedette announced we were going back home, by then an alien environment. I cried because every morning and every night, I felt as if I were meant to stay on that immense farm next to the stream, right there in that big, white house to live happily the long, lazy days of my life.

THE DAWN OF THE BARBARIANS

It was Mother's Day 1957, and I was six months shy of my fifth birthday. Papa went out early that Sunday morning to visit his mother, Angele Paul, whom we all called Grand Angele. He kissed both Viola and me on our foreheads when he passed us playing in the front garden by the hibiscus hedges while Mandedette sat on her favorite metal rocking chair reading a book on the porch, as usual.

On his way, as he did every Sunday, Papa stopped at Peter's Bakery across the street from Champ-de-Mars to buy his mother chicken-stuffed *pâtés*, the small crusty pastries she relished, to better savor their traditional morning coffee.

He drove quickly through the park. Then Papa made a left turn in front of the army barracks onto his mother's street. It was exactly 8:00 a.m. At that precise time, according to tradition, the flag is ceremoniously raised in front of all public buildings. All cars must stop as someone sings "La Dessalinienne," the national anthem. All drivers, passengers and pedestrians must stand erect to show respect for the flag. Papa, who had always been a man in a hurry, forgot to stop. A soldier standing guard in front of the barracks raised his arm high, halting Papa's car, and ordered him out. Papa obeyed. Then the soldier aimed his rifle and shot Papa three times.

Papa crumpled onto the pavement in a thin cloud of smoke.

The gunman in the army uniform turned away fast—very fast—and entered the anonymity of the barracks.

Papa lay spread out on the ground, perhaps feeling his bones disintegrate and sensing his body shake from the thrust of the pain. A crowd gathered around him to provide a thin human shield against the soldiers and their bullets. A witness to the shooting recognized Papa. This Good Samaritan picked up Papa's listless, disheveled body, eased it with the help of others onto the back seat of a vehicle, and drove him down one block to the State University Hospital. Papa must have overheard the swarm of people discussing his prognosis and the wailing of some of the women.

Papa's profession was *hommes d'affaires*, a category that included anyone who gave himself that title in the belief that he ran a business. His was managing a nighttime gambling room where men played poker for high stakes. Everyone knew that Papa's world revolved around money— making money, spending money, losing money. He made it from his cut of the games organized in his gambling room, but also from his luck at the tables, for he was a fierce poker player. Papa's passion was poker—no, it was his addiction. He spent money ferociously as soon as he won it, indulging in the mundane frivolities of life, such as jewelry, clothes, cars, and perfume. He practiced what he preached; money was for pleasure, immediate pleasure. He lost money too, lots of it, for he also knew losing was part of the game.

One morning after a clean winning sweep playing poker, he purchased a car; that same evening he lost so much money and had indebted himself to the point that he had to sell the car the next day. Throughout, he kept his poker face, that inscrutable, impassive expression that hid his true feelings.

That Mother's Day, it was his "poker body" that probably saved his life.

At the hospital where I had been born, the doctors saw that the bullets had missed Papa's heart by a few centimeters but shattered his left arm in several places. Luckily the soldier was not a sharpshooter, because he had fired his weapon to kill. When Mandedette reached the hospital, the doctors reassured her that Papa would live but wouldn't be able to use his left arm ever again.

Early the next morning, Mandedette, Viola, and I sat down in our dining room around the small rectangular table that Marlene had topped with a flowery tablecloth. For breakfast there were our cups of watered-down coffee, the butter dish, the tiny square breads, and the bowls of oatmeal. Almost on cue, Marlene left us to walk to the outdoor kitchen next to her room into the backyard; the prevailing custom was that maids prepared and served the food but didn't eat with the family.

Mandedette's voice at the edge of a whisper said, "Papa has been badly hurt in an accident and needs to stay in the hospital to get better."

I was sad and I was worried about Papa, but Mandedette knew better than to tell us someone had shot him. While everything was falling apart, she tried to hang on by transforming the incident into an *accident* without sharing the exact circumstances so Viola and I could more easily digest it. I fixed my eyes into hers, but as she talked, she repeatedly glanced at the yard to see if Marlene was eavesdropping. She always whispered whenever Marlene was nearby. I never asked why; that's just the way it was. I knew something momentous had taken place, but hung on because Mandedette told us Papa would get better soon. Then we all ate in silence.

The shooting in response to his forgetting in a moment a rule redefined Papa's life. The cruelty of a common soldier, who acted like an obscure vulture eager to show its naked head in the heart of the city, had also toppled our world. Things started to change. Mandedette cut off most of her interactions with us except for a quick *bonjour* and kiss before she went out for the day. Every morning, I saw her rush through her coffee and buttered bread. Her mind was busy with other things; she even stopped reading books on the veranda. She forbade us from playing outdoors; we couldn't even call our next-door neighbor Ginette to come play with us. We had to stay inside all day, so I felt punished for something I hadn't done.

I roamed the house, hoping to see Papa even though it increasingly emptied of his presence; even his ghost was absent because the smell of his Camel cigarette had dissipated. I no longer heard his slight cough signaling his location. A few days after he had gone away, I persuaded myself that his rasping voice was still singing the classic Frère Jacques lullaby to us. I heard him loudly and clearly in my head: "*Sonnez les matines, ding ding dong.*" Papa had created a meaningless ending, "*Kilik kilik poisson cinema!*" which made Viola and me laugh uncontrollably each time he sang it. I was disoriented because he was not home to raise me above his head so I could touch the ceiling. I missed his roguish smile. I missed cuddling with him. I felt like a shaking leaf that nobody saw, but whose shaking was nonetheless very real.

Soon afterwards, Viola and I visited him at the Saint-Francis Salesian Hospital, where Mandedette had transferred him, so he could get more specialized care. I saw the melancholy of the slow walk down the darkened hallway, the nun-nurses going down trance-like in long, white habits and wide, wing-like wimples. In Papa's room, I squealed, the joy of seeing him mixed with the pain of watching his mangled body tucked in starched, white sheets.

Despite visiting Papa, I was sleepless at night. I yawned endlessly. I turned on the side of my small bed next to Viola and wondered out loud when he would be home. I thought of the marvelous, happy times with him—the smiles, the laughter, the tickling. Finally, exhausted, I fell asleep to the lugubrious lullaby of mosquitoes and sporadic gunfire coming from down the street. I woke up often. Even crying didn't diminish my anguish. But sometimes I imagined he was tickling me, and in my child's imagination, I could feel him kissing me goodnight.

Over the weeks that turned into months, visitors ceased coming to our veranda. Mandedette rarely used it anymore.

"When will Papa come home?" I asked Viola one day.

"Why do you always ask me things I don't know?" she replied brusquely. I felt like the baby sister I was.

"I'll ask Mandedette," I said, as I walked away to hide my hurt. Of course, I was scared she would respond, "Beski," so I didn't. As if she was an anxiety detector guessing all our unspoken questions and worries, one day soon after, Mandedette told us Papa had been transferred to yet another hospital. His illness was beyond what the Catholic hospital, where he had had several surgeries, could offer. This third one she found was several hours away but had more modern equipment and better-trained personnel. She had the burden of making decisions for all of us in Papa's absence while also holding down her teaching job.

"When can we go see him?" Viola asked.

"Soon, soon," she replied.

"I'll never see Papa again," I cried. Tears, tears, and more tears. Mandedette simply repeated, "Soon, my girl. Soon. You will see Papa soon."

It wasn't the same after that. Before the transfer, Viola and I visited Papa every weekend, giggling endlessly about the nuns' unusual headwraps. We joked with Papa, and we got hugs and kisses from him. Now we only received news of his progress from Mandedette. She might have wanted to reassure us, but it didn't help. Papa had gone far away, and I missed him terribly.

That year, 1957, was as trying for Papa and us as it was momentous for Haiti because of its "revolving door politics." The state of affairs in the country was chaotic after a relatively peaceful six-year rule by President Paul Magloire; Papa had also worked in his security detail. With profits from a boom in tourism and record coffee exports, he launched a modernization effort by building schools, roads, and other infrastructure. Featured on the cover of *Time* magazine, he was the only Haitian President to address the US Congress, before he was overthrown in a coup d'état for trying to prolong his mandate. The president of the Supreme Court, Nemours Pierre-Louis, assumed the presidency for two months, until judge Franck Sylvain replaced him. Sylvain was quickly deposed fifty-six days later, and followed by an Executive Council of Government, itself dislodged by Professor Daniel Fignolé, a charismatic teacher's union leader and Magloire's former Minister of Education. After a mere three weeks, a Military Council of Government overthrew Fignolé and set elections for September.

These political intrigues and power shifts stemmed from several social movements that came to bear that year. Strikes and demonstrations characterized them, urging more civil liberties and, in the continuation of the *noiriste* movement of 1946, an end to the monopoly of social and political power by the light-skinned bourgeoisie. Both of Papa's bosses, presidents Estimé and Magloire, had made some advances with the *noiriste* policies, but the excluded group of dark-skinned Haitians, including Mandedette and Papa, as well as much of the urban middle class, was restless and demanded social, economic, and political equality, and at all levels. Amidst this turmoil, Port-au-Prince and the country were on edge.

Finally, the day arrived for us to visit Papa at the Albert Schweitzer Hospital in the town of Deschappelles. On that Sunday morning, we made the hot journey, driving northeast over bumpy dirt roads through Haiti's most fertile flatlands. I sat with Viola in the back seat of Papa's car. In front, Mandedette, who hadn't learned to drive, sat stiffly next to a driver. My stomach and head shook wildly as the small car vacillated left and right during the unbearable two-hour trip. To occupy our time, Mandedette used the ride to give both a geography and a history lesson. She explained that a rich American family called Mellon had built the hospital, named it after a famous doctor working in Africa, and still managed it. It had been constructed on the site of an abandoned banana plantation called Standard Fruit Banana Company, which began its operations when the American Marines occupied Haiti from 1915 to 1934. In a wartime effort, Haiti had supplied bananas for sale to the United States, much like other Central American countries did. In fact, the derogatory nickname "banana republic" came from that period. Viola and I stayed quiet and endured the dusty ride and Mandedette's lesson.

The moment we reached the hospital, Mandedette translated the entry sign out loud to no one in particular: "Reverence for Life, Respectez la vie; that's what it means."

I held her hand tightly, and with Viola holding the other, we crossed a courtyard that seemed as large as Champ-de-Mars to reach Papa's room. He was lying on his back with his left arm held up by a metal wire tied to the roof. He opened his right arm wide to greet us. I reached up, and Papa covered me in kisses, as he did Viola.

"*Bonjour Moka, Bonjour Vi,*" he whispered, using the nicknames he had given Viola and me. He complimented us on our dresses, and we told him about our latest hide and seeks and school. I ate his watery oatmeal porridge. I hop-scotched from the door to his bed and back. His hospital room became an enchanted space with the four of us reunited.

Quickly, much too quickly, the time to say goodbye came, and I missed him even before I left. He pulled me up with his good arm to kiss my forehead, then held Viola's head close to his heart. I saw him smiling weakly as if he wanted to prevent the tears from coming out of his eyes. But I wept, and so did Viola. I wanted Papa in our house, not there all alone. Plus, I hated all the thin mechanical wires that seemed to imprison his arm. I slept all the way back home as much out of sadness as exhaustion.

I didn't tell Viola, and I didn't tell Mandedette how terrified I was that Papa was sick and in a hospital so far away from our home. Despite hiding all my fears, I nonetheless felt them, particularly at night: I was scared that Papa wouldn't get better. That he could get shot again when he came back home. That Mandedette might get sick. That Viola and I would grow up all alone. I couldn't say anything to anyone, not even Viola. I just cried myself to sleep each night under my cotton sheet.

Of the summer and fall of 1957 presidential campaign period, my memory is inscribed with the sound of sporadic shooting, an ambient noise that announced nighttime, much like the familiar buzzing of mosquitoes waiting to suck our blood. What was actually happening was this: Four candidates vied for the presidential post in the September 22 elections. Clement Jumelle, a lawyer, economist, former parliamentarian, President Magloire's former finance minister, was one. Two other candidates were the rich landowner and businessman Louis Dejoie, a light-skinned agronomist from the South, and the union leader Daniel Fignolé, whose supporters from the masses in his Bel-Air neighborhood were massacred by the hundreds during the campaign. The fourth candidate was Dr. Francois Duvalier, President Estimé's former health minister, who eventually won the chaotic and violent election, which many commentators denounced as fraudulent.

One night, I woke suddenly, petrified by the noise of gunfire. Outside, the usual shooting continued, but on that cool tropical night, it was different. It sounded like the gunmen were on our veranda, not down the street. I lay still. Viola shook me and laid her index finger on my lips. I followed her to hide under her twin bed. I was trembling, and so was she, but she grabbed onto my hand, as she always did, making me feel somewhat safer. Still, I held my breath. We were completely silent. I thought that the men shooting were coming for us. And I knew there was no one to protect us other than Mandedette because Papa was far away at that provincial hospital. I was petrified that night. And so many others.

I couldn't stop smiling and jumping with joy about school opening in October, which helped take some attention off Papa. The even better news was that I began first grade at Ecole Republique d'Argentine, one of the schools that was part of the government's big effort in the 40s and 50s to provide free education to Haitian children. The effort constructed several new public schools and opened others, like mine, in existing buildings, all bearing the names of countries on the American continent. In class, they told us it mattered that Haiti did meaningful things, like naming my school for Argentina because it was done in a spirit of Interamerican solidarity.

Viola, already two grades ahead of me, held my hand every weekday morning to walk down rue Waag, then we turned right on rue Capois. We crisscrossed students in uniforms different from ours on the busy two-block path to our school, housed in a 19th century building with its distinctive wrought iron shipped from France. Our uniform, a pleated navy gabardine skirt topped with a white shirt with an elegant sailor-collar and tie, was special because the school's insignia—"R.A."—was embroidered on its breast pocket.

Every morning, when we arrived at our meeting place by the stairway, Viola repeated the same phrase: "Go fast. See you soon." Then she went off to her class. And I walked along the narrow veranda that circled the U-shaped courtyard, which was filled with students. It was the first time that I had been around so many other little girls, and classes were strict, almost military style, so I was edgy. Still, I was very excited by the grammar rules, the arithmetic tables, and the names of rivers and mountains I had to memorize. I learned them well because my mind was so thirsty for knowledge. At the end of the morning session, I rushed to meet Viola so we could go eat lunch at home before heading back to the afternoon session. Yet, going home was always sad because Papa was still in the hospital. I turned five on November 2, 1957, a few days before Duvalier was inaugurated President of Haiti.

On the night of January 5, 1958, the New Year's celebrations barely over, journalist Yvonne Hakim Rimpel was home in her nightgown after having put her eight children to bed. A group of *cagoulards,* hooded vandals working for Duvalier, accompanied by three military officers, burst through her front door, ransacked her home, beat her screaming children, knocking out the teeth of one of them, and dragged her barefoot from the house to a waiting car. After kidnapping her, they took her to an isolated, wooded area of the city where they gang-raped and savagely tortured her, leaving her for dead. But she didn't exhale her last breath. Rimpel never backed down; she crawled, half-naked and bleeding, over the gravel and shrubs. Her howls must have torn her lungs. Someone heard her and got her help. It took close to ten hours of surgery, followed by a two-month hospital stay, to bring her back to life. Was it the two editorials she had published to denounce the electoral fraud she had observed in September that made President Duvalier believe she posed a serious threat to his new regime?

"It was the dawn of the barbarians," Mandedette, who rarely talked about the early days of the Duvalier regime, told me one day much later. "That such a brutal rape and torture happened just two months into Duvalier's presidency sent a clear sign that he would rule with an iron hand. There were premonitory signs that the regime would be barbaric."

She paid homage to Rimpel by telling me that Rimpel, who had co-founded Haiti's first feminist organization and become one of the leaders of the successful movement that won Haitian women the right to vote in the 1950s, was silenced; she never published again. Rimpel carried the agonizing secret of her assailant's identity presumably until shortly before she died at eighty years old in 1986, five months after the end of the Duvalier dictatorship. One of her children said Rimpel talked about a beautiful moonlight that evening the *cagoulards* and the army officers killed her voice. With this minute detail, I figured she broke her nearly thirty-year silence and indicated she might have recognized the men's faces shining under the moon.

A few days after Rimpel's gang rape, Mandedette brought Papa home from the hospital. Eight months had gone by, during which Papa underwent seven surgeries in three hospitals and endured excruciating physical pain. We all knew how much he had overcome. And we all shed tears of gratitude for his recovery. I was ecstatic that all four of us had come together again.

But then I realized Papa could no longer lift me above his head because his left arm was permanently bent at the elbow. He found it impossible to stretch the arm all the way down or bring it up. It wasn't as if Papa were content to live with this minor handicap, for he was relentless with his rehabilitation exercises: repeatedly folding his left fingers in a mechanical movement around an imaginary ball. I told myself how comical it was to see an adult playing with a tiny ball toy. But he was training his fingers to hold the steering wheel, a cloth napkin, and more often, a deck of cards. He had been left-handed until the accident. Now, he had to learn to write all over again, this time with his right one. He didn't discuss his arm. Besides, he wasn't a talker by nature, and I was too sad to ask him anything.

Papa abandoned security work and instead got a patronage civil service job at the State Lottery Administration. It was not so much what he did there that was important. In fact, there was nothing of interest in this post; his austere office desk sat empty the few times I visited him with Viola. But having the job meant that people who needed to would know he was a man to be reckoned with. That was his milieu, and like power-connected men everywhere, Papa was *de facto* a powerful man: a commanding presence respected by many, feared by some. He drove a car when most in his neighborhood had to walk, and he always carried a gun. The perception of having power counted, sometimes more than power itself, and Papa knew that.

I didn't ask any questions about the "accident" as an insurmountable wall of silence was erected about it. I never heard Mandedette or Papa mention the shooting by the soldier as if an order had been given or a pact signed not to talk about it, even though it had transformed all of our lives. But then, silence was a language my parents had learned long ago, perhaps before I was even born. They must have had their reasons. I was just happy Papa was home.

SHALIMAR

Papa and Mandedette together: that was the picture I liked to look at.

They rarely went out together, but when they did, it was a major event. I stood by transfixed as I watched her prepare. She sat on the curvy stool in front of the big, oval mirror of the vanity table in her bedroom, her back straight, and began the routine that I reveled in.

"What's that for?" I asked her when she put a cotton pad on the mouth of a bottle to absorb a clear liquid.

"It's to cleanse my face," she responded.

"What's that for?" I queried as she poured a dab of white cream on another. I smiled so I wouldn't be kicked out of the room when she looked at me through the mirror. She had done that before because she wanted to be alone when putting on her makeup.

"It's to hydrate the skin to protect it." I heard impatience in her voice.

"Why do you need to protect your skin?"

"Facial skin is very sensitive because it's most exposed to dirt. It needs protection. Monique, that's enough!"

The mirror reflected her blank stare, meant to get me out of the bedroom. I wasn't ceding any territory, so I kept on playing my favorite game of back-to-back questions on anything. Papa, wearing one of his many fine, cotton-voile shirts tucked into front-pleated dress pants, was pacing the hallway outside.

"What's that for?" I said, shifting my position to her other side, hoping she'd see me in a different light as I watched her put a thick brownish cream on another cotton ball.

"This is makeup. It makes my skin smooth and conceals my small blemishes. Please, get out! I need to finish dressing," she said. It was as if she were an artist delicately painting strokes of color onto a canvas. But then, she always had an eye for beauty and fashion. I could close my eyes and see the photo albums of her teenage years in Cayes, which revealed the life she wanted to show, images of her extensive travels around the countryside during school vacations with friends whose names peopled my life. Her style was a serious one, even for a young woman, as the pictures revealed her wearing shirts with tailored shorts showing her long legs. Her hair was most often rolled up, highlighting her high cheekbones.

"Odette," Papa said softly, contrary to his usual abruptness when he thought he was going to be late. He prided himself on being a very prompt man. He was standing by the doorway, and we both saw him reflected in the mirror.

"Max, please wait outside. I'll be ready soon."

As Papa left, I held on to one leg of his trousers. Then, I followed him to get a pat on my head before coming back to Mandedette.

"Please dab a little rouge on my lips," I begged as she put on her vermillion lipstick.

"You are tiring, and the answer is no," Mandedette said as she slowly folded her lips and rolled them over each other, again and again. I maintained my position and kept asking questions.

"Why are you grimacing?"

"It's so the lipstick adheres to the lips. Monique, really! This conversation is finished."

"Can I have some Shalimar?" I asked, as I stretched my neck, closed my eyes, and held my wrists out, imitating the gestures I had seen her make as she perfumed herself. Shalimar made her smell like a foreign princess. Mandedette was the only person I knew who smelled that good.

"Ok, and then out!" She smiled and her face glowed as she squirted my neck and wrists with the perfume sprayer. I didn't care that she didn't want me in her bedroom when she put on her makeup or dressed. I was willing to be thrown out and didn't even feel shamed by her dismissive attitude, so intense was my desire to be near her and learn her beauty tricks. All she wanted was to be alone to prepare. All I wanted was for her to respond to all my questions and let me witness her getting ready. A clash was inevitable. But I won because I got what I wanted.

"Merci," I said through a smile. As I stepped out of the bedroom, I saw her throw a silky scarf over her head to cover her face to prevent her dress from getting soiled by makeup. Now, I also smelled like a princess and ran to Papa, who was still pacing the floor.

"I am always waiting for your mother," he joked with a proud smile even if he didn't like the lateness one bit.

I waited with him with tremendous excitement. We had to be ready for her entrance, or rather her exit from the bedroom. When Mandedette came out a few minutes later, she looked like a stunning empress. Papa's smile was instantaneous. She had transformed herself so easily to look like the glamorous actresses I saw in the movies. I could spend my life watching her grace and creativity that were as monumental as they were inspiring. I was imbibing her culture of beauty.

Mandedette's scent penetrated my whole being. Then and now.

KENSCOFF

It was that time again. School was over and July was the month for our migration to the mountains, Viola's and mine. This ritual was part of my world every summer from the time I was a year and a half. But this would be my first vacation as a grown-up; I was now five-and-a-half years old, a step up from being considered a baby. Better, this 1958 one was even more special because Papa was driving again following his accident.

Leaving the hot, melting city of Port-au-Prince, Papa first drove his Simca up the paved Bourdon road called Avenue John Brown in honor of the White abolitionist leader, whose crusade to free all the slaves in the United States was inspired by the Revolutionary Army General Toussaint Louverture. The avenue was framed by blazing red and orange flowers of Royal poinciana trees all the way up to the small suburban town of Petion-Ville, a heavenly sight that made me giddy. From there, we climbed more mountains through fields of corn stalks, huge sunflowers, shrubs, and trees. Only one sinuous road led cars up the dangerous, precipitous slopes, deep valleys, and unexpected curves to get to the mountain village of Kenscoff. The sleepy hamlet nestled in the Massif de la Selle, Haiti's tallest mountain range, was suspended at 5000 feet above sea level between the sky and the earth.

My little window to the world was the back seat, where I loved to be during this hour-long journey to this village of farmers, where many wealthy families also had second homes. From there, I could catch sights of marchandes carrying heavy, oversized baskets overflowing with vegetables in the balancing gait they had perfected to hide the pain of walking, at times barefoot, close to ten miles downhill on narrow footpaths or on the main road. They looked tough and muscular, and each woman had a bold-featured, jet-black face topped by a colorful head scarf. I tried to see their eyes, but they never wavered, clearly concentrated on the steep slopes ahead. I saw bony little girls about my age, following their mothers as they apprenticed the harsh life of a Haitian woman street merchant. I didn't think they ever went to school.

"Will she be waiting for us outside or inside?" I asked about my godmother, Lilianne, my mother's best friend, whose nickname was Tyanne. Each summer, with her meager teacher's salary she rented a small, two-bedroom house and invited Viola and me.

"Tyanne will be outside. Stop asking silly questions. You tire me," Viola replied with an older sister's arrogance.

As we gained altitude, my ears filled with pressure. I reunited with the thick clouds of fog that hung over the side of the mountains one after the other, giving life to the proverb "dèye mòn gen mòn" ("Behind mountains, more mountains"). Mandedette and Viola seemed lost in the spectacular scenery outside their windows, while Papa's eyes remained on the road ahead. I saw few people on the road, only more *marchandes*. Every now and then we passed a vacation home made of solid rocks, never far from a grass-covered agricultural worker's hut. I fixed my gaze, determined to see any movement on the mountains, but much to my chagrin, it was to no avail. The higher we went, the more impatient I became to get there, and the colder it got, forcing us to put on our sweaters lest we catch a cold.

The gigantic eucalyptus trees, perfectly aligned on both sides of the road got closer. Next to them stood the very old, giant pine trees and above, the clouds. The tiny wood and brick house was somewhat removed from the street, a few feet away from these massive trees. At last, we made it.

"There she is," I said only seconds later. Tyanne was also on the lookout for us on the front yard.

"*Bonjour la societé*," with the softness in her voice, she pronounced every single syllable like the teacher she was. We all rushed out of the car. Her skinny arms encircled my body, for she was like a porcelain doll with fine, delicate features and a waif-like fragility. I adored her and, to me, she was an angel despite her severe demeanor and her long-sleeved, high-collared, pastel-colored dresses that made her look like a nun without the habit and wimple. Then she kissed Viola, Mandedette and Papa, each one like a long-lost family member.

"After so much time in the car, come stretch your legs. Viergine, please bring some lemon balm tea," she told the maid, a short, stout, black-skinned woman whose scarf held her short braids in place. Tyanne walked Papa and Mandedette through the wooden front door. I heard their voices making small talk and saw Tyanne's wide smile at Papa as she was genuinely happy to see him again after his long convalescence. Then, Viola and I were encircled around Tyanne's dress as she tried to hold our wiggling bodies in place with her tiny hands. She smelled like peach marmalade, which made me happy because it meant she had cooked some for us.

The smell of tea began to fill the room. Viergine had barely finished serving it, when Papa got up abruptly, as he often did, put down his porcelain teacup and saucer, looked at his watch, and said, "Odette, let's go." They never stayed long when they dropped us off because of the long ride, but this time it was an extremely brief hello.

I saw Mandedette's face metamorphose from a smiling one to another which showed her fury as she just stared blankly at Papa. Then, she rushed to say goodbye and planted a loud kiss on my forehead and one on Viola's. I found a brief refuge in Papa's pant legs and scrambled not to fall as he quickly walked away after kissing me.

"*Merci, Tyanne*," Mandedette said in a monotone that was quite different from her effusive greeting a few minutes earlier. Her rigid facial expression showed she didn't want to go, but she followed his lead, nonetheless.

"*Ba-bye, ba-bye*" we said as we stretched the goodbyes. Mandedette and Tyanne embraced silently for a long time, long enough for me to rush back to Tyanne's skirt. I went to her often to cuddle, for she was the cuddling type. Though I loved my parents, I was happy to see them leave so my vacation could finally start.

Kenscoff was where, when the first roosters crowed, the day opened its eyes with light orange tones of tropical sun filtering through the cloud forest. It brightened everything. The scent of coffee was the scent of life, so as soon as I got a whiff of it, I knew Viergine, up since dawn, was along with Tyanne, drinking espresso coffee in her minute enamel cups, not talking, but just being there.

Then Tyanne, Viergine, Viola and I all fell into being a family as the rhythm of each day followed our meal times in the room that served as our dining and living space. The morning ritual started with Viergine doing away with porridges by serving breakfast to be eaten with a fork, a treat usually reserved for weekends or holiday mornings in the city. I loved the thinly sliced sautéed liver smothered with onions and served with boiled plantains, tangy watercress, and the creamiest avocados slices. For lunch, our meal was the traditional rice and beans sprinkled with small pieces of beef or goat. I didn't like the green, leafy vegetables except for the creamed spinach, so Viergine made a bargain with me. If I ate them, she would make my adored *carottes blanchies*, carrots dipped in creamy bechamel sauce. Everything she cooked tasted as good as it looked; she was an artist in the kitchen.

Tyanne was convinced I was not drinking enough water during the day. "Monique, you must drink your water, or you will become a goat" she told me, smiling with her eyes.

"I will not become a goat," I replied, even though I was shaking, afraid I might actually become one. So, every few hours, she offered a glass of water and stood by prodding me to finish it. I was terribly annoyed. Finally, one day she told me sweetly, "Mais non. You won't become a goat!" Only then was I sure I wouldn't be a goat.

In the afternoons, we snacked on fresh fat butter rolls with peach marmalade or ate *pain patate*, Haitian sweet potato bread. For supper, I was the sentinel who made sure the milk didn't boil over when Viergine warmed it. The timing had to be precise to call her to turn off the heat, and I was very proud of that job, done each time without failure. Once she had poured the milk into a large enamel cup, I could dip my buttered bread in it and soak it to my pleasure. I savored it all. I felt grown-up. I had responsibilities.

The trails near our house held no mysteries for me because of our daily hikes organized by Tyanne like army exercise drills. Viola and I pulled our sweaters tight as the mountains hugged us from all sides bringing cold drafts. Tyanne directed my steps through trails winding around immense fields of cabbage, leeks, beets, carrots, and other vegetables. She assured us that this small town formed a major lifeline to the capital city. Kenscoff fed us as most of its vegetables were transported downhill to Port-au-Prince by the market women or in large, overloaded trucks or in Peugeot combis with their distinctive diesel-motor noise. Then there were the pumpkin vines winding themselves along spikes here and there around fences. "*Bonjour*" was the ubiquitous sound with which she greeted all the people we passed; Viola and I quickly repeated it. "*Maa. Maa. Maa*," she belched to the cows who eyed us with total disinterest.

Wild and colorful flower beds dotted the trails. "What's the name of this flower, Tyanne?" I asked as we embarked on yet another hiking trail.

"*Ce sont des ca-pri-ces,*" she said as she pointed to the pink, red, white, and purple blooms of impatiens.

"What about these?"

"These are irises. Over here are jasmine flowers. The fragrance comes from them. Smell them, children. Look over there; they are lilies," she commented. She always found beauty in the mundane.

"Who planted them in the rocks?" I asked.

"Nobody. They just grow everywhere, even in rock crevasses," she said as we walked by fields of wildflowers. "*Respirez, les enfants, respirez.*" The fragrance of the fat eucalyptus tree here, there, and everywhere hit me hard and infused itself in my being. Each moment was a long, enchanting botany lesson, yet she never let us know she was teaching. We also learned how to spell many words from her meticulous pronunciation; that was her trademark.

We called them open market days. They were Tuesdays and Fridays. After breakfast, I followed Tyanne, Viergine, and Viola through the busy, narrow pathways that framed the merchants' stalls up a couple of kilometers on both sides of the narrow paved main road. It all took the allure of a fair, with me passing close by both the buyers and the sellers, never really entering beyond the superficiality of both their worlds.

The very old town's natives looked out to the distance, almost frozen in place and speechless as if they had already said everything they had to say. I stared at the farmers, men and women with strong, ebony faces that expressed both strength and pain, obvious even to my young eyes. They wore traditional dark blue denim clothing as if it were a uniform. The women tied their waists and their heads with wide, multicolored bands. The buyers were, like us, vacationers. They thronged the herb merchants with baskets filled with dried medicinal leaves, which they promised could cure all types of ailments. The butchers were overrun for the choicest parts of goats, pigs and cows killed at dawn. Right then and there, I wanted to lick the tiny, locally grown peaches and raspberries that grew only in the cold mountain air; they looked so exotic for me the city kid. I was at home in this other Haiti, the one with wild gardens, terraces of vegetables, multiple scents, wide-open land, and temperate climate, so different from the hot Port-au-Prince.

When dusk closed the day, the living room became the place where we performed a tea ceremony. We each busied ourselves to choose which leaves to infuse or boil to make our herbal tea. Should it be soursop, anise, mint, lemon balm, verbena or basil, or a concoction of two or three picked in the yard during the day? Then we added some cinnamon bark and sometimes eucalyptus leaves. The scent of the brew permeated the house, and the tea warmed our bodies for the cold night ahead. All had medicinal properties, and a few teaspoons of brown sugar sufficed to sweeten the tea to our taste; but if we were sick, we took it with salt. It was a calming ritual meant to elicit quiet uninterrupted sleep.

Then it was theater time. Lights didn't go out easily in the house as Tyanne and Viergine made the nights come alive. Tyanne was a master storyteller and talked profusely about everything from plants to animals to the stars in the sky, and Viola and I loved this about her. When she recounted the French fairytales I loved, "Cendrillon" or "Le Petit Chaperon Rouge," she worked up great dramatic emotion. Viola teased her: "Tyanne, you missed your calling; you should've been an actress."

Every once in a while, Viergine told us a traditional folktale.

"Krik!" was the call to start.

"Krak!" we called out to signify our interest in hearing a story.

Viergine scratched her head, trying to decide which one of Bouki and Malice's tales—the Haitian version of the dumb and the slow versus the smart and the quick—to tell. "Viergine, come on," one of us was bound to say as our anxiety mounted in anticipation.

In my favorite story, Bouki took care of Malice's old grandmother. After what was a very long sleep, Bouki told her, "Get up, Grandma. It's time to sit up." She didn't respond after several tries. So he threw boiling water on her to shock her into waking up. She smiled and gritted her teeth. Bouki was pleased. When Malice came home, Bouki rushed to tell him about his success. But when Malice saw Grandma, he yelled to Bouki, "Why did you throw hot water on Grandma? She's been dead for a while." I was ecstatic. Laughter reigned until the lights went out.

Those stories seeped down comfortably in my mind, much like water oozing through the cracked soil of a very dry plant. I forgot who I was. Days of hearing words. Nights of listening to stories. Tyanne taught me language, and she and Viergine, the art of storytelling. I was little, but I already sensed the importance of performance, of the preparation needed to receive what the other was offering, whether drama or comedy or anything else. These lessons infiltrated me so subtly, so naturally yet so fiercely, and carved a quiet resting place in me. The distance between them and me impassable until sometime later, when they would prove to be salutary.

I went to sleep every night in absolute silence that contrasted starkly to the sporadic sound of bullets that had become too familiar in the Port-au-Prince city streets. I was wild about feeling so close to the sky because I firmly believed that angels floated on the clouds of fog that hovered over us to the music of the fireflies. Mandedette actually pretended Viola, and I were angels in Kenscoff. She created that myth by sewing what she called "angel nests" to protect us from the cold during our first vacation there. Our little bodies floated in the warm "nest" pajamas she had sewn from a checkered flannel sheet, and our heads and ears were covered in the matching cone-like bonnets that made us look like alien creatures from outer space. Our faces were transfixed by the cold weather, the mist, and the foggy, overcast sky. To me, the stamp-size photograph of Viola and me in our angel nests remained a symbol of the way she protected us from the elements. I knew we were spoiled. We were loved.

As our return to Port-au-Prince approached, the thought of leaving Kenscoff saddened me, for I never felt a twinge of boredom. Rather, I felt the immensity of nature, the hardworking spirit of its inhabitants, the simplicity of life—and I was part of it. I felt as if I were stark naked in front of its natural perfection. I saw gigantic clouds of cotton tightly strung together floating above my head, and my voice couldn't penetrate them. I saw the fog surrounding us in the morning, at noon, or before sunset, depending on how it felt that day. I was a new me who loved to hear the silence of the cosmos, not the one imposed by others, which felt like a prison. Yes, Kenscoff was an exercise in pure hedonism.

One late July morning Mandedette and Papa came to fetch us for the downhill drive back home. Our reunion was joyful and full of loud kisses and tender hugs. But Papa was always in acceleration mode. He repeatedly pulled up the breeches of his pants holding his gun and looked repeatedly at his Longines watch. "Vi, Moka, vite, vite," he told us through the smoke clouds of his unfiltered Camel cigarette. My, "Why are you rushing, Papa?" unfailingly received the same response: an impatient smile and a look that made it clear our imminent departure wasn't negotiable. Viergine scurried to the car with our bags.

The goodbyes were never easy. From the backseat of the car, I watched Viergine rush back to her kitchen as she wiped away tears; Tyanne waved furiously with her face displaying a deceptive smile. The house faded out in a slow, painful haze. When I couldn't see Tyanne anymore, I cried. But I had enough dreams to last me until the next year, even a whole lifetime. I clung to these Kenscoff mountains where my identity seemed to belong to me more than to anyone else.

A couple of years later, I grieved that this paradise was temporarily lost because Tyanne migrated to New York, and the terror overcame all the other spaces where I lived. But then I knew I didn't belong in those other spaces because, in my skin, I knew I belonged in Kenscoff, for it stilled my world.

PLAYMATES

I remember the excitement of getting dressed up when we were going to visit the Jumelle girls. On the drive there, to Avenue Magny near the Champ-de-Mars, I giggled non-stop in anticipation of the heavenly place I'd soon enter. Clement Jumelle may have been a presidential candidate, and Papa's friend along with his three brothers, but to me, his story is linked to his nieces, his brother Ducasse's two daughters. That's because they were our playmates.

The huge, white concrete house was surrounded by a large forest-like yard, probably more than ten times our tiny one. I remember the fruit trees with their wide branches providing much-needed respite from the burning, tropical sun. Viola and I played bones, marbles, or hide and seek with the girls. Maybe we also jumped rope. I giggled with them and Viola. I talked to them, I played with them, and I giggled some more. I came and went amid the majestic trees. I lingered until it was time to go home. I missed that tiny world of sumptuousness before I even left it.

I remember the spacious veranda that circled around the courtyard. Papa and Clement, a dark, serious-looking man, sat back on their chairs and played cards, sometimes with his brothers. And they talked, perhaps, about politics. Perhaps they talked about Saint-Marc, where Jumelle was from, as was Papa's family. Perhaps they talked about how to continue advancing *noirisme* public policies. Perhaps they just joked around.

Then, quite abruptly, we stopped visiting the Jumelle family.

Papa didn't rush us there anymore. Viola, always the more sociable one, asked Papa if we could go play with the girls. My heart raced with joy until he responded that we couldn't. Sometimes, I said, "Allons chez les Jumelle!"

I always heard "No."

I was angry. Despite Viola's and my prodding, Papa never told us why he didn't take us back to that house to visit our friends. Papa wasn't the explaining type. The most innocent assumption on my part was simply that they no longer lived there and had moved very far away from us.

Occasionally, I passed the Jumelle house, which so impacted me with its enchanted little world of four little girls playing. Papa never stopped the car or even glanced in its direction. The sharp twinge I felt in my heart never lasted long, only long enough for me to realize how happy I had been playing with the girls in that huge yard full of overwhelming trees. I just kept wishing that one day I could go back there. Why did I have to lose my friends? Why couldn't I continue to go play with them? Why bother having friends, I thought?

I can't pinpoint the exact moment when I realized that those two friendships had slipped away and that magical space was closed to me forever. Maybe it was when I stopped hearing the name Jumelle at home; I knew it meant I couldn't say it either. On the surface, I had lost two playmates. But those playmates made me happy. It hurt. I missed them almost as much as I missed that tiny forest of fruit and ornamental trees.

Never did I hear of an announcement from Papa of anything about where our friends had disappeared to. And for good reason. Less than a year after Duvalier took office, in the early hours of August 29th, 1958, the lawyer Ducasse Jumelle, our playmates' father, and his brother, the gentleman farmer Charles, were shot dead by *cagoulards* a couple of miles from our home. A third brother, Gaston, a doctor, went into hiding before going into exile in Mexico and then New York. The fourth brother, Clement—immediately sought refuge in the Cuban Embassy. Eight months later, he died there of renal failure at forty-two.

Just days after, Jumelle's supporters stood around the perimeter of Sacred Heart Church, waiting for his funeral procession to arrive. A few blocks away, around the Petit-Four neighborhood, his family and friends in black and white mourning clothes walked in procession close to the hearse. A military vehicle stopped the cortege. An army officer exited the car. He kidnapped Clement Jumelle's body in the casket and the hearse.

Some said the body was taken to the national palace so President Duvalier could do some black magic with it. Others believed it was transported directly to Jumelle's Saint-Marc homestead for burial to keep him from becoming a martyr. No one could really be sure what happened except the one who ordered the kidnapping of a dead man on the day of his funeral and the one who carried out the ruthless and savage deed in plain daylight in front of hundreds of people. The body was never found.

I was a teenager when I discovered what had happened to the Jumelle family; the rage running through my body at their sacrifice frightened me.

MAÎTRE JACQUES

It was late 1958. Dusk had ceded its place to obscurity. The evening ritual was finished; we ate supper, Papa left for his night job, and we went to bed. Quiet overtook the house except for a fearless mosquito dancing petulantly around my head. I was happily wrapped in my cover sheet. That's when I heard voices near the hibiscus shrubs separating our house from our neighbor's. I didn't budge and closed my eyes tightly as if I were erecting a wall to prevent the entrance of a ghost. Eventually, sleep claimed me.

When I woke up with the timid morning light, I said nothing to Viola. I had turned six and believed I had some rights to my own secrets, despite the fear that had become my very cumbersome neighbor.

Over breakfast, Mandedette, dressed for work, was unusually quiet with Viola and me. When she got up from the table, she stepped out to look behind the door of our dining room to confirm Marlene wasn't lurking around and had, in fact, retreated into the outdoor kitchen. I had seen her do the same thing so many times before. Now I understood why; it went beyond ensuring privacy. Ours was a home where suspicion and distrust of servants was normal practice, as it most likely was elsewhere. It was as if a line separated our lives from theirs because cooks, gardeners, and maids could be spies potentially revealing to their friends and family, or to soldiers or *cagoulards*, family matters witnessed, or political opinions overheard that could harm their employers' reputation or put their lives in danger. We were in a world where imposed silence and paranoia marked our survival.

Finally, when Mandedette felt safe and was ready to talk, she murmured that Maître Jacques hadn't come home, and no one had been able to find him. His wife Aniz and their daughter Ginette were sad and very worried, she told us. Secretly, I knew that this news confirmed the urgency of the voices I had heard the night before. I sat speechless. How long had it been since he hadn't come home? Mandedette didn't say.

"Where is he?" Viola asked softly with a puzzled look on her face. She and I glanced at each other, trying to see if the other felt the same way. We waited. Mandedette's mouth didn't utter a sound. Her face was a mask hiding so many things.

"Where is he?" Viola whispered. We were in a stupor and both fell silent, as if we had succumbed to prayer, fate, or more likely, powerlessness. Mandedette was not able to reassure us, much less provide consolation.

Maître Jacques, whose intense brown eyes often looked straight through you, had, in effect, disappeared. This ebony-colored man with a well-rounded stomach and an ever-present briefcase, whom everyone, including his wife, called by his professional title *Maître,* had a small law practice downtown.

His wife Aniz frequently visited our veranda, where she and Mandedette, during long hours sitting on our bright metal chairs, conversed, laughed, and remade the world to fit their dreams. She had a gift for turning my quiet and bookish Mandedette into a carefree, laughing woman. Aniz was a voluptuous, honey-toned woman who strutted on top of spike-heeled mules, wore tight, straight skirts that highlighted her shapely derrière, laughed from her belly, spoke in a deep, husky baritone, and smiled with her small brown eyes. I adored her. I wanted to dress like her when I grew up.

Ginette came to our house almost every day to play with Viola, and I invariably tagged along.

From the moment I heard the news, I wanted to know how a man as tall and big as Maître Jacques could disappear. "Je ne sais pas." "I don't know," Mandedette responded in an almost inaudible voice, followed by, "Don't say anything to anybody about this." At our house, we weren't to repeat what we heard to anyone; keeping secrets was a way of life. Fear was in the room with us, and it lingered in my body for a long time, like toxic waste from a contaminated fish.

That night I went to bed in a daze that would last quite a while. I remembered how I was lost and abandoned and scared when Papa disappeared from our house, but at least we knew where he was, even if the hospital was far away. I imagined Ginette must have harbored the same feelings. I was very sorry for her.

Soon after, our lives changed dramatically.

Maître Jacques didn't come home the next day. Nor the next night. Nor the following day. He vanished. There was no trace of him. At night, I cried in my bed.

Then, Ginette stopped coming over to play. Not only had her father disappeared, but now she did also, staying inside her own home with her mother.

Their house drew in on itself; in the past, artists like Guy Durosier often played the piano and sang in their living room, creating a lively scene quite the opposite of ours, which was almost always quiet with Mandedette reading. I used to love the happy sounds and laughter that crossed the walls and the hedges to reach me in my bed, making for wonderful lullabies. Now, the small gingerbread-style dwelling to our right was noiseless like a tomb.

For the longest time, Ginette waited indoors for her father and Aniz for her husband to come home to the intimacy they shared. Viola and I also waited impatiently, less for him than for our friend Ginette and for my heroine, Aniz.

We so missed playing with Ginette that one day Viola asked if we could go visit her.

"No," Mandedette said.

"Why?" Viola and I asked in unison.

"This is not a moment to be playing," Mandedette told us, and I saw worry in her brown eyes. It was the same story all over again, with adversity engulfing us so soon after Papa had been shot.

"I don't agree, c'est pas juste, it's not fair," I cried, realizing even as a six-year-old that my childhood play area had been irrevocably reduced to a prison that was my own house. It was like a domino effect, with each domino the measure of someone's pain.

Maître Jacques never came back. The magnitude of the immediate shock of his disappearance frightened me. I was lonely because Viola and I lost another playmate, which made three lost ones. For weeks afterward, I lived as if, once again, I was being punished for something I hadn't done.

But I also missed Aniz, who had taken a fancy to me and me to her. She had a laugh that shook her whole body along with the chair she sat on, her strutting, and, most of all, her straight talk. "Odette, she is smart for a six-year-old. She can tie her shoelaces all by herself," she said once in her hoarse voice. Ginette, eleven at the time, still depended on her maid to dress her and tie her shoes. And on one of their leisurely afternoons, Aniz told Mandedette she liked that I wasn't afraid to speak to adults, unlike other children my age: "This little one has spunk." My eyes opened wide, and I burst into laughter from happiness. That woman built up my self-confidence.

There was no public mourning. No closure. A corpulent man who was a lawyer disappeared without a trace. In the city. And all we could do was whisper about it because we were shackled by the perceived— or the very real—state-imposed silence when we should have loudly denounced it from rooftops.

When Maître Jacques left our lives, I lost some of my innocence, and I became more isolated. His disappearance helped root an insidious fear in my life, as if I had a permanent shadow. Over time, it also became obvious that these hushed tones, whispers, suspicions, and sorrow had replaced our friends. With no good-byes.

RUE 3

ONDINE

I was six and a half when we moved to rue 3. I cried on moving day. I felt terrible because I didn't want to say goodbye to the only home I had ever known. After all, in that tiny house I first had big dreams while I lived in Viola's vivacious, generous, and friendly shadow and first learned brotherly love with Serge. It was also where, little by little, I started to absorb, and quite unconsciously, what constituted character and dignity. I discovered how women rose, how women bent down, how women rose again when their menfolk were attacked and when their lives were threatened, and how they instinctively protected their children. Just like Ginette's mother, Mandedette carried on despite the intrusion of barbarians in our lives. And in a subtle manner, she taught us how to resist with serenity and elegance, even though Viola and I were little girls.

Our new, very modest, two-bedroom house stood towards the bottom of a steep incline on a quiet, secluded street with gated houses of different dimensions on both sides. It was a tough hill to climb up and down, but Viola and I did. If we walked fast, as we often did, it would take ten minutes to travel the few blocks to our former home.

Our move coincided with the start of Mandedette's life as a businesswoman. A man came to plant a metal flagpole with an *Ondine Salon de beauté* placard in our tiny front garden. That was the grandiose announcement of the fifth occupant of our new house, the beauty salon. Given her love affair with books, it was somehow appropriate for her to name the salon *Ondine*, after the heroine of a book that had inspired ballets, operas, and paintings. The German French author La Motte-Fouque's Ondine was a dazzling female spirit of the waters who fell in love with and married a knight so she could achieve her double dream: obtain a soul and be human. The writer described Ondine as having delicate skin and long hair; most likely, some of Mandedette's ambitions were to produce those with the salon.

Maintaining a home and business in a narrow, three-room house was difficult, but Mandedette did it. I watched as she converted the living room into two distinct spaces divided by a large folding screen. Closest to the street was what became the salon, with chairs and standing hair dryers, plus assorted accessories. I huddled against the wall as she set up *Ondine* like a temple of beauty with an abundance of mirrors to look into.

On afternoons and Saturdays, wearing a white smock tied at her waist, she worked as a hairdresser and beautician. She had taken a six-month course at a beauty school in New York, just a year after my birth, to give herself a fallback career. She was like a trapeze artist at the matinee, who, by necessity, becomes a magician at night. I imagine that for her, it was not so much the desire to use her beautician's certificate to become financially independent. She was not the kind of person to cross her arms and do nothing when she was confronted with a problem.

Mandedette didn't allow me in the salon, but I found a way for it to become my sanctuary. I had to be invisible, so I was careful not to tip over the screen or be seen by her when I spied on the clients through its folds. I thought each woman who entered was already very pretty. I heard bits of conversations, even though everybody spoke in low voices as if they were in a church. From that little corner, I learned quite naturally from Mandedette that beauty had to be cultivated. I saw her demonstrate it by treating her clients with a very soft touch and doing everything: washing, straightening, and twisting hair in large colored rollers and styling it. She also did manicures and facials. Once, I saw her standing by a cot along the wall of the salon dressed in a light, white overcoat buttoned in the front. Her hands were moist with a white cream. On the cot, a woman lay on her back with her head wrapped in a white towel and flattened cotton balls on her eyes. I was intent on watching what would come next. Mother smoothed the cream on the lady's face gently in a circular movement, back and forth. Both were so quiet, I thought they could hear me breathe, so I slowly walked away from witnessing the facial Mandedette was meticulously giving the lady.

Later, as I took my supper, I asked her, "Why do women go to beauty salons when they are already beautiful?"

She responded with laughter: "So they can be even more beautiful."

She made me want to trade places with the client on the cot. Perfume blew in through the windows and back door, and I sat quietly taking it in as I smiled to myself. That's because our new house also had magic; it happened around dusk as the day went to sleep. That's when I smelled the sweet and fruity scent of the flowers of the ylang-ylang tree in the backyard, so invigorating as they fluttered with the evening breeze.

Mandedette now worked two jobs. Early every weekday, she went to teach French grammar at a public high school. I heard her plaintive whisperings when she'd mention under her breath, "*Ah, Madame Michel!*" Viola couldn't tell me anything about Madame Michel except that she was the principal of the school where Mandedette taught. Whenever I mentioned that name, Mandedette responded, "Beski."

Unbeknownst to me, the political climate in Haiti, particularly in Port-au-Prince where we lived, frightened Mandedette. In the two years since Duvalier had taken office, arbitrary detentions and arrests, political intimidation, and organized repression of people and organizations were *de rigueur.* In 1959, he also formally organized the *cagoulards* into an armed militia. They dressed in blue denim and were named the National Security Volunteers, or more commonly Tontons Macoutes—bogeymen. Mostly men, they covered the Haitian landscape to spy, torture, terrorize, or kill any suspected opponents to Duvalier.

Teachers like Mandedette and other professionals were threatened with job loss if they refused to publicly manifest their loyalty to Duvalier during sporadic demonstrations, I'd learned later. They were expected to attend them. Madame Michel, her school director, pressured her to participate in those demonstrations. Mandedette didn't. Did she and Papa discuss it? Perhaps, but not going could endanger her life; terror was at her doorstep. Not only did she receive several ominous warnings, making it increasingly obvious that her future as a teacher was uncertain, but her refusal to attend those demonstrations also put the director at risk for seeming to harbor an opponent of the regime. What had once been an engaging and joyful job now became oppressive and dangerous. Small things like these school incidents took on political significance as Haiti had become a police state. What was a personal challenge for her had also become a collective tragedy, as the barbarians insidiously took over the country.

In response to the suffocating political atmosphere, which many believed was beyond all hope, cadres of teachers, agronomists, lawyers, and doctors started to leave Haiti to migrate to the newly independent countries of Africa, where they found well-paying jobs and, most importantly, a certain freedom. Others went to Canada, France, or the United States, which effectively began the modern Haitian diaspora— the massive migration of Haitians—first by plane and, decades after, by boat. Mandedette was perhaps looking at such options.

Beyond the salon, the private part of our house was always warm and cozy. Mandedette decorated our living room with the mahogany Art-Deco furniture that always smelled so good, looked so shiny, and felt so silky when I ran my hands over it after Marlene finished polishing it. I loved the greenery of the large plants on the veranda, but I regretted that we had no garden where I could play hide and seek. Viola's and my small room, whose windows had white lace curtains, had our old twin beds. When I went to bed, I felt the potent ylang-ylang perfume surrounding me and permeating my sheets, my nightgown, and everything around me. I slept hypnotized by this fragrance, surely a gift of nature.

On rue 3, it was perfectly quiet, a quiet I felt in my bones. Yet, occasionally, I heard from down the street high-pitched, nasal drawl that seemed to be reciting whimsical, free-style poetry. "*Men bèl zaboka, kawot, pomdetè.*"

One hot and bright morning, Marlene and I ran to the small gate that separated us from the sidewalk. I saw colorfully dressed women street merchants, all with their heads wrapped, some barefoot, and some wearing flimsy brown leather sandals, singing the names of the vegetables and fruits they were selling. The big challenge was that the merchandise had to be seen before a sale; the buyer wouldn't purchase anything if she hadn't seen and touched it. That would be *chat nan makout* or "buying a cat in a bag," and exposing herself to deceit. When they walked away, the marchandes appeared carefree as they went up and down the street, but I noticed that they were carrying baskets weighing up to fifty pounds and sweating profusely. They must have had aching feet and backs and been exhausted since they continued their journey, sometimes taking isolated, unpaved alleys and busy roadways, stopping at huge houses and little ones. I dreaded the excruciating conditions endured by these itinerant women sellers.

That was one of the ways I met the world outside my home. These encounters, though ephemeral, were intense enough to teach my eyes to look at the women's faces, searching for the details that communicated their emotions and lifestyle, so different from mine. I saw that when they weren't working, they were working, just like Mandedette. It was a lot to bear. I was just amazed at these women, whose work seemed to never cease. I wondered if my life would be like that also.

TALES OF CASTE, CLASS AND COLORATION

Children don't know but only feel certain things. On rue 3, I had the impression I was living in another Haiti. I did feel a huge contrast that existed between the marchandes, our family somewhere in the middle, and our new neighbors living in grand houses all along the street. Some looked like the castles I'd seen in the movie *Sissi, the Young Empress.* Most had a floor upstairs and a flower-strewn balcony from which the neighbors could see us below.

One of Mandedette's childhood friends lived in such a dwelling, a mansion at the top of the hill, with her husband and seven children, and Viola and I often played with the two youngest girls. Next to theirs was a grandiose house with a flag sprinkled with small stars floating in the garden. A white family lived there with six children whose hair I thought resembled vermicelli in color and texture. According to Viola, their language was English, which she promised I would learn in secondary school. Mandedette said they were American diplomats.

Directly across from us was the Salgado family's large house, with dense and extravagantly colored bougainvillea cascading from its upstairs balcony. A scraggly, ebony-colored young man who sat on a low stool near the street picking his nose or cleaning his ears with a chicken feather had command of the high, wrought-iron gate, which he opened sparingly. When he did, I could steal a glance at the immense courtyard. Other times, I saw the Salgado children, an older girl with long black hair and two boys, only through their car windows as they passed. They looked so very different from us. Their hair was straight; ours was kinky. Their skin tone was a washed-out beige, whereas mine was dark. Viola and I walked to school every day; they went by car. My house was small and on one level; theirs was huge and two stories high.

We heard their names called and perhaps they also heard ours, but they did not acknowledge our presence by waving at us, as was customary. Viola never took my hand to go to their house nor did they invite us, possibly because they were several years older and possibly not. Of their history, or of why they were as they were and I as I was, I knew nothing.

I discovered that the eye was a powerful muscle. And I exercised it with great enthusiasm, watching the comings and goings of everything and everyone on the block. That's because my favorite pastime on rue 3 was following the automobiles up and down the street. They were quite a symbol. My perspective was necessarily from close to the ground since I was barely taller than the large schefflera at the corner of our porch. Most of the time, I was a pedestrian, so I saw them while walking with Viola or Marlene or as I stood by the front of the house. I found the cars to be wondrous. I also marveled at their enormity, mostly because I knew cars only from my experience in Papa's small Simca in which we seldom traveled, and then only for special events like going to a drive-in movie or to Kenscoff. Its windows stayed wide open to catch a breeze—any breeze—against the stifling heat since typical cars didn't feature air conditioning. Papa parked it on the street in front of our house for lack of a gated yard to secure it.

I vividly recall the shine of my neighbors' cars and the sounds of their engines. The Buick had a powerful one, like a lion's slow roar. I could distinguish it from far away because Mandedette's cousin had a silvery blue one, which he parked in front of his medical clinic next to our former house on rue Waag. The sight of a vintage Buick car still takes me back to a time when Papa and Mandedette were together, when I shot marbles in the backyard, and when our brother Serge twirled me above his head in my attempt to catch some clouds.

Madame Salgado had a big, shiny Buick. Elegant in her sunglasses, she was as cool as the sun was brutal, but she never withheld her generous smile and her waving hand. She followed the custom. From inside a vehicle, the polite greeting was a wave of the hand or a smile. This is what was done—we did it and expected others to do the same when they saw us. The rules of etiquette had to be respected. One of the first ones I learned was to greet people we came across with a *Bonjour*. Mandedette repeated incessantly, "Politeness is a sign of good education."

The American diplomats had a long car always packed with their blond children. The adults never greeted us, but the daughters, each with two long braids, smiled and waved energetically at me from the back window. I often wondered how they knew this Haitian custom.

Then there was Chaton's pink Cadillac convertible. Chaton, whom I knew by one name, seemed to change cars every year. A well-known photographer with a studio located on a lively downtown street corner, he lived a couple of houses down from us. When he drove his car, with the sunlight beating down on his cafe-au-lait skin and Clark Gable mustache that topped a smile I had seen only in the movies, nothing else on the street mattered. It was not as if we could resist, since we were absolutely captivated by him: his teeth were so white and his hair so black and perfectly slicked down. Chaton was the most handsome man I had ever seen in my short life, except for Papa. Even better, Chaton always waved to each of us. He also had me dreaming that he was a Mardi Gras Carnival king on a float, and I was his queen.

That's why it was a mystery to me that certain neighbors never waved back at us from their cars, as if we were invisible while we were clearly noticeable, standing on the sidewalk like two short, black poles in front of the house. Sometimes, I would timidly pull back my hand, interrupting my wave to someone who wasn't responding, afraid that someone else would see my embarrassment. Other times, a car would pass me with my hand in midair, and my smile unchanged. Then, Viola and I would stare at each other, laugh it off, and continue playing. But both of us were keen on being polite, as that was the mantra.

Madame Hogarth, a successful businesswoman who lived next door to the Salgado family with her son and two daughters, always kept her head high and straight when she passed at the wheel of her large black Mercedes. One had to see her. Her car shone as brilliantly as a mirror. She had jet black hair pulled back in a chignon, a perfectly round face, compressed lips, and a full bosom that seemed to embrace the steering wheel. Her younger daughter waved enthusiastically at us as if trying to make up for her mother's indifference. I reciprocated happily.

I wondered why Madame Hogarth never acknowledged our existence. I watched her pass and told myself the reason she was so oblivious to two little black girls waving was that she was busy thinking about other things. At first, it was puzzling, not even a bit hurtful. I surmised that one day she would wave. But as time went by, I started to feel shame at being ignored, as if I were invisible. The shame was deep at the core of my being. It became almost an obsession. Confused, one day I asked Mandedette: "Why is it that Madame Hogarth never greets us?"

"Don't be embarrassed by it. Elle est os-ten-ta-toi-re," Mandedette responded, focusing her wide eyes on mine. I wanted to know what that word meant.

"Os-ten-ta-toi-re," she repeated each syllable slowly like the teacher she was and that word became now ingrained in my brain. Ostentatious.

"It means someone acts as if she or he is important. Don't pay her any attention," Mandedette told me in her strong but calm voice, meant to alleviate my anxiety about our neighbor. With that,

I understood that Madame Hogarth, a widow with financial and material advantages my family didn't have, had bad manners as well as a rigid, unfriendly face.

Madame Hogarth had light skin, and I was a black-skinned girl, which probably influenced both our reactions, except that she was the adult supposed to be wiser than me, the child. To my younger self, she became the symbol of her privileged class. For my age, I wasn't abnormally sensitive, nor was I playing the victim or looking for acceptance, let alone love, from Madame Hogarth or anyone else on that street. In those days, I was not completely aware of there being a "situation" of class or color or ostentatious people to react to, let alone be controlled by; I only sought acknowledgment of my person, of my presence.

Mandedette was not a loquacious person, but she made it clear that we were better than ostentatious people, so I decided to ignore people who acted that way.

That day, dusk seemed to delay its coming, giving us the marvelous orangey light cast by the sun as it prepared to sink on Gonave Bay. Nature knew Madame Salgado's daughter—Michaelle—had her wedding reception across the street from us. Mandedette, Viola, and I watched wedding guests going in and out of the gate, much as today one watches live images of guests arriving on the red carpet of an award show. The gate to the Salgado's house stayed wide open. The music playing loudly in the yard sounded festive. From my front-row seat, I saw women with makeup and fancy hairdos that surely must have taken them hours to prepare. They wore long colorful dresses, all with fringes, pearls, or some other accessory. The men mostly wore white jackets, shirts with ties, and black pants. Everyone was smiling or laughing as they went in. But I was dismayed to see no one who looked like us going into the driveway; all of them had light skin, some even white skin. Apart from our "Ohs" and "Ahs" whenever someone particularly elegant entered the gate, we sat in silence, mesmerized.

I was attentive to the film of events I saw that night: the dresses, the jewelry, the glamour, the crowds, the music. By the time I got to bed, I decided to call my next doll Michaelle, because I believed that if I couldn't have a wedding like hers, I could arrange one for her namesake. But the wedding extravaganza could easily have eclipsed what my eyes also saw—the existence of another world, a white one composed of light-skinned Haitians with money and power living right across the street from me. In essence, they belonged to a caste with its color loyalties and its exclusive privileges. Their gate was wide open, but it was closed to us. I saw that we black-skinned Haitians had no part in their world except to be their gardeners, gatekeepers, and maids.

Light or "fair" skin color was considered a good luck charm, synonymous with wealth and elite social status. A Haitian proverb defines this skin-deep social stratum: "mulat pòv se nèg, nèg rich se mulat," or "a poor light-skinned person is considered black, and a *rich* dark-skinned black is considered a mulatto." This practice of hierarchization of shades of skin tone dated back to the days of slavery. The children of white planters and black slaves, called mixed-bloods or mulattoes, had more privileges and status than those of blacks. They attended Europe's schools. They inherited the land of their colonial fathers. This created a light-skinned elite: "the upstairs people" so aptly described by the French expression *les gens d'en haut*. It signified people such as my neighbors Chaton, Madame Hogarth, and Madame Salgado, who lived in a privileged world; their children's lives protected by high gates, big cars, and strict regimens. Groups were constituted mostly by people's coloration—the amount of melanin one happened to possess. Its accoutrements defined identity and social position and political power.

Those with dark skin, usually of pure African blood from the ranks of the subjugated captives, were purposefully disadvantaged by lack of education, land, wealth, and other resources. This translated into a class at the bottom of the strata—an underclass—systematically hampered over many years by social injustice, inequality, and social exclusion—the "people downstairs" This is not to say that there wasn't the impossible feat of resistance by these men and women left on the outside of the mainstream—the "moun andeyo." They set up their own autonomous system to survive. They dotted the landscape with lakou, a type of communal housing that defined the close social relations reminiscent of their African past. In contrast to the large colonial plantation system, they organized small-scale subsistence farming to ensure their livelihoods. They developed their own language—Creole. They practiced their own religion: Voodoo. People like Grand Angele, like Marlene, like the marchandes, and other vendors—sometimes poorly dressed, most times skinny for lack of adequate food—lived on the edges of society with their extremely limited access to government services, with their very modest means, but also with their own extraordinary stories. Even my seven-year-old eyes could see with absolute clarity on rue 3 the frontiers that divided them from others. The barrier wasn't always dramatic, but my consciousness started there. Was I precocious? Surely not, I simply noticed the obvious, the implacable reality of the class divide determined by the shades of darkness and levels of wealth. These revered values created a pernicious social hierarchy despite the fact we all had the same Haitian nationality. It explained the feelings of entitlement on one side and of exclusion and resentment on the other.

As a little girl on rue 3, I looked at the huge cars, the immense houses, and particularly the light skin color of their owners, without anyone ever having to tell me how to interpret them. I never heard Mandedette or Papa discuss the issue; perhaps they thought that Viola and I were too young to comprehend or that children should not be part of such discussions, so I didn't yet understand the full implication of what I had seen, but I had discovered on my own the chasm that existed between the upper class and the underclass. It literally separated them not only socially but geographically. Everyone also knew there was a marked social geography, with each class living in its own neighborhood, keeping their worlds so very far apart.

And then there was us: unabashedly Black but living in the middle. Papa and Mandedette had, in a certain manner, "integrated" this other world by moving into rue 3, almost like a buffer, hemmed in by the two worlds. We were part of the working middle class. At home, the present was not always easy and sometimes even precarious, but the future could be created. For that reason, the dreams Mandedette instilled in us mostly involved acquiring education, arts, history, heritage, and good manners; they all seemed within reach if we worked hard.

Even Viola had her own dream, which she revealed one afternoon: to marry someone who would give her a car as big as the one Chaton had and buy her a large house. Mandedette listened intently, kept smiling, and patted Viola's hair.

"What would the house look like?" she asked.

"Castel Haiti," Viola replied. It was familiar. Every day, we saw the landmark that stood on the steep hill behind the Salgado house. But to others, it was the tallest building in Port-au-Prince, a hotel with a panoramic view of the city and its expansive bay. That was the future Viola dreamed at such a young age. Even if the possibility of such a grand house was difficult to imagine, the future being so far beyond her reach. Mandedette said with sweet assurance, "My child, it is good to dream. One day, you will have everything you want."

Inspired by Viola, I also started to imagine life outside the borders of our house and our street. But my truth was blatantly simple: I wanted to be like my big sister. In a way she was my mirror, so I dreamed the future she wanted.

Still, Mandedette knew these people on rue 3 were different. She knew the tightropes to be walked. She knew the boundaries that existed. She knew we lived a separate reality from the upstairs people, and not only was she fine with being removed from it, but she didn't have any desire to be part of it. Mandedette's reality at the time was not about being invited to a wedding. People's pretentious attitudes were no more than a mere nuisance to her. She had learned from her father how to fight for justice. She'd spent time with her poet and writer friends discussing the social and political changes needed to make things better for people like her, so she naturally rejected the color and class dynamics of our privileged neighbors and countrymen. Her reference point was always

1946 and the matter of principle: that Haiti's color-coded apartheid society had to end, and black-skinned Haitians be included in state affairs and have the same opportunities as the light-skinned ones. Both she and Papa believed that the time for two separate Republics of Haiti based on the color of one's skin was over.

As an impressionable child, when I complained about Mrs. Hogarth that day, Mandedette understood the need to temper my emotions with comforting words, hoping these incidents that involved disdainful class and coloration issues wouldn't affect my innocence.

Years later, I saw Madame Hogarth again. It was in her home when her son, who had become my friend, invited me for drinks. Early that evening, he drove slowly into the dark metal gate I knew from my childhood. In the living room I saw his sister's large, black piano and an aquarium with lights shining on the angelfish, guppies, and goldfish. A first round of Haitian cola arrived with some peanuts and miniature triangular sandwiches.

Then she entered the room. There was silence. She looked at me and said, "Bonsoir." My eyes wandered to her son's face. I saw his frozen smile before I turned to hers to see the same rigid wall I had seen when I was seven. That incident made me recall the feelings and the memories of this other world on rue 3: Madame Hogarth's morose face in her Mercedes, Michaelle's all-white-folks wedding—the light-skinned, ostentatious one. Sometimes, there is a moment when you realize that you understood everything, even when you were only a small child.

IN THE VIELOT PASSAGEWAY

One afternoon, Viola grabbed my right hand, and we sneaked through the narrow pathway parallel to our house. Earlier that week, she had discovered two girls our age playing in the corridor. By week's end, we waved at them and they back at us. When she told Mandedette about her discovery, Mother forbade our playing there; she preferred we didn't stray from our house and its little front yard. Perhaps she also knew what we'd soon find out.

Nonetheless, after that first visit, the minuscule passageway became our enchanted playroom every afternoon after school. There in that corridor, just along the ylang-ylang tree, in the steamy air, we shot marbles, and we hopscotched, and we jumped rope, and we played bones, and we did the merry-go-around and we just laughed at each other's ridiculous jokes.

Our two new playmates and their five siblings lived with their father in a small, two-bedroom house just like ours. They were the Vielot family. Of their history, I knew very little, and I never saw the mother or the father.

One day, I asked one of the girls, "Where is your father?"

"He is at work," she quickly responded.

"Where is your mother?"

"She went to work in New York," she said.

"Why did she leave you?" I asked because it shocked me that her mother not only wasn't living with her and her siblings but was in another country.

"She went to get money so we can travel there," she told me.

It wasn't that I couldn't understand; the issue was that I wanted an explanation: "Where is New York? How will she get money there?"

"Je ne sais pas." She told me she didn't know, and we quickly returned to our play.

I was deeply curious about the whole thing. Our sneaking around was a great adventure, but I had to lie to Mandedette about it for fear of punishment. So I couldn't ask her where New York was or why people found money there since Viola had made me promise not to reveal our escapades. My fidelity to Viola was non-negotiable because she was my best friend, and I didn't want to disappoint her. She was so boisterous, and I breathed at her rhythm. This bit of freedom to play would vanish if Mandedette knew we had been dishonest and disobedient.

Still, this mother-going-to-New York-to-get-money scenario was a new concept for me because all the other playmates we had lived with their mothers. I thought to myself that I never wanted Mandedette to go away, and even less to a place as distant as New York. I found solace thinking this would never happen to me.

I was too young to comprehend that the Vielot family did these things to prepare for their own elsewhere—their departure from Haiti. It was like a slow, quiet withdrawal, almost like a truce intended to gain time to migrate to the elsewhere because their mother and father could not provide for and protect their children in the Port-au-Prince of my childhood. The Vielot had their own working-middle-class story, which fell somewhere between rue 3 and New York. Like my family, they were among the few exceptions in our street that showed the disparity between us and the people who were more advantageously placed. They were not necessarily looking for a paradise, but rather a chance perhaps to study, perhaps to create wealth, and most certainly to transform themselves from dreaming the future to actually having one.

I could not possibly know that much too soon my life would mirror theirs.

THE POLITICS OF HAIR

No matter what time I awoke, no matter whether the sounds of the day were church bells, French melodies, or the horoscope on the radio, I knew I had to follow a ritual every morning: dressing my hair. The task involved much more than combing; what at first was purely about looking proper eventually represented affirmation, power, and identity.

Viola always went ahead of me; it was her birthright as the first born. I watched Mandedette's long, manicured hands go firmly and repeatedly one over the other, sculpting Viola's thick, black strands of hair; it was like a dance of her hands. When it was my turn, if I sat still on the low child's chair placed squarely between Mandedette's legs, I would get mine braided fairly quickly, but I was rarely still. Mandedette usually started by making three parts in my hair. Sometimes, she pulled it so hard to untangle it that I thought the skin on my head would come off on the comb. At first, I cried, pouted, or complained, but eventually, I just got through it. Then she took the hair in her hands one part after another, one on top of the other, and she slowly, meticulously braided them together. Almost always, Mandedette tied a white ribbon around them.

But once a week, there was a special treatment. It had to be done right. That's why she grabbed her bottle of red Trichoferous liquid and her tube of clear yellow VO5 treatment and mixed their contents for two to three minutes in a small dish to get the exact texture she wanted before she applied the substance to my scalp and hair. She had decided my hair needed these products to grow long, so she adopted this ritual of massaging scalp and hair with the reddish combination, which also made my hair shine. And grow it did and shine it did.

With some variations on the coarseness of the hair and the number of braids, that was the way most little Black girls like me grew up with their hair. For me, dressing my hair became an apprenticeship on how to fearlessly create and frame my look, and ultimately myself. It laid the groundwork, and it wasn't complicated.

But then Mandedette decided that Viola and I should have straight hair for certain events. A boundary was erased, at least for holidays. So hair and holidays became intertwined. I had to have straight hair for weddings, for Christmas, and for New Year's; all such special occasions required that its texture change because she deemed my natural, extra-tight, kinky hair inappropriate. So, Mandedette paid a hairdresser to remove the kink temporarily with a burning hot flat iron picked off the charcoal embers. Put it simply, she fried my hair to make it straight. It was brutal. Sometimes, the iron also fried my skin. I was relieved when I didn't get burned because even though the straight effect lasted only a few days, the pain from the burns could almost negate the momentary pleasure of it. At times, the hairdresser used a curling iron to give me cascading Shirley Temple curls—another very different appearance.

The straight hair style created a huge break from all that was familiar and agreeable, to take me a few times a year to another environment, not entirely uncommon, but certainly not entirely agreeable. In effect, it forced me to exist in another space with its cruel, burning pain, its different aesthetic, and its ambiguities about the natural kinky identity and the straightened hair one—and the truth wherever it lay.

If at first the adults around me imposed the style on me, eventually, I expressed it in my own, almost obsessive manner.

One night, a friend of Mandedette's gave me a doll. I asked Viola to exchange it with hers. "Why?" she wanted to know. Because hers had long, straight, blond hair, and mine had short, curly, jet-black hair. She refused. I cried myself to sleep. In the following days, I asked to play with Viola's doll, and while she agreed she didn't allow me to comb the doll's hair. That boundary was simply too important to be crossed. I was livid; worse, no one said a word or made a gesture of consolation towards me. I was unseen and unheard. It hurt. Maybe this is what led Marlene to try to mitigate my obsession by making a deal with me. "I'll find a way for you to comb the doll's hair if you sit still and let me oil and braid your own hair without fussing," she promised. I knew she was serious because Marlene was our alternate hairdresser whenever Mandedette was too busy.

Having hair like Viola's doll symbolized belonging to a class of people who rode around in cars to go to school, who had large two-story houses with balconies, and who had access to what I had been made to understand I wanted. Frying my hair straight had not made me more beautiful or built my confidence; instead, it had somehow confused me to the point that I identified with the children of the white American diplomats or my very light-skinned neighbors who inhabited those houses and rode in those cars. By then, I had internalized enough of the colorism and hair texture narrative to feel what the French call *appartenance*: to identify with one group or a class, but even more worrisome, to also have a defined aspiration to belong to that group. At that time, I was too young to articulate any analysis. And in my world, no one uttered the obvious: the dominance of whiteness and its close cousin, light-skinned mulattoes.

And here my two stories came together, starkly different in hairstyles and social construct but bound together in one person—me.

One story told what it meant to be a proper little Black girl. On regular days in my normal life, I could assert my natural kinky hair, braided as it usually was, to go to school, play with my friends, and just be my African-heritage self.

The other story described me, the little Black girl approximating the white ideal of beauty. It happened on festive occasions where I would meet other people, and where these people, particularly strangers, would gaze at me. Scrutiny had to be projected on the me with straightened hair. The change in hair style attempted to write the natural out of me—almost like erasing me from myself. My hair had to reflect what society expected of Black girls like me: that we conform to a more traditional, a more prevalent standard of beauty, the very white beauty seen in movies.

A short leap into the future would prove to me that it was a highly efficient construct. When in the 1970s, during the dictatorship of Jean-Claude Duvalier, I vacationed in Haiti from Washington, D.C., where I was attending Howard University; I wore a massive Afro of my own natural, kinky hair. It seemed to touch the sky. A soldier came out of the central army barracks beside which I was strolling—the same barracks from which Papa had been shot in 1957—and brutally accosted me. Point blank, he said: "This hairdo is a provocation. What country are you from?"

"I am Haitian," I responded proudly in Creole, insulted that my nationality wasn't sufficiently imprinted on my face for him to recognize it.

"Haitians don't wear their hair like this," he replied, before threatening to arrest me if he ever met me again with my Afro.

Some years after, when I braided the natural hair into a long Rasta style, I met another soldier, this time near the Petion-ville barracks. He stopped to tell me that my hair was "threatening" and yelled, "You better cut your hair if you don't want to be thrown in jail!"

Both their responses made it obvious that not only did my natural hair tell a truth these soldiers found uncomfortable; it, in fact, seriously threatened them. They both had the goal of silencing me because my hair did not conform, or rather, I did not conform. I didn't even murmur audibly. My inner monologue told me that the ramifications of my hair were life-threatening under the dictatorship, for it equated anything appearing to be a mild dissent with an opposition to be suppressed immediately. Once again, the menace of violence rendered me completely silent. Remaining inaudible and microscopic was my mode of resistance.

The army of these soldiers was the kind of armed forces that at four in the morning on July 27, 1915—thirty-seven years before I was born and at the favorite time of day of werewolves, thieves, whores, and killers—massacred 300 men locked in their prison cells, among them my great-uncle Marcel, a political prisoner. Thirteen days later, his older brother Joseph, Papa's father, committed suicide from guilt over Marcel's arrest according to his honor code: *Potius mori quam foedari*—"better to die than to dishonor oneself." Papa became an orphan at eight years old.

It was the kind of armed forces that in 1940, savagely beat Mandedette's father after arresting him, along with hundreds of others, for his anti-government political activities in Cayes. Straight as a pencil in his values, unrelenting in his demands for justice, press freedom, and workers' rights, Julien Chikel died of complications from the torture a few months after his release. Mandedette became an orphan at fifteen years old.

It was the kind of armed forces that shot my Papa in 1957 for not standing up at 8:00 a.m. for the raising of the flag. Miraculously, I didn't become an orphan at four and a half years old.

So, each time I saw a Haitian soldier it's as if I were once again on the street near the Champ-de-Mars or in Petion-Ville being transfixed into fearful muteness by his potential and also very real violence.

But then, I realized that these soldiers had also absorbed the unspoken law of our culture. These men in uniform, with all their authority and power, were not accustomed to seeing Black girls and women like me wearing natural hairstyles. If this explained their comments about my hair, it didn't explain their mortifying threats of violence. That my natural hair could spark such a multitude of vicious conversations offered evidence not only of all the unconscious biases we—men *and* women—carried with us, but also of the brutal nature of the men in uniform in Haiti.

Time would alter everything, though.

As I got older I stopped following the established script concerning the beauty of straightened hair—even if I couldn't yet rewrite the book on the necessity of accepting the regality of my natural hair. That's why the soldiers perhaps felt the need to crush me for my hair: hair that curled too tightly, hair that stood up proudly to face the sky, hair styled with two braids to make me look like a Taino princess, hair that carried the stories of my pure African-blooded ancestors, hair that had majestic presence and tremendous power. By then I became fully aware that my unyielding natural hair was a political issue as well as a signifier of an identity and a social class.

But on rue 3, my eight-year-old shoulders carried the burden of that balancing act of straightened hair versus natural hair: holidays versus every day, conformity versus affirmation. I didn't know I could resist what defined me.

A SUNDAY AFTERNOON

I had the impression life was perfect for the four of us whenever Papa and Mandedette treated Viola and me to a special outing, always on Sundays. It occurred so rarely, that I might almost be inventing it. We prepared ourselves as if we were going to a party. After all, looking proper and elegant was important to both Papa and Mandedette.

I had never been happier than on that exceptional Sunday afternoon circa December 1960 when all four of us went for a promenade.

Papa put our one and only small bicycle in the trunk of the car and we huddled together as he drove through Champ-de-Mars. Then he entered the harbor area through the avenue that I and everyone else called the *Bicentenaire*.

On the surface, it was just another large road that went straight until it meandered to embrace the coastline around the sweeping views of Gonave Bay. But avenues, much like people, have their stories. It was built by President Estimé as the main thoroughfare of the seventy-acre Haiti World's Fair exhibit city, constructed to celebrate the bicentennial of the founding of Port-au-Prince. Estimé's modernization objective was clear: to show off Haitian culture to other countries and encourage tourism. He also signaled a culture shift by displaying much public art and by celebrating the talent of other black-skinned people. Opened in December 1949, with a parade of soldiers from the U.S. Army and Marines, along with a squadron of U.S. Airforce planes flying overhead, the road was named Boulevard Harry S. Truman in his honor. Very wide and bordered with immense palm and coconut trees, the boulevard went through the little amusement park city with exhibit spaces for over twenty countries. A few months later, the avenue had another day of glory when Estimé inaugurated the World's Fair itself on President Abraham Lincoln's birthday to pay tribute to the man who freed the slaves in the United States. All that history had little importance to me compared to what I found on the boulevard: wind that tasted salty as it touched my face, languorous music made by the soft sea waves, scintillating speckles on the deep blue water; and of course, the multitude of people strolling like ants going after bread crumbs. For lower-middle-class Haitians like my family, promenading on the *Bicentenaire* on Sunday afternoon was like strolling down the Champs-Elysées for Parisians.

Slowly, very slowly, the four of us walked along the pier, passing gigantic passenger vessels and merchant ships. I thought their tops must touch the sky and I would be like a midget next to them.

"How large are they?" I asked Papa. Instead, he exchanged a quick look with Mandedette and stiffened his shoulders.

"Ask your mother," he responded and moved briskly a few steps ahead of us for he had no intention of listening to her answer. Why was he so disinterested? I wondered. Whatever the cause, it didn't mute me.

"Does the ship touch the sky?" I asked Mandedette.

"Of course not!"

"How do you know?"

"I travelled in one when I returned from studying in New York. You two were very little then," she said.

Viola and I became obsessed with the idea of New York as soon as we knew she had been there. I vividly remember both of us questioning her about it, barely giving her time to respond: "How was it? Did you like it? Who did you meet there? What did you do there?"

Mandedette seemed happy to answer our questions and didn't once say, "Beski." We continued our leisurely walk on the pier while passing adults and children talking and laughing. I listened intently as Mandedette explained that it took several days for the ship to cross the sea to its destination. She described its inside as a huge house with bedrooms, restaurants, and even a ballroom for parties. I thought what a terrific adventure on such a vessel; here was my own mother who had gone to New York, just like the mother of the Vielot girls. Even better, she had returned.

I held her hand tightly on one side of her black-and-white, hand-embroidered skirt I loved so much, with Viola doing same on the other. I was in the warmest and most loving place in the world. Then we reached the culminating point: the fountain, one of the world's largest. I wasn't even shocked by the nakedness of the imposing, life-size sculptures of women called the ebony nymphs. I wanted to touch them to be part of their idyllic setting, but they were perched way above my head. Heat-crazed children smaller than I also tried but were restrained by their parents. The enigma of water shooting high up with its full force toward the sky captured my attention. Just as quickly, the water retreated. I walked around in circles to look at the fountain from different angles. The lights shining in different, dazzling colors fascinated me.

The crowds converged there at the fountain. I saw timid lovers seemingly embarrassed to be seen holding hands; children dressed in their Sunday best like us running carelessly to the water to get splashed; young men carrying wooden cases displaying sweet nothings like taffy, mints, and caramels; a middle-aged man with a wrestler's biceps pushing a three-wheeled ice fresco stand; and a couple of skeletal women selling peanuts from small wicker plates. Mandedette held our hands as we stood by the fountain talking, still talking about New York. Papa stayed several feet apart from us. I thought something was wrong but was too happy in the moment to ask him about it. Besides, he had already found a well-dressed man to talk to as he continued to show his lack of interest in our conversation.

While the sun dropped low in the sky, Viola got on the bicycle and circled the fountain, the sea breeze blowing on her face. Time seemed infinite as I waited my turn. I stayed close to Mandedette's skirt and watched other children getting thoroughly wet from playing in the fountain's lower basin. Even though I was entirely sun-drenched, I knew neither Papa nor Mandedette would let me attempt that game for fear of my getting wet, so I didn't even try asking permission to do it. I silenced myself by anticipation. I didn't want to be embarrassed by a "no" uttered publicly.

Just before we headed home, Papa led us to the food stand where a pretty woman with her head wrapped and pearls of sweat running down her forehead served us a small plate of *griyo*—pork morsels and fried plantains topped with *pikliz*, a mixture of thinly sliced cabbage, hot peppers, vinegar and carrots. As usual, Mandedette insisted we finish eating the food before going into the car, for we could never tell how many fingerprints our greasy hands could leave all over the seats. She was mute during the drive home. Papa didn't say a word and his habitual smile was missing. Even Viola and I were unusually quiet, perhaps saturated with happiness.

A triptych image of that afternoon at the *Bicentenaire* has stayed with me: Papa aside, detached, almost melancholic as he pretended to be busy with his friend but with his eyes turned toward us; the second one was of Mandedette, Viola, and me together, and in the last one, Mandedette alone in a foreign land marveling at her discoveries and absorbing new knowledge.

Looking back, it seemed to me our family outing had opened a fault line—a somewhere else represented by the name New York. Perhaps my asking about the inside of the ship was the crack in the sheen of our reality that Papa wanted to avoid.

I didn't know it, but that evening on the *Bicentenaire*, Papa must have known another life full of uncertainties was beginning for all of us— that our days as a four-person family would not last much longer. He either couldn't or wouldn't bring himself to find a way into our conversation about New York because in his mind, as in most people's minds, it meant a place that separated families—in other words, migration, and specifically for him, the migration of his wife. By then, Mandedette had already taken a step away by having discovered New York, a promised land to her and so many others. And worse, both Papa and Mandedette knew that the four of us would not ever be together again. Never. Except for a goodbye.

THE TRIBE OF ORPHANS

The sun was unforgiving in Port-au-Prince but on that same day— January 20, 1961—hundreds of miles away in the bitter winter cold, millions of people celebrated as John Fitzgerald Kennedy was inaugurated President of the United States. Viola and I had skipped school that Friday, but it wasn't for a happy occasion; rather, it was so we could all be together at the International Airport. Papa had driven Mandedette, Viola, and me there, but only the two of us would be with him for the ride back home. In Washington, D.C., the greats of the planet gathered joyfully for this change of power on the national and world stage, but in Port-au-Prince that day was earth shattering for Viola, Papa and me who would soon be left behind.

Our family was at the airport to say goodbye to Mandedette, who was taking the Pan Am flight to her new destiny in New York. With a large hat hiding most of her radiant face, and wearing an embroidered black dress as if she were in mourning, she regally climbed the steps of the airplane, stopping only to blow us a kiss and wave a hand before she disappeared. My world changed forever.

The evening before, as clouds overcast the sky, as birds flew in formation back to their nests, as tidal waves broke in the ocean, and as the sun went down, Papa went to his night job. He left his *Pour un Homme* lavender scent in our bedroom when he said goodnight after supper. "*Kilik, kilik,*" he whispered in my ear to my non-stop laughter. "*Bonne nuit.*"

Then, Mandedette sat on Viola's bed to talk to us. In her soft, velvety voice, almost a whisper, she told Viola and me, "I'm traveling to New York tomorrow morning." I thought, *No, not again.* Not at the pinnacle of my happiness with the four of us.

It took some time for me to comprehend what she was saying.

"What? Why?" I asked, along with Viola.

"Teachers don't make much money. The salon is not making money," she explained. She was going to work so she could take better care of us.

"What's going to happen to us?" Viola asked. We would stay in the house with Papa and Grandma, who was arriving at dawn to live with us until Mandedette returned.

"When are you returning?" we both asked.

"Soon."

I cried. Viola cried. Mandedette cried. Misery hid the future. After a few minutes that were eternity, she kissed me goodnight, did same to Viola, and left our room, slowly closing the door behind her.

Viola whispered that she had overheard Mandedette tell a friend at the salon that she owed a lot of money to various people so she couldn't take care of Viola and me. By then, perhaps Mandedette realized she was living a story different than the one she had married for, but I didn't know any of that. I believed Viola, but she swore me to secrecy. I thought it sounded a lot like the Vielot family story, and I dreaded waiting years to see my mother, like our playmates in the house behind us had for their mother.

I simply covered my whole head with my sheet and wept.

My life as an orphan began that Friday. I had just turned eight when Mandedette disappeared from our lives.

She closed her salon, which made me feel doubly orphaned. Peeking into her world of male and female seekers of beauty was a favorite pastime of mine. It helped fashion the me I wanted to become.

That evening at supper, Papa read us the cable Mandedette had sent him: the plane had landed in the freezing cold of New York, and she was staying with Tante Yolande.

The thought occurred to me that my parents were no longer together. Yet I heard no noise. I saw no detritus. I also noticed no affection. But the change was monumental: we had been four in the morning, and at supper, we were three. It was a nightmare for me. The emotions of the last hours left a deep scar in my being, as if a piece of glass had splintered in my eye, where the shards remain still.

I had the feeling that the farther away Mandedette was physically, the closer she was to my heart. I envisioned her sitting in front of her dressing table, putting on makeup. I saw her on the veranda reading. I heard her heels click on the mosaic floor or her voice calling, "*ViolaetMonique, venez ici!*" I smelled the scent of Shalimar in her bedroom, in mine, in the bathroom, everywhere. That's the way I knew to keep my mother close to me. I didn't want to lose her. I was four years old all over again and retreated nostalgically into my earliest childhood memories of picking mint leaves to make tea, hearing silence, and seeing thick fog in Kenscoff.

I saw no logic in her leaving us. "I want Mandedette," I yelled to myself all the time in the silence of others. If Viola heard my futile whisperings, she kept quiet about them. She didn't complain or show any sign of her most likely unquestionable suffering. I liked that my sister was strong.

The shock of abandonment accompanied my pain and loneliness. The suddenness of her departure made it seem so cruel. This angered me the most. I was livid that she hadn't told Viola and me much earlier that she was traveling. That could have made the shock less brutal since I would've been able to prepare myself against this overwhelming feeling of loss.

"Why did Mandedette leave us?" I asked Viola, oblivious to the fact that she was probably asking herself the same question. She didn't answer; she just turned away from me.

"Why did Mandedette go away?" I asked Papa.

"She went to work. She'll be back soon," he said as he tried to console me with an affectionate pat on the head and a big grin. *Was it because of him that she went away?* I wondered to myself, even though I had never heard either one of them raise their voice at the other. On the contrary, they hardly ever spoke to one another. Was it because of money? But Papa was working two jobs just as she was. *What was it?* I kept wondering.

No answer ever completely satisfied my enormous curiosity or sated pain; all were hollow, even irrelevant.

"Why did Mother leave?" I asked Grandma, Mandedette's mother, who came from nowhere I knew that sad Friday morning with a single, small suitcase to be a surrogate mother to Viola and me. Over the years, she had visited us with gifts of fruits, vegetables, grapefruit marmalade, and thick peanut butter, but she had a hurried walk and never stayed long. Now, she slept on a small cot Mandedette fit into our minuscule bedroom.

Along with *café-au-lait* skin, a large nose, and full lips that framed well-aligned teeth, Grandma had big eyes that could glow like fire. Her medium-height figure was thick-boned, but she was agile and quick on her feet—all evoking her years of constant travelling. Grandma's life was a wandering one. Born Antoinette Laroche in 1903 on a small, hilly homestead in the southern village of Maseillan, she attended primary school and could read and write reasonably well. At fifteen, she and her mother Elisiane moved to live a few kilometers away in Cayes, the capital of Haiti's southern department. That was typical of life in rural areas where people often migrated to the nearest big city hoping to find work opportunities to supplement whatever little they were earning from farming. Two years later, when she met Julien Chikel, Grandma had blossomed into a stunning beauty. How or where Grandma's love affair with Julien started was a complete mystery.

Mandedette was born of that union in October 1924, one month after Grandma turned eighteen.

Much too soon after, Grandma's life was harrowingly disturbed when she learned another woman had borne a child, Anthony, at the same time as she, and by the same man, hers. That threshold of a parallel woman and baby was unsurmountable; it sealed her fate. Rather than accept Julien's infidelity, she made a radical decision that would change the course of everyone's life. Her action was eloquent: at dawn on a spring day, she abandoned Cayes taking her daughter, Mandedette—then six months old—and returned to Maseillan.

Back in 1925, being fiercely independent must have been fascinating for a teenager, but it also came with its burdens, multiplied when one had a child. This was why Grandma, with a baby and few, if any, material resources, turned to the women of the family, who would always be her first and last recourse. From Maseillan, she moved a few kilometers away to Aquin to reside in her aunt ManSissi--Lamercie's house, close to a good primary school Mandedette attended. Grandma had an entrepreneurial spirit and steely determination, and she was a hard worker, all of which could be the ingredients for a successful self-made woman—and that's what she wanted to be. She sometimes worked as a small trader, and then she became a loan shark. But her trailblazing forays into business proved unsuccessful and she struggled through raw, taxing moments to feed and educate her child. With Mandedette in tow, she struggled because of material poverty and moved west a few times to her aunt Chimene's in Port-au-Prince, attempting to stay afloat. While this peripatetic lifestyle opened Mandedette's eyes early to big-city life, these efforts didn't work out either.

Grandma saw no future for herself and her daughter, but she understood all too well the burden was on her to make a radical choice. She wasn't the sort of woman who'd give up on the dreams she had for her only child. So, one late summer morning in 1936 after Mandedette had finished primary school, Grandma tried something different. She grabbed eleven-year-old Mandedette to take the dawn bus to the city of Cayes and left her with her economically well-off paternal family, where she was warmly welcomed. Grandma's wandering days were over; her child was taken care of, and she found steady work as a governess—in other words, a maid for rich people's children.

I thought there was astounding irony in deliberately taking care of strangers' children when you are unable to take care of, let alone nurture your own.

But the most supreme irony was that in New York, Mandedette also took a job as a nanny to four children. Semantics aside—be it governess, nanny or child's maid—Mandedette, just like her own mother before her, had to mother another woman's children to provide for her own. In the realm of possibilities, leaving one's children with anyone was not only a highly difficult thing to do, it was perhaps the most enormous sacrifice one could make. It was obvious that neither of them wanted to make that choice for their children, and each had postponed the decision as much as possible. Perhaps each mother thought if she left her child with her own mother, or in the case of Grandma with her father, it would be a lesser dislocation for the children than if they were left with strangers.

Was it abnegation? Was it courage? It certainly appeared to be a little of both. Mandedette had to defer, or perhaps even mourn, her dreams of teaching, of watching Viola and me grow, so she could be economically independent and provide for us. The dreams eluded her. She made her choice and went to New York. She did what her mother had done. It was Mandedette's experience, it was her reference, it was *the* model she knew and followed when she left us with Grandma.

Perhaps that's why Grandma's answer as to why Mandedette left me was, "She went because she loves you." She knew all too well the burden Mandedette was bearing despite stating the choice as one of love. Yet, it was exactly that love that I questioned. But something else was deeply troubling; their inability to comprehend, empathize or appreciate that they had left their daughters bereft of a mother's presence, which I lived as an abandonment. Neither mother—whether Grandma when it came to her daughter, nor Mandedette when it came to Viola and me—immediately addressed the depth of the trauma their children would face.

But Mandedette knew. Better than anyone. She knew at eleven when she started living without her mother.

Now, I knew at eight. I was devastated, insecure, and vulnerable without my mother.

Grandma marked her territory as a surrogate mother the very first night by coming into our bedroom at bedtime to invite us to pray with her.

"Kneel," she said in a loud, firm voice. She prayed: *Hail Mary, full of grace...* and signaled for us to join her. We repeated each phrase after her in unison.

"Again," she ordered. It didn't feel like an invitation, even less like a choice.

"Hail Mary, full of grace," we continued praying.

"Again," she said. I had to recite the prayer ten times in tender harmony with its corresponding rosary beads.

"Let us continue with 'Our Father, who art in heaven,' she said decisively, yet softly this time.

One furtive look from her sufficed to inform me when I had erred; Grandma didn't appreciate missed words. Mandedette, I thought, had never forced me to pray at night, much less multiple times. But in a way, I was ready for Grandma's prayers. I was studying catechism as a prelude to receiving my first communion a few months later, and I regularly attended Sunday Mass, but her prayers seemed, nonetheless, an imposition. She prayed all the time. Every morning, every night, and sometimes at midday, she asked for God's benediction as she fingered her white rosary. Since he was her savior, she considered it her mission to prepare Viola and me for our religious awakening. It was a ritual I had no choice but to adopt.

Even though her stringent rules did nothing to endear her to me, still, these were moments when nothing else mattered because I was able to detach myself from all thoughts when I closed my eyes. I prayed and prayed and even began to enjoy it. I was alone with God as I knelt next to Viola and Grandma, transported to a quiet place where I believed someone was listening to me. I reached an easy feeling of solitude, of joy, of profound serenity, almost like an initiation.

One night Grandma announced that *Bon Dieu,* the Good Lord, was her husband for he was the only man she loved. The truth was, Grandma had never remarried, because, as she told Marlene one day, "I gave up on men the day I walked out on Julien Chikel." The wound from Grandpa's betrayal was so profound that she took a vow of abstinence from all men, silencing her body rather than exposing herself to further hurt and disappointment. This disenchantment with men must also have hardened her heart, making her rigid and uncompromising, but then that's how she chose to live her life. Middle-aged, bitter from her difficulties, fanatically devoted to her religion, and irritable, maybe because she had to leave her own job to take care of her daughter's children. This was my Grandma.

Things changed in other ways with her arrival. For one, I woke up at dawn every day, not because I wanted to but because of the commotion she caused when she prepared for the daily 4:00 a.m. mass she attended nearby. After church, she spent her day in our backyard, which she claimed as her territory. There, in the outdoor kitchen, she planned our meals which rarely varied from a few pieces of meat with boiled plantains followed by delicious red kidney beans served on top of rice or corn meal, all cooked by Marlene. They chatted all day about God, about food, and about their respective families.

When Papa was home, she laughed and shared jokes with him. At first, I found it strange, but I easily understood their camaraderie after Papa told me that he was a mere two years older than she.

My universe before Grandma's brusque arrival consisted of quiet times and practically no punishment because we were generally well-behaved children. Mandedette saw to it. Viola and I were not familiar with strict discipline. Mandedette showed her authority with her presence and her firm voice, which she rarely raised and then only when her silence or the fury showed in her eyes didn't work. Then we immediately obeyed. Papa's authority arose from his tall, dominant stature and the strength of his smiles. Mandedette and Papa both believed their eyes and facial expressions alone had the power to right any of our wrongs. I don't remember any corporal discipline by my parents except for a couple of times when Mandedette had me kneel for a few minutes, or Papa pulled hard on my ears. Now force, loudness, and fear had entered my life with ferocity.

Some of my fear of Grandma owed itself to her domineering ways with us but some of it also came from what I saw one day. She was doing her *toilette de chat* with water dripping from a bucket when I secretly glimpsed her enormous breasts, which drooped to her waist. She threw one breast over her shoulder to wash her torso, then dropped it and repeated the same movement with the other. It was not an illusion. It was the first time I had seen such gigantic breasts, which occupied her whole stomach as if they were two small beasts. They appeared so unusual that they made me terribly afraid of seeing them again.

Despite Grandma's presence, I felt like a motherless child.

Regardless of what she said, and Papa echoed, I felt Mandedette went away because she neither wanted nor loved me. My body ached as her absence had dug a road in me; it destroyed my insouciance. I cried myself to sleep every night. My infinite sadness returned her to Haiti like a shadow attached to my stomach, as if it were a Siamese twin, impossible to let go yet lifesaving. I wanted to comprehend my situation and had many questions. If she loved me, why did she abandon me? How was being without my mother "best" for me?

Still, nothing could compensate for my broken heart. Nobody replaced Mandedette in it. I simply closed it down, like a turtle pulling its head inside its shell to protect it from a predator's clutches. I had a taciturn, sour look for weeks, since most of what had brought smiles to it had disappeared with the cloud of dust left by the Pan Am jumbo jet on that Friday morning. I didn't allow anyone to get close to me other than Viola and Papa, who must also have felt abandoned. Viola was the only one to occasionally retrieve me from my isolation. At the time, I didn't have other friends in whom to confide my misery; she was the only one. She continued to hold my hand more firmly when we walked to school, as if she were assigned to be my protector because I had become a member of the tribe of orphans.

One morning a few weeks after Mandedette left Haiti, Papa announced we were moving.

"Where?" Viola asked about one second before I did. Silence. Papa managed the soft smile I knew him for. Nonetheless, I happily got in his little car and saw Grandma waving at us with a half-smile and muttering something that sounded like a prayer. Papa said Grandma was returning down south to Aquin and Marlene would look for another job. That's how I left rue 3.

RUE OSWALD DURAND

THE LAKOU

Papa took us to his house. By abandoning the arrangement Mandedette had made for us to live with him and Grandma, Papa made it audaciously clear that he, alone, was in charge.

When I moved to rue Oswald Durand, the natural order of things as I knew it changed; it was yet another radical shift.

I can place the address of Papa's family compound on any map of Port-au-Prince, almost blindfolded. It was 114, rue Oswald Durand. The street had the honor of being named for the first known Haitian poet, whose lyrical work "Choucoune" was sung by Cuban superstar Celia Cruz and translated into the international hit "Yellow Bird" crooned by the civil rights activist Harry Belafonte. Located in the center of the new and expanding area of the city, migrants from the rural countryside settled there in the mid-1800s to early 1900s. Many would become the carpenters, masons, seamstresses, and other working-class people of the capital.

The compound was a small lakou—a traditional African-style rural courtyard filled with homes of extended family members—with three independent houses clustered inside a low brick wall enclosure. Except this one was located in an urban area, the Morne-a-Turf side of the Bas-Peu-de-Chose neighborhood of Port-au-Prince. It was around the corner from the State University Medical School hospital where Viola and I were born, an easy five-minute walk north from the National Palace, a fifteen-minute one to my school or south to the cemetery, and two blocks up from the stadium named after Sylvio Cator, the Haitian long-jump track athlete who won the silver medal at the 1928 Olympic games in Amsterdam. The sounds, scents, sights, and occupants of what Viola called "our magnificent and supernatural voyage into the lumpen proletariat" slowly became part of me.

The lakou was a world of small businesses, constant radio music, and card games. Continuous movement, like a ballet, defined it. Everyone knew his or her place to stand, to sit, to move on silently, because a furtive glance or a name called were known codes to all. The lakou transported me to a universe that was different in colors, people, and activities. I felt as if I had left a country of stark black and white hues to travel to another with vivid colors and continuous noise.

Even the language was different. When I lived with Mandedette and Papa, I spoke French, and only uttered Creole with Marlene. In my new home, everyone spoke Creole, not only to each other but also to me. At first, I resisted and held on to what I had—to this small detail of my former life—and responded only in French. That didn't go well. Sometimes they rolled their eyes at me or exchanged smiles with each other while mocking me; other times they simply laughed at me. I felt small again, as I had when the wealthy residents of rue 3 had ignored me. I had tremendous difficulty navigating that change, which Viola found a little easier perhaps because she was older. I was overcome by an immense feeling of not belonging, almost like my identity or a prized possession was taken away from me. Still, they said things such as, "She is acting like a star," and "She thinks she is better than us." I was at war with everyone who said that; though angry, I said nothing.

After a few weeks, they decided I was brooding and aloof and left me alone. Eventually, I gave in and started speaking Creole, except to Papa, to Viola, and in school.

Still, I felt suspended somewhere between New York and Port-au-Prince, learning to understand the back story of Mandedette's letters while also apprenticing the language of my paternal family. I remembered the values mother had instilled in me while discovering new ones. I appreciated the virtue of silence while distinguishing the music from the noise. I recalled happiness with four while managing my solitude in a crowd.

I didn't know whether Papa was caught off guard by Mandedette's departure or simply didn't have enough money to finish his house because it had the monotone grey of unpainted concrete. It was a quiet oasis in what used to be the lakou's backyard, cool because air circulated through the latticed cement blocks and somber as if bathed by dusk. I loved its narrow balcony and spent hours there looking down in fascination at people passing through the tiny corridor or singing off-key, to no one in particular, Dalida's "*Papa, buy me a husband.*" Various scents made their way to our home as the distant cacophony from downstairs filtered in: coffee roasting, codfish cooking, red beans boiling, and most of all, the burning of charcoal, since it was the only fuel used in the outback stoves.

While it stood unpainted for the longest time, the house suited Papa. No one came to visit, as if he told everyone to stay away, except for us and Anna, our new maid.

I liked to think that Papa moved us there to be close to my grandmother, Grand Angele, the matriarch of our family and the owner of the lakou. She was born Angele Paul in 1877 in a large, extended family in Charlier, a village of mud houses topped with grass roofs, located on the banks of the Nippes River, near the southwestern port city of Miragoane. The family had deep roots in the Yoruba and Igbo tribes of West Africa and in the Kongo one from Central Africa through invisible and mysterious spirits or gods called *loas*. The *loas* had made the journey on ships that carried human cargo—African men, women and children—victims of macabre human trafficking to Haiti. The centuries-old separation and enormous distance between Africa and Haiti did little to alter the rites celebrating these spirits, which survived through brutal slavery on sugar, cotton, indigo, and coffee plantations and through the war of independence. Through the practice of their religion, Voodoo, Grand Angele's family remained in communion with these ancestral spirits. Sometime in her teenage years, her father had initiated her in Voodoo.

I loved Grand Angele's favorite place in the lakou. It was the minuscule pink and yellow-hued brick *boutik,* or convenience store, which fed her family for many years. Grand Angele built it in front of the main house so as to face the street, the psychiatric hospital, and more importantly, the majestic ceiba tree. Her customers could order peanut butter by the spoon on dry, crackling biscuits, canned milk, bread, cigarettes, kerosene, candles, balloons, and thread—almost anything. Grand Angele sat like a queen on a throne in her traditional bar-high chair, her back framed by the vine canopy and hidden behind the big glass jars that contained varieties of multi-colored candy. Imagine having a grandmother who made her living selling sweets!

I liked the mints, caramels, lollipops, and Bazookas; I loved the blue taffy best because it was long, and I could make rings with it until it disappeared down my throat. My second favorite was the long, white mint that stuck on my back teeth for the longest time. Grand Angele let me choose whatever candy I wanted except for the chewy, brown caramel. It was as precious as the Holy Eucharist, since Grand Angele gave it to me only on special occasions—a birthday or a good report card or just to show me some extra love. My eating all these sweets was curtailed when I went to see Dr. Argant, the dentist. From his immensely tall body with white hair and slightly bent shoulders, he admonished me for my sweet tooth and promised to see me often. I became a regular at his clinic for the months it took him to repair all my cavities.

At times, Viola and I played make-believe customers at Grand Angele's boutique. "Bonjou Madan Paul," I said, mimicking an older woman's voice. She always recognized our little fingers from her high counter and asked what we wanted, "Kisa nou vle, timoun?" Then we'd rush out to hide.

Even today, the most prominent image from that period is of Grand Angele on her large, high-backed rocking chair, sliding back and forth like a slow dance with time. Despite being frail, almost skin and bones, she retained her regal demeanor. She had the darkest skin and the whitest, kinkiest hair my eyes had ever seen. I liked to touch it; it felt like the rough cotton I had seen on a bush, but so much brighter.

My lips fell softly somewhere among her infinite wrinkles when I bent down to kiss her, with a "Bonjour Grand Angele" in the morning, and when I came home from school. She looked like she had earned every one of her eighty-eight years.

"How is the body feeling?" I asked, in one of the traditional greetings.

"M ap kenbe," she responded, "I am holding on." I was too young to understand what she was holding on to, too scared to ask for what she might tell me. Sometimes, I saw a faraway look in her eyes, as if she saw something in the distance that neither I nor anyone else around her could see. Other times, I caught her gazing absently at her lakou. I felt her fatigue and every day she seemed a little farther away from me. But her wide, brown eyes were always filled with love and kindness.

"Bring me a little coffee, please," was her refrain morning, noon, and afternoon, right after she greeted someone. Coffee defined the day in Grand Angele's lakou. It provided rhythm to every event, every moment. It was as if a coffee-tasting ceremony started anew with every visitor, and she received a steady stream of them, all feeling compelled to visit her with their demands, problems, and affections.

Each cup of coffee was a creation, and it didn't really matter how much time it took for it had to be done right. That's why I decided to learn how to make coffee. Viola wasn't party to my decision, and I didn't tell her or anyone else. My style was to beg, watch, and help. It always worked. I would rush to the small kitchen out back to beg Anna to let me help while she put the beans in the *chodyè* or pot, to grill them, while breathing in air thick with smoke. I hurried to put my small hand over hers on the wooden spoon to turn them over, for they had to be evenly grilled on the small charcoal stove she hovered over as she hummed a song. Then, she put the beans in the small drawer of the hand-cranked coffee mill to be ground. Sometimes if she wasn't in a hurry or in a bad mood, she, with sweat on her brows from the heat, allowed me to turn its handle while waiting for the pot of water to come to a boil. Afterwards, she pulled the tiny drawer to reveal the ground coffee and poured it into the burlap percolator.

"Hold it tight," Anna said as she gave me the thin handle twisted from a metal hanger. Then it was time to pour in the boiling water and watch the coffee seep through into the enamel *cafetière* or French press. By the time Anna served the hot, black liquid in the small, white enamel demitasses, every corner of the house was permeated with the scent of coffee. Grand Angele's mouth twisted slightly as she took the first sip of the blazing hot coffee. "Pakèt afè. Mesi wi," she always said, "Big deal. Thank you," after tasting it with a smile of satisfaction.

After multiple trials and as many tastings, I learned to make a perfect cup of Haitian Arabica espresso. For me, it was a way to be part of Grand Angele's family ritual. I giggled as I realized Mandedette would never have let me get so close to the boiling water, because I might get burned. She was probably right, but with her in New York, I had more privileges.

Indelible in my mind was the centerpiece of the lakou, the small, two-bedroom, Victorian-style house built of wood and decorated with lacy facades that seemed infused with love. I imagined the paint had probably shone brilliantly in the sunlight at one time, but now it was colored a dark green that had gradually lost its luster yet still contrasted well with the tall, white louvered doors that everyone called *jalousie*. The house had the tough soul of a place where many lives had intersected, and destinies been determined. The family living room had a white wood chair set with a matching table on which stood a vase of colored plastic flowers that functioned mostly as a dustbin. It was the least-used room in the house, despite the steady stream of daily visitors. It served primarily for important visitors deemed unworthy of the informality of the veranda or when two adults needed to hide or whisper. I disliked that but had my way around it: I pulled back the louvers of the interior doors to eavesdrop. Viola did the same and remembered it was there she first saw a couple make out.

Papa first really moved into very sharp focus for me then and there in the centerpiece of the lakou. That's when I learned that details were terribly important to the stories of Papa's family. The predominant one was high up above our heads on the wall of the living room: two gigantic, poster-sized photographs. The one of a white man with a slight moustache caught my attention with his serious expression, straight black hair brushed back, dark eyes fixated on the camera, and wearing a military uniform with braided highlights. He looked very much like the Army general that he was. Next to it was that of an ebony-black woman whose kinky, salt-and-pepper hair was neatly rolled back. It was Grand Angele with her high cheekbones that were the mark of pure African blood because her family had never mixed with any other race. My gaze was full of amazement as it went from one stunning image to the next. I recalled a rare conversation with Papa about these photos.

"Who is this white man?" Viola asked him point blank.

"It's my father Joseph Clesca, your Grandpa," Papa replied, after looking over at her and then at me, wearing a smile that hid as many things as it revealed.

"How did Grandpa Joseph ever meet and fall in love with Grand Angele," I asked Papa, wondering how I fit in that puzzle and desperately wanting to open a window onto the past lives of the men and women who shaped the life of the little boy who would become my Papa. After all, without them, I wouldn't exist. I should have also asked Papa about his grandfather Alexandre Lambert Bruno Clesca, born exactly a hundred years before I was born when Faustin I was crowned Emperor of Haiti. I should also have asked him about his great-grandfather Jean Joseph Clesca, Bruno's father. These were among the lost souls of Papa's family.

When Grandpa Joseph and Grand Angele met, close to a century after Haiti's independence, mulattoes were most likely theoretical abstractions for Grand Angele and her poor, black-skinned, rural folk. Perhaps those differences are exactly what led her to become the long-time companion of a rich, near-white landowner general. She made it very far from home, considering that in addition to the social dynamics she couldn't read or write.

Although Papa's parents, Joseph and Angele, differed strikingly in color, origin, and social class, I knew their bodies smiled to each other because the love between them produced five children. Papa and his twin brother Herman were the first born in February 1907, but Herman died at age two. Carlo, a son who died as a teenager, followed, then a daughter, Carmella, who died soon after birth. Tante Yvonne was the last born.

Yet in the real story lived by my grandparents, there were no winners. Grand Angele was brutally and prematurely widowed. Perhaps that's why her lakou was always filled with people, to assuage her loneliness?

Dead bodies littered Papa's story—the past was torture, with an uncle massacred, and his father dead by suicide. Papa must have lived an indescribable torment, having to bury his father at eight years old, leaving him as the only man in the family. Papa and I, when Mandedette left me, became orphans at the same age. Could his memories echo the sadness I felt? Would his trauma pass down to me, to my generation? His precocious entry into manhood was surely fundamental to understanding him. But did he ever grieve his father and uncle? Could his permanent smile speak for the pain he probably buried deep inside?

With Viola and me in the living room, Papa continued to speak. "When a light-skinned man is in power, I point to my father's white complexion and military uniform, and they serve me well. When a black-skinned man is leading the country, I show the picture of my ebony-colored mother."

Papa created that self. Whatever the past, that's how he chose to define himself in the present; that was his identity. That was also his genius; a practical balancing act that exposed how he had internalized the class, color, and power issues so prevalent in the country. But Papa had revealed his truth as well; he may have been the intersection of many things, but he had a cold, strategic, calculating mind to claim legitimacy with both mulattoes and black-skinned Haitians in order to survive, or better yet, to succeed. They were also part of who I was. Generations are fate; this was a circle of family, and I heard Papa's words about ours.

Then, there was the lakou's veranda which served as a miniature city where everyone converged. It extended along the front and side of the house and was covered with a canopy of huge, cascading grapevines, giving it an exotic, tropical cachet. The veranda and vines shaded us from the glare of the midday sun and provided both a sanctuary from the heat and a haven for constant conversation. The breeze, when it whistled through the vines, made the mosaic-tiled space the coolest place in the lakou. In season, an abundance of small, chardonnay-type grapes hung over our heads. Then, whenever I sat in the "*galri*," as we called the veranda, I picked them and gobbled them down while Grand Angele rocked in her chair.

When Mandedette left Haiti, the big challenge for me was overcoming my memory of her scent, her image holding a book, her devastating smile and the softness of her kisses. I tried to forget her and fill that void by observing everything that went on in the veranda, continually filled with music from the radio. Some people played cards—either *bezigue,* a traditional French two-or four-player card game from the 19th century, or poker, usually when Papa was present. Still others talked and laughed loudly at each other's jokes. The neighbors lived so close to us that they could talk with us from their porches. One lady, TiKam, even ran a beauty salon on the veranda where people lined up to get their hair pressed and curled.

In the afternoon, family members migrating north from Grand Angele's Nippes rural homeland and staying for a time in her lakou, dozed off in rocking chairs. Each came with huge baskets of vegetables and fruits and was greeted with deep warmth and effusive joy. Nobody could ignore that they came to escape the barren earth and rivers that could no longer feed them and to find work and a better life in the city. At night, in the dry season, some even slept under the vines on green army cots.

Close to half a dozen young women from Grand Angele's poverty-stricken backcountry boarded with her while looking for work in the big city. So many lives. So many ambitions. So many relationships. I was told some were family and others just treated as if they were. All had one title, cousin. While I never fully understood how they were my cousins, ultimately it didn't matter. Each, no matter how remote the link, had value and a place in the family. The term "cousin" was sufficient. Later, I learned that in Africa where adults are called Aunty or Uncle, such a title didn't necessarily represent a family connection but rather respect.

That was Grand Angele's philosophy of life. Her body was in Haiti, but her mind and value system were in Africa. She learned early that family was sacred. Family defined us; it was visceral. And for family, Grand Angele had to provide a roof, food, solidarity, a haven; and always, coffee.

That's why Papa, while in his twenties, went north to fetch his half-brother George. Once he discovered his late father had left a young son in the city of Saint-Michel de Lattalaye in the Artibonite he travelled there, brought him home, and found him a job so he could become independent. Every weekday, I ran joyfully into Uncle George' arms when he came to eat lunch in the lakou.

Still, the main activity of the veranda and the lakou during the day remained my aunt's sewing business.

Tante Yvonne, Papa's younger sister, who shared his fine angular features, was the lakou's other matriarch. If Papa was the showy debonair, she was an earth-mother type, extremely pretty in a subdued, matronly manner, fitting the norms for a married woman. Her A-line dresses with belts wrapped around her waist accentuated her enormous buttocks and ample breasts. Yet, she had a smile as girlish as it was mischievous and an omnipresent measuring tape around her neck. Her immaculate feet, the result of a weekly pedicure done by a child servant, furiously pedaled her Singer sewing machine. Somehow, she single-handedly controlled space and time to manipulate grown men and women alike. Tante Yvonne was immensely cunning, and her name as a master of intrigue was attached to every important event that occurred in the compound. There was no doubt in everyone's mind that she was the queen bee who regulated the lives, affairs, and unity of the lakou.

Her husband of a decade, Uncle Sylvio, sixty to her forty-seven, was a prisoner of liquor. It had eaten him alive, rendering his handsome body spaghetti-thin, yellowing his hollowed face, saddening his small, green eyes, and ruining his kind heart. Whenever I kissed his forehead I smelled his strong, repulsive alcoholic stench. He was the first person I met who had that odor—all the time. I hated the smell, yet he didn't frighten me because he was such a soft-spoken, handsome, unerringly polite man. He had a sincere smile, proper manners, and a hesitant walk. Uncle Sylvio was the eldest of three children of an Italian father and a wealthy, light-skinned Haitian mother who probably had big dreams for him and his two sisters. Falling in love with and marrying Tante Yvonne, who came from a lower-middle-class Black family, was most likely not one of them. By choosing to live in her Morne-a-Turf neighborhood, Uncle Sylvio had in essence become "Black." At the very least, his family considered him a provocateur, or worse, a traitor who turned his back on his bourgeois social class. Maybe that was the source of his incurable melancholy.

Tante Yvonne was an independent businesswoman who had a large clientele, from the rich ladies of Pacot and Bois-Verna to the middle-class ones from modest neighborhoods like Carrefour-Feuilles. They surrounded the two foot-pedaled sewing machines to look at the oversize dress catalogues, place orders, or try on clothes in the privacy of the living room. It was as intimate as it was public, and most clients left the veranda entranced.

Very quickly, Viola and I became members of Tante Yvonne's group of assistants. It never occurred to her or anyone else that I was an unpaid child laborer or that I might not be interested in the job. Still, I happily joined the cousins doing the hand sewing and learned by observation. I had much fun being part of all the excitement while I sewed hems, put on buttons, stitched buttonholes, and removed loose threads. So did Viola. It was obvious from the seriousness with which we had to properly finish our tasks that we were apprenticing with a master, but Tante Yvonne avoided saying anything about a future career in the field. Later, the skills I gained from her helped me pay for several semesters of university by selling dresses I had sewn myself.

Tante Yvonne was at the core a true fixer who strongly believed in marriage. She set up couples whether or not they were compatible. I loved it because Viola and I were bridesmaids in every wedding she arranged. We also benefited from the ample side benefits, like fancy organza or lace dresses, getting our hair straightened and curled, and being put on a pedestal; if only for a few hours. Because the lakou was also a transit point for family and friends trying to journey to New York or elsewhere, it provided ample opportunities for Tante Yvonne. The game of fixing requires that one have a sharp eye for them and absolute disregard for people's previous commitments. And so it was that one day Tante Yvonne's keen spy eye paid off. She saw an investment opportunity with eventual dividends for the whole family. That's how her brilliant strategic mind functioned, for if anyone had one in the family, it surely was she. After drinking one of her endless Arabica coffees, Tante Yvonne broke the news to her godson, a family member.

"You are going to marry her."

"But I already have my fiancée," he dashed to reply, although he should've known something like that couldn't deter Tante Yvonne's plans. "She has a visa for the United States. She travels to New York in a few days," she explained. She knew this because she had given permission for this demure, soft-spoken, extremely pretty nurse with an engaging smile to board in the family compound while waiting for her visa.

He knew what she represented. People with visas were more than golden opportunities—they were a long-term investment, being the entryway for emigration of their families to the United States. No discussion was necessary. He heeded her injunction, not because he wanted to marry this young woman—after all, he had only recently met her and had his own promised bride—but his relationship with his godmother left him no choice other than to say yes. Where and when the wedding ceremony would take place were mere details. It happened so quickly that no one in the lakou could talk about it simply because they weren't present.

Afterward, I remember seeing the godson's newly married face look like a banana leaf battered by a hurricane while Tante Yvonne's smile was as large as her buttocks. In the cool breeze of the veranda, the cousins often loosened their tongues to tell the story of the new husband having sprinkled his finely chiseled nose with pepper so he could sneeze and cry at the airport when his bride flew to New York after the visa wedding, as I called it.

Long before I grew old enough to know about romantic love between two adults, I learned from Tante Yvonne that marriage was a contract, a deal, an arrangement. No one mastered it better than she, no matter what the impediment.

Underneath her steely core, Tante Yvonne had a big heart for those she loved, even though not overtly affectionate. Even as she pampered me, making me feel confident about my skinny black body, she protected me despite me being defiant to every concept of obedience. She nurtured and showed Viola and I love the way she knew best, by pushing us as bridesmaids, creating gorgeous dresses for us, teaching us sewing skills, and quietly developing our sense of beauty, worthiness, and pride.

One of Tante Yvonne's invaluable lessons was how she made me understand the power she exercised as a woman without ever raising her voice, in a culture that adopted men as the viable face of power. In fact, her authority always transcended any notion of gender.

WILD FLOWER

Tante Yvonne held power under the watchful eyes of her son, my cousin Fritz, a lanky, chocolate man with a chiseled, stern face who was well into his twenties. He rarely spoke and smiled even less. His cold personality, which some mistook as a sign of privilege, gave him the aura of a distant, brooding, dark prince although he was a homebody who spent his days playing cards on the veranda because he didn't have a job. Several of his childhood friends were closely tied to the regime at a time when President Duvalier's dictatorial grip on power solidified, but he never spoke against the president in my presence, whether from indifference or just plain self-preservation.

My heart beat like pounding drums one afternoon when he described me as a wildflower. I saw an opening and asked him: "Why do you call me *Fleur Sauvage*?"

"When you moved here, your sorrowful but beautiful face reminded me every day of a wildflower. The first time I called you by that name, I got you to smile," he explained.

Beyond his powers of description of my affliction, despite his well-known inability to talk with other people, it was the attention he paid me, the most I ever saw him pay anyone, other than his mother and card-playing buddies that impressed me. He kept calling me *Fleur Sauvage*, and the nickname stuck. It set me apart from the others; it made me feel special and important. I also felt secure near him for no one laughed at me when I was near him.

On the surface, me starting to fit in seemed simple. But it was my discovery of *bezigue*, a card game related to pinochle, and the Mexican music that composed Fritz's world that made it possible. Every afternoon after school, I rushed to change from my uniform and finish my homework to watch him play. And being his soft spot, I stayed close to him every day until sunset like a kitten to its mama. He sat with his back to the louvered doors and facing the iron gate and the street beyond, his wide shoulders embracing the chair across from three other master *bezigue* players. I stood behind him, my eyes moving quickly from his hands to the cards laid down on the small, rectangular wooden table.

I watched his sharp brown eyes dart from side to side, scanning the faces of his adversaries. I saw how he held the cards close to his chest, which ones he kept, which ones he played, and when. He would often turn to me and say, *"Fleur Sauvage*, you are so pretty but too wild and unpredictable." His words watered my scorched earth of a heart, still reeling from the loss of Mandedette's attention and affection.

I grew so confident and proud that every now and then, I glided on the mosaics from him to the other players, all of them bowing their heads and analyzing their cards as if the clue to some earth-shattering mystery was hidden in them. I sometimes thought I was cheating because they knew I was rooting for Fritz, but no one minded me or told me to move, for I knew my place and stayed mute. Even better, I started to fit in.

Under the grapevine, the sound of the radio continuously played the songs of Miguel Aceves Mejia, a popular Mexican singer and actor that Fritz was passionate about. I still remember how the hit

mariachi song "Koukouroukoukou" enlivened the veranda, I liked to repeat it, imitating his falsetto. I enjoyed the sharp guitar notes and understood some of the Spanish words sung, like *Hermosa, cantar, corazon,* or "beautiful, sing, or darling." Fritz swayed ever so gently from side to side, and I wondered sometimes if I was the only one who saw him dancing.

I loved *bezigue,* and over the course of a few weeks, I became an ace at the game simply by scrutinizing Fritz. I won sometimes when I played with Viola who had also learned by watching. I memorized Fritz's moves to uncover the tricks of his game, which provided him with constant wins. He stayed focused and invested endless hours in the game. I saw him communicating his love of the game and music with minimal, wordless gestures. He believed it was best to be quiet and soak it in like a sponge. I gradually underwent a metamorphosis, starting to feel privileged from this second, though unconscious apprenticeship. The girl who had constantly frowned was left behind as she absorbed what she witnessed at the card table. Fritz's admiring and steadfast gaze awakened me.

I also began to take pleasure in the long days spent at Grand Angele's lakou, where I felt a certain kind of freedom, as if on furlough from mother's strict rules. I had freedom to do things I had never done before.

ANNA'S LOVE LETTER

Her small almond-shaped, tamarind-colored eyes were as easy to remember as her humility and tenderness. Her name was Anna. I cannot remember if in the letters I wrote each week to Mandedette, I told her the truth about my love for Anna or about Anna's love letters.

But then I rarely told her the whole truth about my life in Papa's house. If I had, I would have told Mandedette that when the morning light bathed my bedroom and I didn't hear her deep, smiling voice saying good morning, I fought back tears. I didn't want sorrow to paralyze me. I also would have told her about Saturdays, my favorite days. Tante Yvonne never failed to send us a large plate of her special breakfast of rice colored pink by crushed tomatoes and flavored with bits of codfish. It tasted as delicious as it smelled; the salty, tangy scent of dried cod filled the house for the rest of the day. As a side order, Anna added thick, creamy avocado slices.

On Saturday afternoons, Anna grabbed Viola's and my hands and walked us a few blocks to the outdoor market. In the tiny park nearby, I passed Carl Brouard, a short, light-skinned man drunk with both rum and poetry, who recited verse after verse to no one and everyone. Some paid him no mind; others smiled, but there was nothing more loving towards him than Anna's tender smile. It showed compassion. That was Anna. I learned to haggle from observing her work magic as she negotiated prices with the vegetable and fruit sellers. She had metamorphosed into a powerful woman, having gotten the best deals and won over the toughest negotiators.

If I neglected to tell Mandedette all of this, it's because Anna, only in her mid-twenties, was my *TiMaman*—"little mother." All of which belied the fact that she was our maid. I thought Mandedette might be jealous of her. Anna combed our kinky hair, cleaned the house spotless, and cooked delicious meals. But I pitied her when she was in the kitchen, a cramped concrete slab with a tin roof, barren except for a couple of charcoal stoves and a water bucket. It was like hell with its toxic fumes and overwhelming heat. She hated it and often complained the fumes were the source of her headaches and sore throats.

In the morning, Anna looked tenderly at me: "*Ti Chérie*, little darling, you are lucky to be going to school. Study, please." No one ever said it quite the same way that I remember, and I liked the nickname: "*Chérie*." It made me feel loved.

I did a brisk fifteen-minute walk from the lakou to school with Viola every weekday in my uniform, clean and well-pressed because of Anna's washing and ironing. Prior to leaving the house, I sometimes sneaked into Papa's bedroom to take coins from the neat stacks on his dresser. There were so many different heights and circumferences that I thought it didn't matter how many I took. I had become a thief, though I never told Anna or anyone else about it. I felt guilty for stealing from my father, but I was also proud that I had outwitted him. Years later, Viola confessed she had done the same. I spent the coins on a few small dreams of glory, which were simply a good supply of taffy and caramels, grilled peanuts, and ice frescoes for school break. From rue Oswald Durand, Viola and I zigzagged up the sidewalk to avoid the furniture displayed by our neighbor, the cabinet maker BossMémé; then we cut through the stockpiles of merchandise in the large open-market, Marché Salomon, and walked two more blocks of small, private homes mixed with businesses. With my hand firmly in Viola's, we rapidly crossed a main thoroughfare crowded with uniformed students. We were out of breath by the time we reached the courtyard, but we did it four times a day without a single pause or a wasted step.

Anna was taller than Viola by a head and so thin that I once teased that her body would break if she laughed too hard. She'd spend what seemed like hours sitting in a low, child-height chair combing her very short hair into countless minute braids. Despite all the effort, whenever she went out, she adorned her head with a multicolored scarf as if her hair had to be hidden. She walked with her head bowed, making it difficult to see her eyes. These things conspired to make her appear anonymous, but to me she was as sweet as taffy. And whenever I kissed her after coming home from school, her brown face was soft like butter melted in the heat.

When Anna spoke, her voice was barely audible, low and slow. But a will of steel lay underneath it, along with strong principles and clear boundaries she had set with us and others in the lakou, telling things straight to your face, telling what she didn't want to be part of, telling what her priorities were, and telling it without a trace of anger.

"I don't want to get involved in all the gossip here, because the only thing I care about is *my* God," she explained.

The way she said *Bon dye mwen*, "my God," struck me the first time I heard it. It was not at all like Grandma or the priest at church, for they sounded like they were evoking someone quite far away. When Anna said it, it was intimate and affectionate, and her use of the possessive gave credence to her close relationship with God.

Anna had great expectations of love and money. "I am a poor lady from Jacmel passing through to save money for my marriage to Lucien," she told us.

But she was careful never to mention a wedding date, saying only that preparation for her future required her physical labor. She talked about the pretty, small house they would build. They would sell rice, flour, candy, and cigarettes from the front room, which would be their little store, and the veranda would serve as their living room. She mentioned the children they would have together, at least three. At times she stood up, looked into space, and whispered his name in adoration, as if he were standing there looking at her. Then she just grinned like a little girl. Anna never finished a conversation without mentioning Lucien, God, or Jacmel, the city closest to her hillside village. She was so crazy about all three of them that she made me want to know them all.

One day she threatened to quit. Perhaps she felt homesick; perhaps she tired of complaining about the toxic fumes. Whatever her reason, I ran to Papa and begged him to stop her. He knew that Anna was like a mother to me and filled a large void left by Mandedette's absence. Papa kissed my forehead, tenderly patted my shoulder, and promised Anna wouldn't leave us. And she didn't.

The most lasting image I have of her comes from those ordinary afternoons when Viola and I sat around the dining table, whether to do our homework or just to talk. Anna sat away from us by the door, and every now and then looked out into the dark hallway as if she had to stand guard against something to protect us. But we could still hear the constant noise coming from the veranda. The soft light streamed through the small window and drapes fluttered in the soft breeze, which mercifully tempered the effects of the tropical sun.

One afternoon Anna eyed the floor and asked Viola for a favor: "Viola, I want you to help me write a love letter to Lucien to tell him I am sad without him."

"A love letter," I screeched, unable to contain my excitement at the prospect of witnessing the first love letter of my life.

"*Ti Chérie*, calm yourself," Anna told me.

"I want to write it," I offered, even though I knew nothing about such letters, much less about writing them.

Anna laughed loudly, but she was adamant, "No, thank you. Viola is older."

Viola showed surprise as her gaze went quickly from Anna, who was smiling widely, to my eyes filled with sorrow. She responded quickly: "A love letter? I will write it for you."

"Please, Anna, let me do it." I still believed I could influence the situation.

Anna shook her head at me and tied us together in purpose: "Viola will write it, but we will keep it a secret among the three of us." Viola grabbed the writing pad we used each week to write to Mandedette and quickly tore out a blank page.

I sat there expectantly as if I were about to witness history.

"*Mon Lucien bien-aimé, kè m grenn paske ou lwen m,*" Anna dictated in Creole to Viola.

"Anna, slow down. You forget, I am translating it in French so I can write it," Viola remarked. At the time, the Creole language was not widely written nor learned in school, so we wrote in French.

"*My beloved Lucien, my heart is so empty without you,*" Anna repeated. "*Lucien, ou nan lespri m tout tan.*"

"What does that mean?" Viola asked.

"It means I think of him all the time," Anna explained as I watched her fidgeting with her fingers. When she smiled, I saw someone different—a happy woman beneath the tired face of an overworked and lonely domestic worker. "Lucien, you never leave my mind. You never leave my heart, which is sad because you're far from me," she said.

I knew exactly how Anna felt about Lucien. As she continued to dictate the letter, her words reflected my thoughts about Mandedette. I could no longer bear to listen. It seemed Mandedette, with her stunningly beautiful face, was before me, her upturned hair parted in the middle. She wore her white cotton embroidered shirt and full-circle black skirt. I pictured her sitting in her metal rocking chair reading a book. I sensed her Shalimar perfume and felt the warm, unconditional love at the corners of her mouth and eyes.

I hated Mandedette for not being present, even though she sent two letters—one each for Viola and me—every week in one envelope. She gave us news of her diametrically different world clearly written in her distinctive script. New York was very cold, with dark clouds that gave it an austere face, lit only when the sun shone on the white flakes called snow that covered the trees, the rooftops, and the streets. She wrote of her plans to get a better job to make more money so we could be together soon, right after she graduated from her secretarial and translation courses. When I read her letters, I was confused because though I tried to remember her, I started to feel her slipping away from me. Writing to her had become more of an obligation than a pleasure. But I kept writing.

"How do you know your heart is sad?" I asked Anna.

"*Ti chérie,* please let Viola write the letter," she said. I felt slightly guilty for interrupting them but needed to assert my presence.

Viola—undoubtedly aware that this moment was, if not historic, very important—carefully wrote Anna's words on the white page. No one had ever talked that way in front of me before, so I thought the phrases were funny. But I had to be serious, for if Anna thought I was laughing at her, she would stop dictating, or I might be banned from ever watching Viola write another letter.

Anna's voice trembled as she continued: "I can't wait anymore to place my head on your heart and to hear you say you love me. I want you to know my heart will forever belong to you, my beloved Lucien. " She was deep in thought, for she was no longer with us but with Lucien.

I became interested. I wanted to know why Anna, a grown woman responsible for our food, our house, and our well-being, asked Viola to write a letter for her. "Why didn't you write the letter yourself?" I asked her in a near whisper. I didn't want Viola to hear me, fearing her wrath if she were to lose this exciting new job.

Anna looked at me with surprise. The smile that had taken over her whole face disappeared as if she needed time to respond and regain her composure. I had touched a sensitive, perhaps even an unpleasant subject, and I saw shame on her face.

"I attended school for only two years. I didn't master reading, and I didn't learn how to write."

"Why only two years?"

"My family pulled me out for lack of money. Besides, my mother needed help with the chores," she answered.

"What chores?"

"Fetching water. Cleaning the house. Taking care of the small ones. Planting before the rains. Harvesting, everything." She looked at me as if any bitterness she might feel about being deprived of schooling was erased by the pride she took in being part of her family's workforce.

A long silence followed before she grabbed her chest. Holding it tightly, she said: "That's what we do in *andeyo*." I listened attentively; so did Viola.

"Where is that?" I asked as I watched her every move.

"*Andeyo* means small villages outside city limits," she explained, waving her hands animatedly. "We are peasants who farm our own land. I am the first one in the family to travel so far to find work."

All of us grew silent.

This encounter precipitated a change in me. I was breathless with the shame of my privilege of knowing to read and write when she couldn't. The tradition of taking children, particularly girls, out of school to help the family survive was due to the cruelty of poverty and deprivation. I learned that the country separated us—some in villages, others in cities—with vastly different circumstances. I also discovered not all of us were equal since in villages like hers, children didn't have the opportunity Viola, and I had to go to school. What for us was a given was for her a struggle. I could see the ambiguities and inequalities of our two worlds in the wide gap between her life and mine; where we slept, where we bathed, where we ate.

As a child, I couldn't yet take the full measure of what it meant. Later I would discover that much like Anna, Mandedette was the granddaughter of peasants and great-granddaughter of peasants; the women of her maternal family had all been born "*andeyo.*" And except for her mother, none knew how to read or write. But Anna, like Grandma and Mandedette and lots of other women, understood that she had to work, in her case with physical labor, to realize her dreams of starting a family with Lucien, and for Grandma and Mandedette to raise their children. I felt somewhat guilty because I couldn't obliterate my genealogy any more than I could separate Anna's injustice from my own legacy. Anna's story was also mine.

We had become accomplices from all the time we spent together. I knew her tender stares, her quiet generosity, and her parade of smiles well; all were lessons written in me.

Finally, Viola handed Anna the love letter to Lucien and told her she would continue to be her writer. Anna clutched it tightly with both hands. In the dim and quiet room, I felt an uprush of love for Anna because Viola had pulled her out of her illiteracy, if only temporarily. I saw her smile and understood. She walked away quickly and stopped at the door to look at us as she held the letter to her heart.

EXIT VISA

In the lakou, we had a direct link to the National Palace through my cousin Edith who worked in President Duvalier's office. She rose with the sun, styled her short, straightened hair, and put on her strict official uniform of a crisply pressed, straight blue skirt, and white short-sleeved blouse. Then she walked the few blocks to the Palace.

I would see pictures of her boss, by then a full-fledged dictator, with the dark top hat and round, black-rimmed glasses, pasted on walls and on banners hanging from electricity poles. On April 30, 1961, just three months after I moved to the lakou, almost four years after his election, and two years before the end of his first term in office, President Duvalier, organized a presidential referendum with only one candidate: himself. He wanted Haitians to prolong his constitutional term by six years. What was extraordinary was not that he received over 1.3 million votes, but rather that not a single vote against him was registered. The *New York Times* reported in its May 13, 1961, edition: "Latin America has witnessed many fraudulent (fake) elections... but none will have been more outrageous than the one which has just taken place in Haiti." Duvalier figured this "unanimous" re-election gave him a mandate to carry out all the "reforms" he wanted with this perceived *carte blanche*. He immediately dissolved the Parliament, therefore silencing all other official voices. With that, the grand illusion of democracy died.

On the veranda I heard cousins quietly discuss tales of his brutality. No one dared speak openly about it; most, gripped by fear, retreated into silence. Some talked about Edith's work in Duvalier's office, others said it functioned bizarrely as a second immigration service. Duvalier set up a system by which any person wanting to leave the country for any reason needed an exit visa. It meant he had to authorize the trip personally. While most countries required entry visas, few demanded exit ones. Passports had to make their way up to Edith's unit for Duvalier's approval. The wait was unbearably long, either from the sheer number of people eager to escape the rising terror or the lack of sufficient staff. In ordinary circumstances, it would be annoying, but in the current climate of fear, it was deplorable and worrisome.

People tried to find back channels to learn if they were approved to travel. Word spread that Edith had a job in the palace, so she quickly became one of them. In the late afternoons and early evenings after work, when she had visitors, I walked back and forth across the veranda, among the army cots that served as couches, to spy on them. I often heard people ask her, "Eske non m desann? Has my name come down?" meaning, "Did I get the obligatory clearance from the President to leave the country?" He had made himself a higher being.

I witnessed the eruptions of joy, but mostly of disappointment, and sometimes tears of desperation from people who had waited weeks or even months for the visa, sometimes to have it denied. I saw first the humiliation on the faces of those who received exit bans, but then the enormous strength they showed as they left the lakou with their dignity intact. Suddenly, I knew Mandedette had to have gone through this system, and I hoped her wait had been neither painful nor too long.

THE VOODOO PRIESTESS

One night soon after I moved to Grand Angele's lakou, I woke up abruptly to what sounded like distant music.

Tap tap. Tap tap tap. It got louder. Then, the drumbeats became deafening.

Patap tap. Patap tap tap. I wondered what it was.

I glanced at Viola's bed a few inches away. I saw her contours through a flicker of light coming from downstairs; we locked eyes for a few seconds. I was scared, so I crawled slowly from under my cover and slid under hers, my head fitting perfectly just below her armpit.

"Dilelo." That one word whose meaning I didn't know came from far away but sounded bluesy. It rose above the drum as it gained momentum on the final *o*. "Dilelo" was said like an a capella choir. Yet, it sounded like the rhythm of a badly strung guitar. Then came the muffled sound of feet fluttering. From my armpit perspective, perfect harmony existed between the music and the dancing.

The drums were climbing up the stairs slowly, very slowly, to our bedroom. I was afraid because we were alone; Papa had said goodnight much earlier, when he left for work, and Anna was asleep downstairs.

Curiosity tempted me to rush down the stairs to the music, but I knew Viola would have stopped me, for she was also my disciplinarian. I could imagine her saying, *It's the middle of the night and we go to school in the morning.* The songs of the women and men pulsated in my ear, and I had the faint sensation of my body slowly dancing itself to sleep with angels floating above me. I sighed in Viola's armpit. *I am not going anywhere*, I thought.

The next morning the sun rose luminously bright and pitilessly hot. Two cousins were talking when I passed by the veranda on my way to school about the prayers and drums of the Voodoo ceremony held the night before. So that's what it was! I wondered if *Voodoo* was the religion of Papa's family why, he didn't let me follow the services. We had never been a church-going family. I had never seen Papa, or for that matter Mandedette, go to Catholic church. But Viola and I did when we went to Sunday morning Mass in our school uniforms with our teachers. I also wondered why the Voodoo prayers happened in the middle of the night after I went to sleep.

"Bonjou Mademoiselle Viola. Bonjou Mademoiselle Monique. You heard the drums last night during the ceremony?" Gaston asked, chuckling, as he followed me to the lakou's gate. At fourteen, only a few years older than I, Gaston was Papa's valet as well as the houseboy who cleaned everything Anna didn't, including the floor, the bathroom, and the car, much like in other city households. His family had sent him from a mountain village near Jacmel to work and to have one less mouth to feed. Short, muscular, and dark-skinned, Gaston had a talent for giggling. It helped that he never took himself seriously, except when one of the adult cousins gave him a two-finger smack in the back of his shaven head, just for the "fun" of it. Then Gaston screamed in pain and cried, making a masquerade with his large, round face and intelligent, brown eyes. No one came to his defense. I saw firsthand this type of violence, all too common in the lakou. Gaston crawled through the bullying because of his youth and his status as a domestic. He was totally powerless to respond. So was I.

Despite it all, Gaston relished putting on his widest smile and showing his perfect bright-white teeth whenever Papa noticed he had shined the car so brilliantly that he could see the reflection of his face. Gaston spent most of his time in the cult of Papa's car: washing it, shining it, and protecting it with his watchful eyes so that no one touched it. The wide branches of the ceiba tree across the street did the rest by screening it from the glaring sunlight and overbearing heat. "The car is cool the moment you step in." Gaston made sure of that. Taking care of Papa's car was Gaston's own, very personal triumph.

"Gaston, you can tell me about the ceremony later," I quickly responded, knowing his knack for storytelling, and we left for school.

By night, the heat had dissipated, and quite unexpectedly, Papa announced he was taking us somewhere special. In near-total darkness, he led Viola and me, wearing our light cotton nightgowns downstairs. Walking into the veranda, I was immediately struck by the intense light reflected by the white worn by everyone. The veranda shrank because each face radiated familiarity since I recognized most of the women—I was at home among this society of women in white. Many were my cousins; others I had seen visiting Grand Angele. Some sat on low chairs, others stood idly; all wore dresses with intricate lace details. In contrast, I saw a kaleidoscope of faces of all shades of black and brown, each topped with a white headwrap as if a hairdresser had styled each to look exquisitely like no other. The men wore white shirts and pants. They seemed to swirl around Grand Angele in a semi-circle as if they were protecting her.

Papa sat down and motioned for us to sit on his lap. Viola claimed one knee and I the other. Some people smiled at Viola and me. I bowed my head respectfully at each face in a subtle attempt to salute without disturbing the prayers for what sounded like an invocation to Bon Dieu/Good God rang in my ears. It originated from a short, stout lady. Everybody stayed in place and nobody knelt down, as I had learned to do when praying. The others responded in what became a call-and-response prayer.

Then I heard the name "Papa Legba." It was another lady, this one tall and big-shouldered, who led the worship. Instead of holding rosaries, she shook a *chacha,* a calabash with pebbles that made a catchy sound. A skinny, somber man was writing something on the mosaic floor with a white powder. It was an intricate design, which consisted of crosses and circles. A secret writing code, the *vèvè,* along with its corresponding drum beat and prayer, was a call to the spirit of Legba. Still, each spirit had its particular *vèvè*, a symbol that embodied the deity.

Then they all sang to Papa Legba:"Papa Legba, Louvri baryè pou Atibon, Louvri baryè pou mwen, Papa pou mwen pase. "

They asked him, as the guardian of the gates of the mystical world, to open them to clear the paths so the spirits could pass through and join us mortals.

For Papa Legba was a wise old man who had travelled from Africa to Haiti, Cuba and Brazil with his people. He helped them survive slavery, start new lives, and bless their journeys.

That night on the veranda, there was not even a hint of a breeze. Tap Tap. Tap. Three men played drums, each a different height, each with its own colorful design. The sound felt like a big wave crashing into my body as it got louder and louder. I wanted to dance but Papa held me in place by the waist.

After the Legba song, the women dispersed and moved away from Grand Angele. She was now fully visible, sitting on a low chair, her head wrapped, and her face showing a peculiar tranquility. Tante Yvonne sat slightly behind her. My heart pounded with the excitement of being out with Papa and the family that night even though we were just on the veranda.

A woman's a capella voice pierced the night and, when I heard her melodic soprano, I knew it signaled the beginning of something important:

"Papa Loko, ou se van, Wa pouse m ale, mwen se papiyon, ma pote nouvel bay Agwe" Papa Loko, you are the wind, push me forward. I am a butterfly; I will bring the news to Agwe.

Then the drums picked up again and everyone sang together the same refrain.

The women in white were dancing and singing. I gazed at them. Some were dipping, some were swirling, others were shaking their shoulders in rhythm with their feet along with the drums, and still others were prostrating themselves. I read in their faces what I couldn't understand. Their eyes were far away; each was talking to herself or to someone who was not present, perhaps someone long gone or some divine being only she could see and feel.

They remained in constant motion. I liked how they prayed with music, singing and dancing. I was learning a new language. I thought of my own praying when I had to be alone, close my eyes, and kneel in one place. Here, everybody prayed together.

Papa beamed at us. I hadn't seen him this happy since Mandedette had left.

Grand Angele came into my view again as the women backed away from her. They lined up, each prostrating herself, twirling, and doing a curtsy while holding Grand Angele's hand for what appeared to be a respectful salute to a divine leader. They were curtsying to Papa Loko, for he had taken possession of her.

One woman swirled wildly away, her engorged eyes looking into the distance as if something or someone had taken control of her. Another spun furiously after touching Grand Angele's hands. They behaved as if my grandmother had magical powers. She helped them reach this other world, where they were in a trance.

I didn't comprehend everything, but I noticed the respect shown to Grand Angele. Overwhelmed by my curiosity, I whispered in Papa's ear to ask him what was happening. "Moka, Grand Angele is the Mambo. She is like the priest when you go to Church," Papa explained quietly. "This is how they pray. They are possessed by spirits who give them strength." I felt special, powerful even sitting on Papa's lap in the front row looking at Grand Angele as the priestess officiating at this Voodoo ceremony.

The grapevines cast shadows on the dark veranda. The ladies in white, all of them, sang and danced in a group communion, responding to the mystic sound of the drums. The men in white shirts joined them in a kind of continuous ballet; their bodies were also possessed by the rhythms. I wanted to sing but didn't know the words. The space, the time, the sight, and I, were all under a spell.

Papa walked me to Grand Angele. She pulled me gently towards her by taking my hand from Papa. He went back to his seat and Viola to his lap. Grand Angele's eyes looked at me, but they weren't really her eyes. They belonged to someone else's whom I didn't recognize, but who knew me. I realized then that Grand Angele was not my grandmother anymore; she appeared to be elsewhere as if someone else had taken over her whole being. For Papa Loko was in complete possession of my grandmother's body and mind. I gasped for air, and only when in a soft voice, she called me by my nickname, Moka—the one only she and Papa used—could I relax.

Grand-Angele spoke slowly, in another tongue I didn't understand. Her voice was low and deep and resonated with the soft drawl of people possessed of enormous power and courage, who are listened to because of the sheer force of their words, their demeanor, and their aura of spirituality.

At that point, a lady in white brought her a live chicken. Grand Angele grabbed it by the head and wrung its neck. Like everyone else, I watched as the chicken swirled uncontrollably like a spinning top. One, two, three, more drops of blood spotted the mosaics. Some fell on her hand. Then she put the lifeless and disheveled chicken on the ground.

Ever so slowly and lightly, she passed her red-hued hands tenderly downward on my face, intending to transfer energy to me. This blooding, tradition in many cultures, felt so warm. I didn't say anything because Grand Angele often stroked my face, except this time she did it with blood-soaked hands.

She whispered words that sounded like an invocation. The women in white chanted. I felt secure. The strange and beautiful memory of being in Grand Angele's hands but really in Papa Loko's never left me.

Tap tap tap. Then patap tap. The feet went back and forth on the ground. The drums never stopped beating. The voices became one as the congregation—for it was one—swayed back and forth. Voices, drumbeats, words, dance steps, all poetic gestures inscribed centuries ago in their bodies and souls.

Embodied by Papa Loko, Grand Angele called, "Vi," Viola's nickname. Papa brought Viola to her for the same ritual and took me back to his lap. Papa lowered his voice and told me: "Grand Angele blessed you with luck and success. She asked the gods to watch over you."

I smiled, knowing immediately that I would no longer be the same. This exceptional new change was almost as if I had been baptized all over again. I was now blessed by both the Catholic God and the ancestral gods. During a lull in the drum beating, I asked Papa why Grand Angele had killed the chicken.

"It's an offering to the *mystères*, like the wine and bread of the priest. The *mystères* are what we call the spirits, the divinities of our ancestors, the elements of nature—water, earth, air and fire," he explained. I knew the meaning of the word *ancestor* from studying the slave revolt in history class.

Leaving the ceremony felt like being torn from Grand Angele. I wanted to stay with the drums, the singing, the dancing that was still engulfing the veranda, but Papa walked us up the stairs and said goodnight.

A little blood, a few words, a night filled with spirits from another world.

I curled up under my cotton coverlet in the darkness with the blood on my face. I beamed, thinking that I liked God's nickname *Bon Dieu,* and that Papa Loko had made me feel as light as a butterfly. I hummed: "Papa Loko, Ou se van, Pouse m ale, Mwen se papiyon…"

The morning after we did not waste any time getting an explanation of the Voodoo ceremony because, in Papa's house, Gaston knew everything—sometimes, it seemed to me, even before it happened.

"Last night, Papa Loko gave you everything: good luck, protection from evil spirits, and blessings by the family divinities. *Pakèt afè!*" Gaston told us using Grand Angele's favorite expression.

"Your grandmother is a powerful Mambo," he commented through a wide grin while he rubbed his bald head. "You two have divine protection now. *Pakèt afè!*" he repeated.

I knew that the quiet order of my first eight years was now very much in the past because I had seen with my own eyes how Grand Angele had metamorphosed into someone else. I was astounded and mystified; I had been hypnotized.

From then on, I could not stop looking at Grand Angele. She was also possessed by other spirits, for when the drums spoke in the Yoruba, Igbo, or Kongo sounds of her ancestors, they resonated with her. When the spirit Erzulie, the goddess of love who came from Guinea in West Africa, danced in her head, Grand Angele the seductress twirled like a young woman flirting, the skirt of the bright-yellow dress she loved to wear billowing around her. Legend has it that Erzulie shared a passion with Ogou, who also loved Clermezine, the sad lady who always lost in love.

She was most often possessed by *Général Vaval*, a name given by the family to the Yoruba god Ogou, god of war, thunder and fire. An ancestor who knew the ways to her mind and body well, he came and went at will in her head. When Général Vaval took control of her consciousness, she became him. She was fierce with his power, put a machete in the belt of her red dress and scared all who needed to be scared. She also decoded dreams. Papa Loko, the wise old farmer who had blessed Viola and me, was also a master of her head, as spirits are sometimes called.

Years later, I talked to Tante Yvonne when I became acutely aware that I also needed for Papa Legba to open the gates for me to better comprehend Grand Angele, the family history, and the symbolism of this religion that is so fully connected to the natural elements. She quoted one of Grand Angele's favorite lines about her spirits: "They are my *mystères*, the masters of my intelligence. I must celebrate them regularly."

I also went to Voodoo ceremonies. I had missed these ancestral rituals, which deeply connected me to my paternal family. The larger story started to emerge: Grand Angele was more than my grandmother; she was a *poto-mitan*, the central anchor of our family. She belonged to all of us because she carried a special legacy and was guardian of our heritage. I felt a certain invincibility, even a degree of legitimacy from being part of that legacy. I finally understood my family at the most profound level. Through the spirits that possessed her and the rituals she carried out, Grand Angele transmitted the positive, tolerant, and benevolent aspects of the Voodoo religion. She formed part of an unbroken chain of transmission starting in Africa and passed from father or mother to son or daughter.

Even her name, Angele, identified her role. It came from the Greek *eggelos*, which meant messenger. She had brought the past from Africa to us.

THE CEIBA TREE

Then within a few weeks, Grand Angele lost a great deal of weight and lay in bed all the time. She was a shadow of her former self, and even my childish eyes saw her health had dramatically worsened when I went to say *Bonjour*. She looked tired, yet she still received many visitors in her small bedroom, kept cool and dark to prevent drafts.

When I looked at Grand Angele, as dusk was falling on her very old body, she mostly seemed alone in her thoughts. Despite being surrounded by her extended family, she was present but somewhere else, in the passage of time. I thought of asking if her voyage in this world had been a good one, but I just stood by her and slowly rocked her crinkled body back and forth. Her presence was enough of a response.

"Pitit mwen. My child, get me a little coffee," Grand Angele said, often as she caressed my arm and looked up at me. Coffee was comfort, it was what she knew. Once, I gently leaned on the arm of her wide rocking chair, in which her small silhouette seemed lost, and curled my hands into hers despite the heat. I so loved spending time with her. It also filled the emptiness of Mandedette's absence.

"She has a problem with sugar," Papa told us. But something seemed to be weighing on his mind, and everybody else's, for that matter. I overheard the words "diabetes" and "cancer" whispered on the veranda, but everybody stopped talking when I approached. I, for one, believed she was suffering from old age.

One morning, Papa and Tante Yvonne sat close to Grand Angele's bed, as if they wanted to hear her breathe. They knew. They were waiting. They called in Fritz, Viola, and me. I could hear the whispers of cousins from the next room.

Grand Angele made a very loud gasp, then a noise like a hiccup. That was her last breath.

Tante Yvonne leaned over her, gently slid her fingers over her eyelids to close her eyes. Then she kissed her goodbye. So did Papa, Fritz, Viola, and me.

Tante Yvonne was quiet for a few seconds, the absolute silence that follows the moments after the earth has shaken. Then I heard a visceral, piercing scream from deep inside of her. That shriek, I have since realized, comes only from a person who has just lost a mother or a child. Tante Yvonne's scream was the signal that Grand Angele had died and allowed everyone to release the pain of her loss. Tante Yvonne started to cry, Viola followed, as did I, and all the other members of the family started to screech.

"Woy! Woy! Woy!"

Screams pierced the wooden walls of the house.

"Woy! Woy!"

Bodies convulsed in fits of pain.

"Woy!"

The mosaic floor of the veranda shook as if death had caused a seismic shift.

"L ale. Li travèse. She is gone; she has crossed over," a trembling voice yelled. The day I lost my grandmother is engraved in my memory. She was eighty-eight, I was eight. It seemed to me the sun went down very early. Just closed the day.

White shadows walked through the lakou but became clearer as I recognized they were people in white clothes. I was frantic, but for once the adults didn't care because no one told me to go rest. Innumerable visitors, tearful sighs, distraught faces, uncomfortable silences, far away looks, and a soundless ballet of ebony bodies in white sleepwalked throughout the house and on the veranda. There was no intimacy. There was no privacy. Everyone was there. In Haitian homes, guests are welcomed with coffee, which also perfumed the day as it was continually roasted, ground, filtered, and sipped.

I was happy not to go to school and mingled freely through the white skirts and pants. Some visitors bent down to kiss and console me with "Condolences."

Later that day, I watched as the cousins bathed Grand Angele with water scented with bitter orange and other leaves. Each time their hands gently stroked her body with a wet cloth, it was a testimony of love.

Inside the house, Grand Angele's old, decrepit body, wearing the simple white dress Tante Yvonne had selected, lay on her bed for the last time with her white hair braided around her jet-black face. Tante Yvonne, whose large bosom seemed almost flat compressed as it was in a demure white dress, sat by Grand Angele's head, crying softly. Papa stood next to his sister and mother; his eyes filled with tears.

Soon after, her body was moved from her bedroom to the living room, where she lay on huge blocks of ice purchased by Papa. The house was totally silent as if no one was breathing. Tante Yvonne stared into space with red swollen eyes. I stood by the door and peeked in every once in a while, not sure if I should enter. Finally, with a trembling hand, she waved me in.

"Come, come. Look at her," she urged me with a whisper as if she didn't want to wake Grand Angele up. I did and stayed in Tante Yvonne's loving arms for a while.

The next evening, Papa and Tante Yvonne arranged Grand Angele's wake, according to tradition. I watched as small groups of family and friends gathered throughout the house. Men with reddened eyes drank *klerin*, a local alcohol, while others played cards, surrounded by those anxious to replace them. Still others told jokes and folktales. Hushed voices filtered from the louvers of the living room.

I sat in a quiet corner observing everyone and listening to conversations about Grand Angele. One man said: "Se yon mapou ki tonbe la wi. Angele Paul, sete you gwo mapou." That man's metaphor comparing Grand Angele to a gigantic ceiba tree that had fallen entered my consciousness very deeply. I tried to imagine what would happen if the ceiba tree across the street fell. So immense was its base and the circumference of its shade that I simply couldn't. I had heard about the ceiba being the symbol of the strongest spirit in the Haitian mystical universe. Whenever we went to the countryside, Papa told us not to get close to its huge roots, because they had life in them as they were used to store the accoutrements of Voodoo ceremonies.

Grand Angele's was the first funeral I ever attended. Just before her casket was closed, Tante Yvonne took Viola and me to kiss her. She looked as if she were sleeping. Viola kissed her first. Then, it was my turn. My soft, wrinkled Grand Angele with the smiling face I had kissed so often was now cold as ice and rigid as a brick. This was neither Grand Angele nor Papa Loko. I froze. I was scared of her. That was my biggest nightmare: I saw what death was and I hated it.

Papa, Tante Yvonne, Fritz, Serge, Viola and I sat in the front pew at our majestic Saint-Anne parish church, the men in black suits, and Tante Yvonne, Viola, and I in black dresses. Inside the church, mourners sat dressed in black, grey, white and purple mourning colors. I remember the large wooden box in which Grand Angele's tiny body lay, the voices whispering prayers, the cousins with their tearful eyes, the slow procession down rue l'Enterrement to the cemetery, the pelters with sweat pouring down their foreheads as they dug a deep hole for her final resting place, my faltering knees as she was slowly lowered in, the man with the hoarse voice reciting the last Catholic prayer, the sound of earth and tiny pebbles hitting the casket. Then, an utter void.

Fortunately for me, death didn't prevent Grand Angele from coming back to her lakou. One night soon after she died, she visited us.

"*Kote Moka? Kote Vi?*" she whispered, her hand touching Viola's face and arms, then mine. After a while, she silently covered our heads with the sheet. Viola, a light sleeper, told me about it in the morning. I looked straight into her eyes as she said: "I smelled her scent." That's when I believed her.

Calmly, we agreed it was our secret to keep, thrilled that she missed us as much as we her. Did Viola have special powers to speak to the spirits? Perhaps. Grand Angele may have been gone, but she was everywhere. In a way, this made her immortal.

Another day Viola and I saw a black butterfly as big as my hand on the wall of the veranda. I thought it so beautiful that I called Tante Yvonne's attention to it. In a serious tone, she told us, "It's Grand Angele visiting us."

"How can Grand Angele be a butterfly?" I asked incredulously.

"Black butterflies either announce death or mean death is visiting," Tante Yvonne told me without hesitation. She paused and smiled at the butterfly.

Viola and I laughed so much at the idea that Grand Angele had turned into a big black butterfly that Tante Yvonne got upset and asked us to leave. We continued our laughing upstairs in our room.

Later that night, when we saw a black butterfly in Papa's bedroom, we didn't laugh. Viola and I talked to it as if it were Grand Angele. I told her how happy I was to see her. Later, I experienced a mix of apprehension and comfort whenever I saw a large black butterfly—apprehensive about who was going to die and comfort to think it might be Grand Angele visiting or maybe the other lost souls of Papa's family.

In our lakou, the loss was immeasurable. A wholly different way of life suddenly started for us. The tangible proofs of Grand Angele's existence gave me no solace, whether her empty rocking chair or the locked doors of her store. No one wanted to speak, no one smiled. The sun seemed hotter, the days longer; even the vine leaves over the porch were so tired they started to fall, as if they too, were grieving.

Except for the occasional drums beating fiercely downstairs in the middle of the night during Voodoo ceremonies, people no longer played music in the lakou. After the burial, color stopped being part of our lives because all the adults in the family wore mourning clothes for two years; Viola and I for six months, including a black school uniform skirt that replaced my navy blue one.

I had become accustomed to Grand Angele's sweet love. Nobody stroked my face with blood or otherwise as tenderly as she had. I missed her bony body in the big rocking chair she let me push back and forth. On the onion-skin paper I sent every week to Mandedette, I wrote that Grand Angele had filled the emptiness left by her departure and how I now felt doubly lost. A second light went out of my life. Her disappearance imposed my silence. I relived the wake, the funeral, and the burial ceremonies overcome with tears and overwhelmed by sadness. I had gotten close to her only in the last few months; now I wanted to extricate her from the earth in which she was laid. I wanted to have my grandmother back alive. I revered her: Grand Angele was my totem.

Everyone in the lakou looked sad, everyone, that is, except Papa. Whenever I asked him about her death, or said anything about her, his response was an endearing smile. It was unnerving. Had he also mourned his father that way, when he was eight years old? Me, I would keep on crying my loss.

I kept thinking about the comparison of Grand Angele being like a ceiba tree. That's how I came to learn of another Haitian proverb, "mapou mouri, kabrit manje fey li," when the ceiba tree dies, goats eat its leaves. Maybe that's why I wanted to compensate as a goat eating her leaves; to become, in a way, a repository of some of her wisdom. Only then could I hope to have a role in transmitting her ancestral legacy to others.

I thought life couldn't get any worse.

It did.

Uncle Sylvio became violently ill and was rushed to the hospital. It was all predictable, but nonetheless unavoidable and yet so very heart-wrenching. I was shocked, standing by his bedside, to see the terrifying manifestations on his body; his long, slender frame had ballooned to three times its normal size as if he had been inflated. I couldn't bear to hear him moan with pain.

Frightened, I asked Papa, "Why is he so big?"

He responded with his habitual smile. Tante Yvonne's face showed gloom. She knew, but she wouldn't say. She rocked side to side in a slow cadence as she sat close to him. Her strong hand patted his continuously as if she were transmitting life. Uncle Sylvio was no longer in my world. Amidst the brouhaha, as we left, I overheard someone whisper a little too loudly: "Too much alcohol equals cirrhosis." Alcohol, I understood, but not cirrhosis. Back in the lakou, there were murmurs of spells put on him by werewolves. When nighttime fell, I was very frightened the werewolves would also come get me.

The next morning, Tante Yvonne's wailing woke everyone in the neighborhood. She came back home. Alone. Uncle Sylvio had died before the sun rose. His death transformed Tante Yvonne into another person. The sparkle in her eyes disappeared and she retreated into inconsolable silence, the only language she knew for the pain she was living. I recall her looking through me rather than at me. I thought her condition was surely better than if she had lost her mind to folly because the piercing screams from the psychiatric hospital's patients across the street did little to reassure me. Just like that, Uncle Sylvio was gone, proving that liquor has a good memory and kills those too intimate with it, and I became afraid of it then.

The rainy season came. Every night at dusk, rain flooded the streets and hid the stars. The wind whipped through the land in a desperate attempt to demand that we confront nature's blunt force.

JACMEL

That summer, jubilation was resuscitated. I successfully completed my school year. I survived the loss of Grand Angele and Uncle Sylvio. I became more comfortable with Mandedette's letters from New York; even if they didn't completely abate the hurt of our separation. So when Papa said he had planned a surprise trip, I was overjoyed. Tante Yvonne, Viola, and I were going to Jacmel, and we could stay as long as we wanted. Instantaneously I liked the musical sound of Jacmel, this new world I was going to discover.

At sunrise, Papa drove us to the bus station. The colorful vehicle was, in fact, a large truck with rows of benches installed on its flatbed. Close to fifty passengers had packed themselves like sardines into the back along with goats, chickens, suitcases, cases of cola, baskets of fruits and vegetables, and huge bags of merchandise. I heard the noise coming from there and realized it would last until we reached our destination. There was also a throng of people at the sides of the truck, most selling food and drinks, others stretching their goodbyes, and I felt insignificant around all of them.

Papa went to see the driver to confirm the seats he had reserved in the driver's cabin, considered to be the first-class section, before he kissed us goodbye. I sat between Viola and Tante Yvonne and at our feet was a large, tin container with cooked food and a thermos filled with iced water. Papa waved as the bus departed, and I waved back with tears in my eyes. It was the first time I would be away from him since we moved to Grand Angele's lakou.

The three of us were unusually quiet for the start of the ride from Port-au-Prince. Tante Yvonne still suffered from a visibly distressing and worrisome melancholy, as if death had become a predator in the lakou. She walked aimlessly and stared with lost eyes at her sewing machine. She held a demitasse of coffee all day long as if it were a lifeline. With this trip, she was leaving the setting of her misery, even if only for a few weeks. She looked straight ahead as if her courage could falter if she smiled or talked.

Viola had decided to take a positive attitude to deal with the change in our lives. So she smiled in the truck, as she did all the time. Like Papa. She was calm, sweet and nice, and everyone in the house took notice. I, on the other hand, was suspicious of everyone and everything. I most definitely didn't smile. I often silently cursed people who looked at me in a way that made me uncomfortable, and I kept a safe distance from almost everyone. I was called a *fille à Papa,* a "Daddy's girl" because I took my place behind him when he played cards on the veranda. I never knew if I stood there to scratch his head, which he loved for me to do, or just to feel close to him, although I never figured out how to play poker, his go-to-game. I was going to miss Fritz, Serge, and Papa terribly. I didn't know what I would discover in Jacmel, but I was thrilled to go to Anna's hometown. I also relished the chance to see the paradisical beaches Papa had always raved about. Jacmel held the promise of a summer of magnificent discoveries.

The wild ride to Jacmel, along a winding road through mountains and valleys, took a little over an hour. The driver twisted the truck through the thin corridor going south along the coastline with the sunrise in front of us. I liked everything I saw: the sky-high coconut trees; the vast sugar cane plantations; the huge baskets of mangoes by the roadside; the sweet, pungent smell of molasses; the small, multi-colored houses with thatched roofs and wood lace trim; the deep valleys in all shades of green; and the mountain peaks standing one behind the other as if in formation.

When we finally reached flat lands after an hour, the driver made his first stop on the bank of a wide river.. From my elevated front seat I saw the road on the other side of the river, but I couldn't see how to cross it. Strange, I thought. Either the government hadn't thought of building a bridge or didn't have the resources to do so. The whole town of Jacmel and the villages to the east of it were simply inaccessible unless one took a boat, swam, or walked across the river.

How to get to the other side? I wondered. Fortunately, my puzzlement didn't last long because the driver yelled for everyone to get down from the truck; we had to cross the river by foot. He needed to lighten his truck's load so it could pass through the water.

Viola, Tante Yvonne, and I hurriedly stepped down into the refreshing, bright, early morning light. Passengers from the back spread out across the riverbank. A couple of *passeurs,* young men with body-builder shoulders, walked up to Tante Yvonne and proposed carrying us one by one across the waterway. These local experts knew about the undercurrents and the location of rocks and crevasses in the riverbed and made a living taking people to the other side. Tante Yvonne negotiated a price with them, and we would be among the privileged to pay a *passeur.*

I huddled against Viola, terrified, but realized this was the only way to get to Jacmel. She bravely decided to go first. With that, I followed her movements intently as she straddled the passeur's back. The man crossed the river as easily as if it were a street. A few minutes later, Viola smiled and waved as she arrived on the other bank. I was thrilled of her achievement. It dawned on me that for the first time, Viola and I were apart, each in another universe. Our separation scared me even more than the river, so I clung to the back of the passeur like a baby on the back of its mother when it was my turn.

"Hold tight," he said.

"Please, please, please, don't let me go. Don't drop me," I yelled.

I trembled with fright that my small body would end up in the deep blue sea to meet *La Sirene*. She was the languorous and powerful fish-woman divinity who, for centuries claimed sailors and lost bodies in deep rivers and the ocean according to the folktales of her exploits that I had heard since I was little. Yet, I saw lush green vegetation—tall palm trees brushed the sky, and mangoes, big and small hung low on tree branches. Birds flew just above my head in the liana-filled tropical area. I held my breath and closed my eyes as my feet dangled over the passeur's back and splashed in the water. It seemed like forever, but in fact lasted only a few minutes. Once on the other side, I knew I had also won over adversity and smiled triumphantly with Viola. I noticed other passengers straddled on the backs of passeurs, but most dared the currents and rocks by walking like Tante Yvonne. She bunched her skirt around her hips so not to get her clothes wet. And though she was overweight, she moved agilely by others also braving the waters.

When every passenger stood on the opposite side of the river, I watched the driver maneuver his empty bus across the water with a lot of hesitation, but without our extra weight as a hindrance. We continued on the road, and minutes later, we came upon the second river, then the third one. Each time, we repeated the drill.

Finally, we arrived at the buzzing entrance to Jacmel. Tante Yvonne led us across the street and after a few steps we came to a large two-story, concrete house with a balcony.

Agosta, a lithe, copper-colored, beautiful child-woman of sixteen, with a shapely body and wearing her long, wavy black hair down her shoulders, opened the door. I wanted to look like her, but of course, I never would. She rushed to kiss Tante Yvonne and help her with her bag. Then she looked at Viola and me and in a girlish voice, said: "*Bonjour les enfants.*" The kissing continued when Tante Yvonne introduced us to the owner of the house, Madame Rochelle, a large, light-skinned woman with a very wide derriere. She was Tante Yvonne's long-time friend and Agosta's grandmother. The maid and the gardener handled our bags and Agosta led Viola and me to an upstairs bedroom where we lay down on the beds for a quick rest.

When I came down the stairs, I discovered Tante Yvonne had arranged everything, so our vacation started on her terms. She sat at the head of the dining table and announced her surprise. The smile on her face was a lure. "Come take the medicine," she said with some irony in her voice about the *lòk* she had given instructions ahead of our arrival to prepare.

Lòk is a medicine as potent and effective as it was foul-tasting and smelling. Its name alone could repel even the kindest of souls. It's composed of castor oil—an antioxidant known for its antibacterial, antiviral, and antifungal properties—spiced with nutmeg, mashed garlic, and crushed atiyayo leaves to make the remedy.

I hoped Tante Yvonne would change her mind, but she filled three large enamel cups with the dark, thick cleansing mixture. Agosta took her cup easily. I thought of hiding behind Viola, but she defiantly took hers from Tante Yvonne and quickly gulped down her *lòk*. She looked disgusted. I reluctantly took my cup, drank it fast and considered myself brave as the slimy mixture passed over my tongue and down my throat. Tante Yvonne gave each of us a couple of orange quarters to eat, saying they would take away the acrid taste, but they didn't. Nothing did. That day, Viola started hating oranges, and I found an easy enemy in castor oil, except to massage my hair and aching bones. By sheer necessity, we stayed indoors all day to be near the toilet as the medicine made its way down to our bowels. The next morning, Tante Yvonne gave us another cupful.

Once purged of harmful bacteria, worms, and other toxic creatures that inhabited our bodies during the school year, we received a *rale*. This was a deep-body massage done with the same castor oil, this time mixed with bitter orange leaves, both known for their extraordinary healing abilities. The *rale* scared away my aches and fatigue and left my body soft, smooth, and perfumed. When we finished, Viola and I rubbed our hands on each other's arms to see who had the silkiest skin. Over the years, I've tried to recapture the *rale* feeling of a floating angel by booking massages wherever I traveled.

Having survived Tante Yvonne's traditional cleansing purge, I finally became a vacationer with a mission of prolonging summer pleasures. I soon discovered nothing about Jacmel would be unpleasant. Waking up there was special because the fragrance of fresh bread baking wafting across the street propelled me out of bed. Although the July heat was merciless, the clouds gathered like white ruffles in a deep blue sky. With Agosta as our guide, Viola and I strolled around her city, discovering grand, colorful, almost-gothic 18th century, Victorian-style houses embellished with lace-like woodwork on their broad balconies, windows and doors. We marveled at the open market in the middle of the city for its food sellers and its same lacy scroll design but in a rusty red and green painted cast iron.

We climbed stairways that were in fact small streets connecting the high-plateau neighborhoods to the sea-level ones. Hearing the hurried steps on the pebble stone alleys that led to the main streets made me feel as if I had stepped back in history. Little children peered from behind half-opened doorways, playing hide and seek with their faces. Even the dogs barked for our attention.

I often traced the aroma of bread by crossing the small, paved road to walk down the narrow dirt pathway to the one-room bakery owned by a burly, chocolate-colored man everyone respectfully called Monsieur Metellus. Once he honored us with an invitation to visit the big, brick oven in the backyard and the little front room where he sold his tasty bread and biscuits. Whenever we passed, he was working, and I wondered when he found time to sleep.

We finally braved an unexplored area, which quickly became an obsession, the Raymond-les-Bains beach. Agosta, Viola, and I often took a public bus there for impromptu picnics. I immediately ran to the water to feel its temperature on my skin. The waves were strong and broke hard, showering me with seawater. They hit the sand like thunder, close but yet far. From my perspective the sea was infinite, enveloping the space to the limit of my view. Better yet, it changed from celery green to azure, depending on its mood. The sun covered the water with sparkles. The wind was soft, and I inhaled the salty scent quickly. I smiled. I laughed. The sea at Raymond-les-Bains symbolized timelessness.

"Timoun, this sea is dangerous. Do not venture farther than here," a lady dressed in street clothing told us one day while we sat in our swimming suits. She bent down to show us an imaginary line a short distance from shore. I couldn't imagine why because, seen from the distance, bright white clouds created delicate lace designs above the clear water.

"Even when the sea looks calm, don't be fooled. Underwater tornadoes can swallow you very quickly and take you far away," said the woman calmly, with a kindness that contrasted with her ominous declaration. She walked away without looking back, as if she was forever finished with her guardian angel mission.

By telling us about this sometimes furious and savage sea, this stranger had brought the idea of death much too close. I felt totally helpless, wrapped around *La Sirene's* arms in a colorful, blissful underwater world. I was fascinated by the imagery of the deep sea where this stunning fish goddess lived. Yet I was also terrified when I heard her tales because I knew that to meet her one had to transition from life to death. And I didn't want to die.

Agosta's voice brought me back to earth. She explained that Jacmel's sea was well known for the ferocious, even monstrous, and sometimes deadly hidden undercurrents. Its stillness was deceptive, and she often heard misogynistic people say, "Women are as treacherous as Jacmel's sea." So I started to associate anything vast, deep, and seemingly motionless like the sea with the possibility of treachery. It was all there: the sacredness of the sea; the deceptiveness of the sea; the power of the sea; the beauty of the sea; the serenity of the sea. It was good that I learned early to savor it, even when I never completely trusted it.

Suddenly, I saw the young man in swimming trunks leaning against a tall coconut tree. I was intrigued by this thin but muscular feather-weight boxer man who directed his intense, piercing black flirtatious eyes at Agosta. I was blinded by his perfection but was also chagrined that the first boy I really looked at didn't even see me.

"Come talk to me, Agosta," he said as he walked towards us, as if he were bouncing on quicksand. I was impressed, not solely because he was older than I and terribly handsome, but because he was almost cocky and full of brazen confidence, so different from the men I saw sitting idly or playing cards on Grand Angele's veranda.

"*Les enfants,* he knows my name," Agosta whispered to us, got up as if he had snapped his fingers, and galloped towards him. They talked for a few minutes, and she came back with him. From then on, whenever we went to the beach almost daily, Ged spent his time with us until we left before sunset to go home.

Ged was a seventeen-year-old high school dropout who scraped by living as a store clerk. Agosta told us he was an Arab. I had never heard that word, nor was I aware of ever having met an Arab. His family had migrated to Haiti from Lebanon in the early 20th century, along with hundreds of other refugees from that country and Syria. Haitians called them Arabs regardless of their nationality or whether they were born in Haiti. After that, I wanted to know all about Arabs. Did his family eat rice and beans like we did? Was the inside of his house like ours? He spoke the same language as we did and looked like us except for his lighter skin and curly hair. While we saw Ged as a tall, friendly young man in Jacmel, he grew up as an outsider. Agosta told us, "They are foreigners who keep to themselves, work from dawn to dusk, and marry within their small circle of family and friends. They live in their own world right here in Haiti." Moneyed mulattos contemptuously considered them to be just a step above the mass of poor, black-skinned people.

By the time I left Jacmel a month later, Ged and Agosta were in love. They eventually ran away from their respective families, rented a room in a boarding house on the outskirts of Port-au-Prince, and lived as a couple. Then he had the brilliant idea to ask a rich cousin in the Middle East for a loan. He used that money to purchase a huge Mack truck he called *L'oiseau Bleu.* With his Blue Bird, he started a transportation business and over the next forty years, always with Agosta, he expanded into other arenas with raging success, becoming a multi-millionaire. That's not nothing. I admired his brash ambition, and I'd say to myself that I needed to believe in myself the way he believed in himself.

Too quickly the vacation was over. Leaving Jacmel became a grieving process for me. During my month there, I felt free as if the chains around my legs and even my heart were broken. I knew life with Papa, Grand Angele, Tante Yvonne, Fritz, Anna and the cousins on rue Oswald Durand had already changed me to a more confident and sociable self, but Jacmel added to the mutation. Fretful me became calm me. At eight years old, I found some peace of mind and harmony in its air, its sunshine, its infinite blue sea, its sand.

Later, no matter how intense, chaotic, or frightening the noise of Port-au-Prince, that hypnotic coastal city of Jacmel was my solace and refuge. When the sirens of my mind were deafening, when I insulted the universe for its inattention to the misery of my countrymen, or when I was in need of renewal--I smiled, thinking of Jacmel.

I didn't want to leave Jacmel. I couldn't wait for the new school year to start and end so I could go back. I didn't want to say goodbye. Leaving meant abandoning it, so I daydreamed about living there in a small, wooden house with a lacy-scrolled veranda built on a rock off the main road facing the beach. I would fall asleep to the continuous music of waves that gave such a joyful rhythm to my life.

BIRTHDAY

On All Souls' Day, a pilgrimage to the tombs of departed family members was a duty. Papa led the call. That's why he woke Viola and me at sunrise and told us to dress quickly in mourning clothes. He drove Tante Yvonne and us to the cemetery a few blocks away to pay our respects to Grand Angele.

At the gate, he purchased flowers. In the soothing, early morning sun we slowly walked down the narrow cobblestone road of the sacred geography of crypts and headstones. It was not a sterile or even a static place where the dead rested peacefully forever after, but rather the site of perpetual movement at the crossroads of life and death. We passed throngs of people wearing the mourning colors of white, black or purple, walking, standing or kneeling and whispering prayers by the tombs, large and small, all along the sinuous trails.

As we arrived where Grand Angele lay in the stark-white family crypt that bore Papa's name, Serge and some cousins were already in communion with her. Tante Yvonne swayed side to side, in an effort to contain her pain. Papa, the dutiful son immediately ordered cemetery workers idling nearby to freshen the crypt with bright white paint and urged Viola and me to place the flowers on the tombstone.

I sneaked around Papa's leg to an empty space for a private moment with Grand Angele and prayed for her soul to rest peacefully.

At the same time, I tried to maintain a certain calm and pretended not to pay attention to *Guede*, the spirit of the Dead, who had possessed Cousin Viergelie who stood a few feet away from me. *Guede*, dancing in her head, was gyrating wildly. Filled with the spirit, Viergelie yelled obscenities right there in front of Grand Angele's tomb in the middle of the Port-au-Prince cemetery. Proudly, unabashedly, she contorted her waist and hips to a drum rhythm that only she could hear, but to the unknown might seem obscene. But in the Voodoo religion she practiced, along with so many in my family, *Guede* perpetually made fun of death and reveled on All Souls' Day.

The Viergelie of any other day conveyed beauty with all her resources, including her soft-spoken voice and her immaculate, charcoal-colored skin. Her permanent smile showed off her exquisite magenta gums and the stunning small gap between her two front teeth, both cultural beauty symbols of which I was quite envious. I used to stare at her whenever she came to visit Grand Angele because I admired her strikingly unique beauty and enjoyed her cheerful presence. She charmed all of us with her killer smile.

That early morning, at that unsettling moment in the cemetery, I looked at Viergelie's face. My curious gaze confirmed that she, my cousin, was a perfect and most wondrous metaphor for a dance, a belief, a spirit from centuries ago which was in front of me. It was a mystery to me how she managed this duality—the spirit and her real self—much like Grand Angele had. It was one of Viergelie's deep truths. She was family and that's who we were.

As it happened, there was a happy subtext: my birthday coincided with All Souls' Day.

In this completely incongruous setting, in front of the crypt, Cousin Wilfrid bent down to plant a kiss on my forehead. He was Uncle George's affectionate and loud oldest son. Devoted to physical prowess, he regaled in performing exercise routines which shaped him like a middle-weight boxer with well-toned muscles. Wilfrid wasn't in school, as he should have been, nor was he at work, as he should also have been. He amazed me with his supreme indolence. Wilfrid gave the impression of being an extremely confident man but underneath stood someone barely out of his teens. He was the family's adorable and intoxicating bad boy with his brutal honesty, not much appreciated by the other cousins.

In his own way, he lived as a rebellious poet who stood up for the downtrodden. He was vocal about his intense and fierce dislike of Duvalier, his restrictions of freedoms and the atrocities of the bogeymen who terrorized people in his name. His outspokenness was almost to the point of being ridiculous, so much so that others were incredulous he could say such things and survive. He was the only one I heard cursing: "Duvalier se vagabon. Duvalier se kriminel."

He inspired me with his undeniably obvious bravery. For me, Wilfrid had a mythic quality, and I wanted to have his irreverent personality and be as debonair, as honest, as incisive and as exuberant as he when I grew up. But I could feel he had to be that way to exist; if not, he would be disloyal to himself. He had to be jarringly different to attract attention in the fiercely competitive lakou, which was just too small for too many men as strong as Fritz and Papa.

"Happy Birthday, Moka," he said and handed me a small present. It was magic, my ninth birthday. His was a small gesture, yet to me remarkable. That was Wilfrid. Whatever he did, he did it boldly. One of the narratives on the veranda was that Wilfrid was, in short, too brash for his own good and would always be consigned to irrelevance. But here, with his priceless nod towards me, the other cousins followed his lead and drifted to me to express their birthday wishes.

Wilfrid affectionately patted my short braids before stalking out of the little city of sepulchers. We had decades of so many sweet, loving moments like these before I had to speak of him in the past tense.

THE OTHER PROGENY

It was now melancholy season. It drifted in and out of our lives in my grandmother's lakou, becoming a sentiment I knew well. It was after Grand Angele's death had broken all of us. It was after Uncle Sylvio had painfully ballooned to the point that his death was a relief for us who so loved him. Melancholy set in after I started to understand that death meant that Grand Angele and Uncle Sylvio would never wake up again and after I started to doubt Mandedette would ever come back from New York.

A few weeks after Grand Angele's death, I heard the rumor that Papa had a secret daughter. I was under the grapevine, listening to my cousins' habitual talk about everything and nothing. And one of those nothings, which would become an everything, was Gladys's story.

When Gladys arrived in the lakou to visit Tante Yvonne, she offered us a timid smile. Dressed in her school uniform and carrying a large bag of books, she had a roundish, fifteen-year-old face and limped a little on one side as though one of her legs was shorter than the other. She wore her long, curly, black hair gathered in two long braids that rested on her small breasts like Maya women, and her sad eyes seemed to crave something.

"Gladys is your sister. Gladys is your sister," a couple of cousins teased Viola and me in singsong after she left.

I laughed in disbelief, unable to fathom how she could be my sister because she lived outside my private world. Obviously, Viola and I were spoiled in comparison to Gladys because we lived with Papa in a concrete house, albeit unfinished, while she only came to visit, and even then, not entering our home. We also had the privilege of carrying Papa's last name, with whatever little pedigree was attached to it, but Gladys didn't.

Still, I had doubts because the cousins' tales always had seeds of truth. If it were true, I asked myself, why had she never played with us like Serge? Then again, why hadn't Papa ever told us about her? When I went to bed that night, I pressed Viola about what she knew and hadn't told me. She said the rumor was false: Gladys was Tante Yvonne's goddaughter.

I saw Gladys a few times afterwards during her ephemeral visits. Even though she carried a generational difference of seven years over me, she greeted me properly with a "*Bonjou. Kouman ou ye?*" Or "How are you?" Out of the corner of my eye I watched her sit close to Tante Yvonne at her sewing machine, hands clasped together, and feet crossed at the ankles—the image of a proper young lady. Enigmatic on her best days, Tante Yvonne smiled and kissed her warmly and whispered to her as if sheltering her from the rest of us.

Each time Gladys came, the cousins' tongues wagged. But then, nothing, no one was immune to the *teledjol*, the given name of any informal channel of gossip, but it was particularly inspired by Gladys. Everyone knew the cousins possessed an exceptional gift for gossip and derision, so persistent in the lakou as idleness flavored the days. We exchanged banal civilities on the veranda, where everyone whiled away the afternoons after school and on weekends, talking and listening. The family had grown, and there were always too many people for any privacy, so everyone heard everything in this, our only outdoor space.

I personally couldn't understand their fascination with Gladys or Papa or their reasons for spinning tales about them. I was a child so I often walked away without bitterness, knowing silence was better than a futile argument the cousins would always win. Children's memories exaggerate time, but it seemed like the buzz about Gladys lasted a long time. When she left the lakou, she looked trapped, as if she had entered a wasp nest. Over time, hearing the gossip might have affected her, for she was shy, almost speechless, as if in her own world separate from the cousins. It finally got to me, and when something began to bother the me of that time, I acted.

One day immediately after one of Gladys' visits, I mustered enough courage to walk over to Tante Yvonne. I folded my hands and defiantly looked her in the eyes, clearly conscious that children didn't ask questions of adults and almost begging for punishment.

"Is the rumor about Gladys being my sister true?" I asked.

"Talk to your Papa," she told me brusquely. Her eyes made me fall silent and confirmed that this story mattered. Her answer didn't satisfy me, but I walked away. She left me no other option but to talk to Papa. That's when I learned I wasn't the only one intrigued by the mystery because one day soon after Viola asked Papa point blank, "Is Gladys your daughter?"

He looked straight at her, coughed a bit as he removed the cigarette from his mouth, and said through his smile, "No, she is not. Haven't I introduced you to your siblings already?" If Papa had lost credibility in my eyes with the ambiguous reply Tante Yvonne had given me, he regained it with his response to Viola. Not only had he introduced us to Serge, but every Sunday, Papa brought him to our home to play. We were Papa's three children. We had a loving relationship with him. These details counted. So, I believed Papa with his big smile, his aura of assurance, and his constant presence, and not the gossip.

Yet, I still harbored a lingering doubt about Gladys's origin story.

Around dusk a few weeks later, I noticed a handsome, dark-chocolate sixteen-year-old with perfect white teeth as he stood behind the lakou's iron front gate. Despite his frail body, he had a strong physical presence. His sorrowful eyes and obvious timidity caught my attention in the faded light of the early evening. I remembered smiling at him. He smiled back.

The next day, I woke to a rooster crowing as the scent of coffee crept upstairs. As I lay on my bed, Viola whispered: "Jacques, the young man we met last night, is Papa's son. He is our new brother. A cousin overheard me say he was handsome and told me the truth after he left."

My blood froze at the distressing swiftness with which my new half-brother Jacques entered my life.

In the early morning quiet, I whispered back about the strangeness of accidentally discovering from someone other than Papa the existence of his child. It was my second intimation, after Gladys, of another hidden subtext to Papa's story. What I did not understand was why Papa wasn't telling us about his other progeny, first Gladys, now Jacques; both known to others but surfacing only now to Viola and me.

While there was delight, though not in Jacques himself because he had never told me jokes or hugged me, much less ever talked to me, but in the promise of a new relationship, I still couldn't believe that Jacques was my real brother.

From then on, my shock turned to curiosity as I scrutinized him the rare times he came to the lakou. It was always around dusk as if he were avoiding the visibility of the harsh daylight. I didn't know why no one invited him to enter. He stood outside on the sidewalk and me inside, physically separated by the gate, as if the time for brotherhood hadn't come. He often stuttered when he asked to see Papa, who was rarely willing to see him. The few times Papa did, Jacques' stutter became so profuse that I feared words wouldn't come out or he wouldn't be able to breathe. Whatever he had to say was short, but it took him an extraordinarily long time to express it. The meetings ended with Papa reaching into his pocket to give him money before walking away.

It was supremely stupid, but without Papa's benediction and Tante Yvonne's approval, Jacques was excluded from the family. In reality, there were no parentheses for him: Jacques was a *pitit deyo*, a child of unmarried parents, without his father's legal recognition as his kin, although born several years before Papa married Mandedette. He was almost invisible, since he was left to live in the family's shadows. I already knew all too well how it hurt to feel invisible.

I was conscious that Papa dreamt of having a son who was an engineer, but he denied another son's dream of properly acknowledging his father. While Papa was tremendously attentive to Serge, he was totally dismissive with Jacques. Sometimes, I imagined Jacques's fear of his own father who refused to assume responsibility for his actions. I imagined Jacques' despair at having to stand outside his own father's house, waiting for some meager handouts as though he were a beggar. I imagined Jacques' confusion at not having the same last name as his father. It was all torture for me, and I assumed even more so for Jacques, for in his own unobtrusive way, he was fighting to exist. I realized later that in the process, Papa showed Jacques core elements of his personality that no charm and polish could mask, namely cowardice, absurdity and meanness. But ultimately, the sustained denial and insidious exclusion of Jacques proved as futile as it was toxic.

I was also confused by that vortex of Papa's children. I longed to untangle the whole buried back story, not only of Jacques, but of Gladys. I was angry. I was unbearably sad. It was no singular event because, once more, no family member was providing me coherent answers despite my relentless questioning. They were commanding my complete silence.

A few weeks later, one late afternoon after school, I heard Tante Yvonne's slide heels stomping the mosaic floor as if she were at war with it. She had crossed the minuscule pathway that separated our house from hers to walk into our living room with a very skinny man. She found me picking at my supper of bread with guava jelly and warm milk. The fact that she rarely came over, much less with a stranger, made her visit all the more ominous. Their faces were blank canvases, as if smiles or frowns were useless.

I rushed to fetch Papa as she ordered and hid behind him as he faced them. The man uttered his news as if it were a death announcement: Papa's car had rolled upside down on the hilly Bourdon road full of precipitous curves. Its four tires faced the sky. Serge, who had borrowed the car earlier, was in the hospital with the three friends he had gone out with.

Papa's already long face seemed to drop to the floor, and he rapidly dismissed the man. He rushed out of the house, and I lost sight of him as he quickly turned the corner on foot toward the University Hospital, one block away. I feared for Serge because, for me, hospitals evoked loss and death.

A few hours later, Papa returned wearing his customary, wide smile as if the accident hadn't happened. Viola rushed to ask about Serge, with me anxious at her side.

"He is fine," Papa said and explained the accident. It turned out Serge and his friends had been slightly hurt when the windshield shattered. All were released from the hospital after treatment of their cuts and bruises, and Papa had taken Serge home to his mother's house.

At barely nineteen, Serge represented possibilities Papa never had. He was about to graduate with a French-level baccalaureate degree, whereas Papa had not finished secondary school. Serge was set to enter the university to fulfill his dream of becoming an engineer—a future Papa never even imagined for himself. I looked up to Serge, not only because he was so much taller than I, but because he had purpose—he incessantly talked about his studies and his future career in engineering. I wanted to be like him, as well as like Wilfrid, when I was older.

When Serge came to visit a few days after the accident, his tall, lanky body was erect as if held up by a baton. He moved directly towards me, then bent slightly to kiss my forehead. "*Bonjour Monique*," he said. His thick lips hardly moved when he said my name in an odd, mechanical way. His eyes looked through me to some unknown space far beyond. All he did was stare at the wall in total silence. He sat down stiffly, his face inscrutable and without even the faintest smile, let alone his customary happy grin. He didn't utter another word.

"*Bonjour Serge*," I said. I wondered if he were playing a new game, pretending to be dead. I tried to detect a sign, a smile, a movement, anything, even as I allowed myself some comfort in knowing he had not forgotten my name. I missed him terribly when he was right in front of me. Did the accident cause some internal damage the doctors couldn't see? Anyway, it seemed to me that something in him had died.

"Will Serge ever talk to me again?" I asked Papa when he came home.

"Yes, of course," he responded, and I believed him like I did everything he told me. Serge will get well soon, I convinced myself.

Over the next few weeks, whenever Serge came over, he remained catatonic, looking downward as if he no longer wanted to see me and the family. He recognized me, called out my name, but the brilliance had left his amber eyes, and the verve had gone out of his movements. It broke my heart because the distance between us seemed insurmountable. It didn't matter what Papa said. I thought something horrible had happened to Serge. I dreaded his visits in those days and the thought of his haunting silence frightened me.

My nine-year-old spirit missed his arms lifting me to the sky and twirling me until I couldn't laugh anymore as I rushed to him each Sunday morning when he came to visit. I missed his playfulness that made him plot with Viola against me to make me do stupid things and provoke wild outbursts of laughter. I missed his ability to make me happy to be his toy.

At the same time, Papa stopped smiling as much and his shoulders stooped as if his shirt barely hung on his body. His lips were tightly pursed, and he smoked ravenously as if he wanted to eat his cigarettes.

Shortly thereafter, I overheard a conversation between two cousins about a she-devil using her magical powers to bewitch Serge.

"Everyone knows Marie's mother is a *loup-garou*; she is the one who put a spell on Serge," one cousin said.

"Now, why would she do something so mean?" the other cousin retorted.

"Payback. She hates the way Marie is treated. Talked about like a dog, cast aside by the others. Somebody's got to pay," she explained.

I was not surprised because in the lakou werewolves and their curses explained anything bad, whether big or small. Yet, I was somewhat relieved that others were concerned about Serge's health as well as the cause of his brutal entry into silence. My sweet light of a brother with intense wit, captivating humor, and pure enthusiasm had turned into inexplicable darkness. I simply didn't know what to believe in this incredible supernatural story. I was extremely lonely under the grapevine, even though I was surrounded by people.

A few days later I sat hemming a skirt while Tante Yvonne talked to a client. With her elbows standing squarely on her sewing machine, she told the lady that Papa's girlfriend, Olga, had taken Serge's soul. The client looked blankly ahead and didn't say anything.

As if I hadn't heard any of the previous explanations for Serge's illness, I mustered enough courage to ask: "How did Olga take Serge's soul?" I had learned recently from the cousins that Papa had a girlfriend named Olga.

"Hush, child," Tante Yvonne told me.

"What will Olga do with his soul?" I persisted, hanging on to the hope that Serge's soul could be restored to him so he could be normal again.

Tante Yvonne sent me a look of fury. I shut up as ordered and made myself small, becoming almost invisible to continue eavesdropping. She told the woman Olga took Serge's soul because Papa preferred Serge to his other son Jacques. She explained that Olga and Jacques were blood relatives with the same last name; Jacques happened to be her dead sister's son. I stayed still with my anxiety from hearing these two interlaced stories, less because I wanted to than because enduring these tales of Papa's love life shut down my senses.

"*Jalouzi wi. Jalouzi Sergo*," Tante Yvonne, with a solemn expression, castigated Olga for putting the curse on Serge because she was jealous of Papa's love for him.

And, just like that: Olga had sucked the life out of Serge but nonetheless kept him alive as if he were a zombie. I understood the manifestations because I was experiencing Serge as a person whose soul was taken; he didn't smile, and didn't talk; he had lost his vivacity, his wit, his intelligence. Serge simply existed without a soul.

I looked absently at Tante Yvonne and asked her, "Where did Olga put his soul?"

"I don't know," she said, exasperated by my persistence.

Despondent that Serge was in the throes of a mysterious illness, I waited for Papa to come home to try to get some coherent answers that neither the cousins nor Tante Yvonne would give me. I took a desperate chance while he played a poker game and went to ask him: "Who can put Serge's soul back in him?"

He looked lethargic despite a timid smile because after all, Papa's hopes and dreams for Serge and for the family's future slowly eroded. Although Serge's illness was life-changing for everyone, Papa was obviously the most affected. He couldn't face the possibility his son might be that way forever. He couldn't bury his dream for his first son, the one he so cherished and envisioned as his heir. I had overheard him tell Tante Yvonne about his discovery of doctors giving electric shocks to people's brains to stimulate them back to normalcy. "Big White American doctors gave me the use of my arm. I know they can cure my son," he told her.

Annoyed at me and perhaps at the world, Papa answered my inquiry loudly enough so everyone could hear, "Serge will be somebody. He will be an engineer or a doctor. He will be somebody." Papa measured success for his son and for himself by Serge's future. So, he rejected the suggestion that Serge's condition was incurable. He simply refused to believe it.

Papa, usually quasi-mute, especially when concentrating on his card playing, seemed quite voluble as he stalled the game to talk about the miracle of his recovery. "I endured seven surgeries. Touch it. Come on, touch it. It won't hurt me."

He was talking about the metal that protruded from the shoulder of his shirt. That was the tip of the steel rod that the surgeon had inserted from the shoulder to the elbow to replace his shattered humerus, transforming him into a mechanical man. After a moment on the veranda bathed by sunlight, Papa even started to undress, something I had never seen him do in public. He removed the left sleeve of his starchy-pressed shirt to show what he clearly, by then, considered to be his trophy: the discolored criss cross lines where he had been sewn up. It looked like a long flat tattoo of suture points and yellowish skin on the upper arm. I had seen it before, but seeing a partially undressed Papa in front of people was a moment matched only by the shock of hearing him brag about his endurance.

Despite his mangled left arm and almost useless hand, I never heard Papa mention what he couldn't do—he simply did not set any boundaries for his life. Pity seemed useless to him; he wasn't made or brought up that way. Yet, there was surely an emotional price for having the disabled arm. But I saw him act normally, like everyone else. Everyone thanked Papa for his explanations and a couple of the men even commended him for his bravery. Essentially, Papa's very public undressing and bravado were to show that recovery was possible if one had the right doctors. That's what he was betting on for Serge.

"I am going to New York with Serge," Papa told us repeatedly. Weeks turned into months, and he didn't go. Even though he said his stay would be brief, I worried I would be orphaned again, since both he and Mandedette would be gone. But I kept quiet, not to appear selfish, particularly because I really wanted Serge to get well again.

Papa never stopped fighting the good fight—until he couldn't.

One day, he simply stopped talking about taking Serge to New York. I never knew why they didn't travel. Was that dream deferred for lack of money, or perhaps was it simply too ambitious to achieve, even for Papa? He held on to the idea of the trip for such a very long time it became the most he could do not to lose face in front of everyone, perhaps even himself. Whenever he faced adversity, Papa looked for options and found solutions. This time, none worked. For the first time in my life, I saw Papa powerless because he couldn't do what he wanted; in this case, cure his son. Serge's misfortune disrupted, even shattered, something in Papa. I felt tremendously sad for him, for Serge, for all of us.

In the lakou, melancholy had sucked us all into its realm.

THE MISTRESS TOUR

New Year's Day was celebrated everywhere, but in Haiti it meant much more than the first day of a new year; it was Independence Day. Papa added yet another dimension to it: he took Viola and me on a city tour to wish Happy New Year to his friends, practically all of them women. He said it would be a great occasion to meet them and wish them well since they often asked about us.

Although we had no say in the matter, our outing with Papa that particular day was a major event for us since we could show our very best selves. Like Viola, I wore a stunning white lace dress that I chose from the considerable wardrobe Tante Yvonne had sewn for me from her clients' fabric waste. Tante Yvonne was happy to see us so elegantly dressed as we were walking advertisements for her talent. Our hair straightened and curled for the holidays, each of us wore our favorite gold chain, bracelet, and earrings; all gifts from Papa's ephemeral visits to jewelry stores following his sporadic wins. These important details showed Papa, as a bachelor dad, taking good care of his two daughters; he projected us as his successes. Papa wore one of his pastel cotton shirts, superbly pressed by Hoo Koo Wawa, the very short laundryman who from behind the counter of his little downtown shop, claimed to be the only Chinese living in Haiti, along with his wife and children. Papa splashed on more of his *Pour un Homme* perfume that day, I thought perhaps to attract more of these women's attention.

Eating our pumpkin soup for breakfast on New Year's Day was not a luxury but a necessity. I had learned that during colonial times, only slave masters could eat it, so to celebrate Haiti's Independence, the revolutionary generals ordered that all formerly enslaved captives eat the soup to mark their freedom. This idea that a soup carries a heritage of freedom became part of a Haitian collective consciousness in 1804, and still today, most Haitians cling to this tradition of pumpkin soup on New Year's Day and also on Sunday mornings. The soup was magic. Created with mashed-up pumpkin, the soup becomes even thicker and tastier when it's enriched with potatoes, carrots, leeks, turnips, chunks of meat with bones, spices, and a few macaroni. The sweet, earthy smell of this patrimony filled the house. Because our pumpkin soup was enshrined with a noble purpose, searching for a meal's back story became a favorite pastime of mine.

Once we finished, it was time for the oranges sectioned into quarters by Anna. Actually, it was less about eating them and more about preserving the seeds as good-luck talismans. For me, it meant guarding my family from curses that might throw a werewolf in our path and ensuring abundance, so that Papa could take us to the restaurant and jewelry store.

"How will orange seeds bring us good fortune?" I asked.

Papa ignored me, suppressing a sly smile. Anna didn't respond. I didn't understand how saving a few orange seeds could confer these things, but I found no one willing to explain the wisdom of the practice. Children had to stay in their place, which meant we also had to keep our mouths shut or face the consequences if we were bold enough to speak up. Viola hated the oranges and the ceremony around them. But I ate them and kept the seeds, just in case.

After breakfast, Papa drove us first to Premiere Avenue Bolosse, located in a middle-class neighborhood that bordered the southern entry of the city's cemetery.

"Whom are we going to see now?" I asked Papa multiple times as we climbed a long uphill road in his car, but he was mute.

Through my window, I saw people in their Sunday best walking the shoulders on both sides of the street. After a sharp U-turn, Papa stopped the car, and I noticed a very pretty forty-something woman waiting for us by a short stairway that led to a narrow veranda of a small house overlooking the sidewalk. Her up-do chignon looked as if it had survived a night's sleep because of an abundance of hair spray. The sunlight on her eyes made her blink when she saw us. But as we got out of the car, she gave us a look that to me meant she possessed some secret knowledge of us.

"This is Viola and this is Monique," Papa said, touching each of our heads in the affectionate way he always did.

"Bonjour les filles," Papa's friend greeted us with a welcoming smile. I kissed her hello; so did Viola. Papa didn't introduce her, but she grabbed our hands and walked us to straight-back chairs on her porch and offered cookies with colas. He followed her into the house with the greatest ease and good humor, as if he were familiar with the surroundings.

When we were alone, Viola whispered, "Do you think she's his mistress?"

"How should I know?" I retorted.

They came back giggling and their complicity was so obvious that Viola and I exchanged a quick glance. I saw Papa's triumphant smirk disappear because he knew we knew. He brusquely rushed us out of the house as if he were a man with other pressing business. I remember seeing the woman like a marble statue, holding a silver platter of Danish sugar cookies and two tall glasses of *Kola Couronne*, as my lips touched her cheeks for a quick goodbye. I wished she'd fought our departure to allow us to enjoy her offerings, but she didn't. Only then did I understand her initial, excessive enthusiasm; she had a keen self-interest in Papa and didn't want to disrupt him in any way.

Papa then took us to visit another woman. He was a master of discretion because she, like the previous one, had no name. He called her "*la pèsonn*," "the person."

"You see that all his women friends are very pretty," Viola said. Her comment was more a confirmation of a relationship status than an observation of beauty, so I said laconically, "Yes, I see."

The scene was replayed a little later when we went to see *la pèsonn* on Ruelle Alerte and then *la pèsonn* on Rue Bonne Foi. Papa didn't cite the name of any of the women. I could not help but believe he meant his discretion to make us think he was faithful to Mandedette, to whom he was still married, even if she had migrated to New York a year before. He wanted to put some distance between the women and us.

Sometimes, *la pèsonn* had children our age, although it never crossed my mind that they could be our siblings. Their gazes toward us were hesitant because, much like us, they had no choice except to pretend to be good little boys and girls for their mother's satisfaction during our visit. On rare occasions, Papa and *la pèsonn* left to go to another room and soon diffused echoes of their voices reached us. None of these visits lasted long. Papa was not a man who wasted time, so very soon after his tête-a-tête, we left to see the next woman.

Then there was "*la pèsonn*" on Avenue Magloire Ambroise. When we reached her house, he ordered us to stay in the small car. We waited patiently, sometimes scrutinized by passers-by.

"Do you think all of these women are his girlfriends?" Viola asked with a giggle.

"*Je ne sais pas*," I shouted, understanding she was implying he was a philanderer taking us on a mistress tour.

As for me, I had a type of awakening and actually wondered if these women were concurrent or successive girlfriends. Fortunately, I had realized early that my path to knowledge was paved with listening to the *teledjol* as well as keen observation since I was rarely told anything directly by the people who knew those things. That's how I had overheard cousins on the veranda gossiping about Papa's women friends and inferring they were his mistresses. They adopted the term *la pèsonn* as though it were an accepted code, except for Olga, which I heard once.

This was the way Papa took us to discover his predilection for beautiful female friends. Papa wanted to show them his world: Viola and me. He took special pride in exhibiting us to the outside world; I knew that. It was tricky for me and for Viola, too. At each stop, we exchanged glances at the strange eccentricity of our tour. I grew bored when we had to get in and out of the car for his adoring females to ogle us like pretty objects. When they complimented us, Papa grinned because they actually complimented him for his groundbreaking role as a single father of two girls. Men as primary caregivers were a rarity in the Haiti of the 1960s. The norms of masculinity dictated that children were the business of women, who nurtured, fed, and educated them, in the presence or absence of menfolk.

But looking back, there was more to it, for during these visits, the intangible fact was that Papa was not a father. He was a seducer with a half-smile for the benefit of the hostess. He had a gleam in his eyes that expressed desire. The women, each different in the degree of her curvaceousness or in her manner of dressing, had two things in common, obvious even to my young self. One was a generous smile and a hint of wonder in their eyes directed at Papa, as though they looked at him as a savior. The other was an air of silent bragging as if they had already succumbed to what he could offer them: his charm, power, or money—or all three—and bravely claimed him as theirs. I never knew what their dreams or authentic selves were, but they in turn validated him, and he basked in that. That was his fuel.

I fully recognized my Papa.

THE GUN

I was enthralled.

The sunlight sparkled in the deep blue sea of the Caribbean. On my right, through the car window, the greenish mountain ranges peppered with tall acacias and sculptural cacti stood majestically as a backdrop. I thought of heaven, the one I would find when the car finally stopped, and I walked into the divinely warm sea. I went so frequently to the beach that I knew exactly the number of steps from where the car parked to the smooth pebbles that carpeted the beachfront.

Midway to our enchanted destination, Papa stopped the car on the side of the road. He opened the doors on the mountainside so we could stretch our legs. The spot was totally isolated. Then, alone, he walked down a footpath that was like a vein in the woods. He stood there watering the shrubs since there were no public bathrooms on the road.

Standing idly by the front door, my feet resting on leaves burnt by the sun, I decided to do something different to pass the time. Something brave. There was only one step left to take. A test for conquerors. Drunk with adrenaline, I opened the dashboard, took out Papa's gun, and held it to Viola's head.

I knew how to do it from watching men aim guns at people's temples at the drive-in movie.

At almost that exact moment, I felt Papa grab the gun from my hand. My eyes were on Viola's frozen face. "Never touch it again," he said almost as a whisper. I turned to look at him. This time, contrary to his habit, he was not smiling.

Papa's powerful gesture ended my bravado, blocked my move, and saved my sister's life. I was as terrified as I was surprised at the speed with which he disarmed me. Shame was indelible. I disappeared into the silence of the back seat to ponder my self-inflicted misery.

I'd spent my whole life surrounded by the shiny, dark gun, even if I hadn't paid attention to the way Papa interacted with it before his accident because I was so young. But after he left the hospital, I saw him regularly hitch up his pants on the right side and put the gun under his belt as if it were a makeshift holster, just before he put on his perfume and picked up his car keys to leave the house. Only then was he ready to face the street. Before taking the wheel of his car, he put it in the glove compartment. When he reached his destination, he ceremoniously tucked it in his belt again to arm himself as he got out of the car. Sometimes I saw him raise his right side from the shoulder, almost like a nervous tick, enacting a power move, which was a precise show of the gun. When he came back home, he placed the revolver out of our reach on top of his dresser. Sometimes, parts of it reflected the sunlight as it lay idly there.

But this begged the question: isn't that why someone carries a gun all the time, to kill something or someone he or she doesn't want around? Few things were harder for me to believe than Papa being a fearful person. So, why was the gun his most loyal companion?

My relationship to violence was intimate because, despite being very young, I had had to live without Papa's affection and presence for several months while he was recovering from the accident. Perhaps because he had been shot so many times, he felt it necessary to be on the defensive if he ever ran into the soldier who tried to kill him. From time to time, when I observed Papa exercising his hand with a small plastic ball to regain its elasticity, I wondered about that soldier.

One afternoon when we were in his bedroom, I asked him, "Papa, what happened to the man who shot you?"

He glared at me, and I understood his fierce stare to mean, "How dare you ask such a question?" But since I was glaring back at him, he whispered: "He was punished." Papa was visibly weary, but I was stubborn if only because I didn't understand how an adult could be punished.

I insisted: "How was he punished?"

Papa continued to stare at me, except this time a smile formed at the corner of his eyes before he said brusquely, "I took care of it."

His smile spoke to me, and instantly we both—I almost ten and he at sixty—understood that, in his own laconic manner, he had revealed the punishment to me. The defiant smile on his face told me without a hint of a nuance what I have since believed, and this sentiment has never wavered; that Papa had obtained revenge for his shooting by having the soldier who had maimed him killed or had done it himself. He had the means and certainly the motive to carry out the punishment. The thought terrified me, but I was equally sure Papa was not capable of killing even a fly. Standing near him that afternoon, I also thought maybe Papa had the gun because he carried a lot of money for his gambling business. But I knew it was a lie. In that moment, I also thought it was best sometimes not to know things. I regretted my curiosity, but I couldn't even be sardonic, so I simply shut up.

During Duvalier's time, I observed many men in civilian clothing with prominently placed guns routinely standing near storefronts and on street corners, most likely government agents spying on people. Some wore very dark sunglasses—their omnipresent accouterment. Others walked with their heads up in the air, never smiling. But to my child's eyes, it all looked like intimidation. They were trying to scare people, and they succeeded with me. I wanted to hide when I saw them. Like everyone else, I understood showing the gun mattered almost as much as possessing it, as if the mere sight of the weapon announced danger.

But then, for many having a gun meant one was a Tonton Macoute in uniform who killed people, that brutal paramilitary force that Duvalier had created and that answered only to him. Sometimes I wondered if Papa was a Tonton Macoute. Yet Papa looked so different from them— and not only because he never had or wore their blue denim uniform, but because he never owned, let alone wore, sunglasses and he always smiled. I worried silently because the thought was so scary that I never contemplated expressing it to Viola, even after I met some of his client friends one evening.

I went to say good night to him in the poker room he had installed in Grand Angele's storefront. Dressed in my white cotton nightgown, I opened the back door and came face to face with ten or so men wearing sunglasses and sitting around a large table covered with green felt. I saw the halo of smoke above their heads. I saw their dark faces showing faint amusement at the nervous pre-adolescent girl I was. I saw their large fingers holding playing cards. I saw their shiny black guns resting on the table in front of each.

I lost all my senses and trembled with panic.

Ashamed for my intrusion, I backed up while telling Papa I came in to kiss him goodnight. His eyes spoke to me, and I quickly remembered what it meant to be an obedient girl respectful of the rules of etiquette I had been taught. Like the proper little girl I was, I dragged my feet along as Papa's voice introduced each of the men. He said names like *Boss Peint* and *Clement Barbot*, which I was familiar with from the veranda's gossip. These deceptively common names masked that they were those of much-feared henchmen and killers of the regime. I whispered, "Bonsoir. Bonne nuit," and lightly kissed the forehead of each poker player. When I finished the rounds,

I hurriedly kissed Papa's temple with my trembling lips and left the suffocating room.

On the way to bed, I thought mostly of the dark sunglasses worn by the men, for it was the first time I saw people wearing sunglasses inside a house and *at night*. I wished I had not seen these men, and that Papa had simply walked me back to my bed. I was breathless with fright as I crossed the veranda and the hallway to go upstairs. I couldn't sleep. In the magical space that was the lakou of my family, nights always had their secrets, some of which would always be enigmas. Gossip, innuendos, even werewolves were the norm among my intriguing family members. Now, the nights held men with guns and sunglasses.

Just after seeing Papa's poker-playing friends that night, I started avoiding even looking in the direction of that room. At the time it was my secret, but that incident convinced me to shun, at all costs, men in crowded, smoke-filled rooms, with or without guns.

Once Papa made it clear to me that I had no business ever touching his gun, I became fearful of them. The end of the gun as a prop was the beginning of my dislike of it. So shaped was I by this incident that it forever framed my vision and my politics.

Papa, Viola, and I all got back in the car and never talked about it again. As though it had never happened. But the gun grew in importance, its might forever confronting my vulnerabilities.

THE DIVINE CONFIDANT

Finally, after months of studying catechism, I was ready for the last hurdle before receiving my First Communion: the solemn and terrifying exercise of confessing my sins to the priest. He sat behind what looked like bars of a prison cell in a dark, wooden booth designed to hide his identity. But carefully, the words came out. I whispered about my sins: I didn't like Grandma. I stole Papa's fifty-cent coins. It felt good to admit to all that, to free myself. The priest punished me in a barely audible voice. I was to repeat Hail Mary and Our Father prayers over and over and over again ten or twenty times. By the time I left the tiny cubicle that imprisoned me for several minutes on the eve of the big day, I knew God forgave me and I had the divine love of Mary and Jesus Christ before receiving this sacrament.

It was on Wednesday, June 6, 1962. I was five months shy of my tenth birthday. In the predawn darkness, the cocks crowed as if they wanted to announce the day long before it was ready. When I rose from my bed, I was short of breath and couldn't stand straight, as if the ground were shaking under my bony body. Noise came from outside the walls despite the early hours as if everyone in the compound were involved with the preparations. It was cultural, whether Voodoo or Catholic practitioners or both at the same time, as with some in the family, First Communion was a significant rite of passage for a little girl like me to transition to a practicing Catholic.

I could see only floating white when Tante Yvonne came through the door carrying the dress she had sewn for me. I slipped it on and immediately felt angelic, shaped as I was by its extravagant, imported lace and the three-tiered skirt that flirted just below my knees. Then Viola placed the flower-trimmed white tiara on my straightened hair, leaving a couple of curls dangling on my powdered forehead, and neatly arranged the veil around my shoulders and back. I was silent throughout, for I missed Mandedette's face, smile, and perfume on what was to be the most important moment of my life. But Anna quickly interrupted my introspection when she helped slide the see-through white organza gloves on my hands. She gave me the large prayer book Mandedette had sent me the week before in which I had delicately put the images of saints with prayers, received as gifts from my cousins. Viola handed me the new white rosary with the wide cross. I was ready.

Papa, dressed in a new, elegant suit and with his hair waved to perfection, gave me an adoring smile, grabbed my gloved hand and moved me cautiously through the house. The cousins lined up in a human corridor on the edge of the veranda and waved timidly, as if the occasion were too solemn for expressions of joy. I felt like I was being passed hand to hand through an honor guard.

Outside the gate, Papa guided me to the passenger side of the car, and I got in the front seat for the occasion. Through the car window Gaston had cleaned to perfection, I watched girls and boys my age dressed in white walking to their churches. I wasn't alone but I had the intimate conviction that something momentous was about to happen to me; a special magic was in the air.

As I entered Sacred Heart Church to join my classmates, I struggled to walk straight. The church was suffused with a soft, colorful light that shone through its stained-glass panels. Tall, large vases filled with white flowers gave it an allure of abundance. I was in an immense sea of black girls impeccably dressed in variations of lace as if we were small, ebony statues, each with a frilly white covering.

Mass started. Songs came from the nave above and the sound reverberated all around me. Then, with my head bowed, I walked slowly in a line with my classmates toward the altar, as I had practiced so many times. I knelt carefully so as not to trip on or dirty my dress. I knew the priest from catechism classes of the last few months: lean, middle-height, soft brown eyes, handsome, and a serene, chocolate-brown face. As he approached me, I closed my eyes and opened my mouth. I will never forget the moment the holy sacrament touched the tip of my tongue, and the priest whispered, "*Que le Seigneur soit avec toi.*" I feverishly recited my prayer to God as the tasteless wafer melted away, much, much too soon.

Coming out of my trance, I floated back to my seat. I timidly glanced at Papa, Tante Yvonne, and Viola, who had done the same ritual two years earlier, as if all three were my landmarks within the mass of faces in that vast space. I was thankful for their large, proud smiles. I knelt and whispered the prayer, "Our Father…" over and over again.

I sat with my classmates but was really elsewhere. My heart was racing, for I started to understand that something profound happened to me. That was it; I had found God. I was now part of something bigger than myself or my family; I had someone else in my life. I felt less alone. I prayed with ferocity to my divine confidant.

After the ceremony, I settled into the front car seat, leaned against the window to rest a moment from all the emotion. Papa drove to Chaton's photography studio. He never missed an occasion to have me or Viola photographed to send pictures to Mandedette. I suspected that deep down he wanted to show her how well we looked and take credit for being an exemplary single father. A few days later when we picked up the prints, I signed my name on the back of the photograph, just below my dedication, "A souvenir of my First Communion."

I had become a mere souvenir for my mother. My eyes filled with tears.

SAINT-MARC

Every two or three Sundays, Papa took Viola and me, and sometimes Tante Yvonne, to Saint-Marc with a basket filled with creole chicken and white rice that gave off a pleasing aroma. Then, Papa's small car became the happiest place in Haiti.

On one particular Sunday after my First Communion, I told Papa I didn't want to go. I preferred to go to mass with my school. It was hard to imagine him not agreeing with me after his stewardship of the event. His response was as prodigious as it was unequivocal: "The priest says God is omnipresent, so he is everywhere. This means he is also in Saint-Marc. The priest says God is omniscient, so he will hear all your prayers from Grosse Roche Beach. Let's go." His reasoning freed me from the guilt I felt about skipping church.

The gateway to going home to Papa's ancestral city of Saint-Marc was the passage from Port-au-Prince to the L'Artibonite region. Papa drove north for an hour while Viola talked endlessly, helping us pass the time and shorten the distance, but he told us to scrutinize everything, to remember everything.

I sat as close to the window as I could to catch the first sight of the sea and feel the salty breeze on my face. And no matter how many times I had seen the deep indigo sea, whenever it appeared on the horizon through the car window, my heart raced with joy. The road curved, offering a hypnotic spectacle of the coastline, its water a sheer turquoise as it lay over a bed of small rocks as if landscaped. That day, the sun had wrapped its rays around all things, so hot it seemed as if it could break the pavement in two. Beads of perspiration glittered brilliantly on our bodies like sparkles on the ocean. Fat, white clouds danced behind us. The sky in front got bluer and bluer as the car sped down the highway. To my right rose majestic mountains, some thinly covered, others generously so, with all possible shades of green. On the lower hills, mighty acacias and bayahondas stood above the shrubs and grasses adorning the rocky landscape. Various types of cacti and aloes hung on to the rugged terrain.

Halfway to Saint-Marc was the Stinking Spring, from which natural sulphur gas poured out its familiar but nauseating odor. Some used it for therapeutic purposes; others embraced it as a mystical site, but I recognized it only as a disgusting milestone on the way to our destination. I often watched surreptitiously, even if I could hardly bear the hundreds of tiny flies making a hard landing on the windshield. Even the butterflies left their colorful fluff on the transparent but efficient wall of death. Then, rice fields scattered on both sides of the road in perfect rows.

I viewed Saint-Marc with its twenty thousand city dwellers, surrounded by thousands more villagers in its towering mountains, as legacy. And although Papa hadn't been born there, Saint-Marc was home to him, and the soil was fertile with his ancestors, who for the most part laid in the cemetery. One of them had even saved two shiploads of sailors from a cholera epidemic and gotten the French medal of honor from Napoleon for this heroism. He was the one who started the family after his arrival in Haiti in 1848 at thirty-three-years-old from France. He, Jean Joseph Clesca, born Giuseppe on Italy's Elba island became a trader in the rich Artibonite valley exporting precious woods, and then the commercial consul of France. Before he died at fifty-three, he fathered at least ten children—including Papa's grandfather Bruno—with at least four different women; the children continued to live there. Today, every member of the Clesca family is connected to this man. The visits to Saint Marc, and to Gonaives further north once in a while, introduced Viola and me to the family. Now these towns and these landscapes were home for us also.

At the city entrance on the main street, before the gingerbread-balconied houses, we visited great-aunt Mathilde. Slight and fine-boned she looked like a little girl lost in the convenience store that also served as the living room of her small, dark green, one-story house. I kissed her cheek, soft and cool like polished mahogany. This exchange of affection repeated itself at each impromptu visit to a family member. Only when all the courtesies were rendered did Papa finally drive us through the city square.

One Sunday just before Fat Tuesday, the beginning of Lent, Papa continued north past Saint-Marc to Gonaives. Once there, Viola and I left the adults talking and joined a group of girls for a walk in the main square. They wanted to see people in disguise. I held Viola's hand tightly as I looked around hesitantly at the girls laughing and talking nonchalantly. The square seemed infinite to my eyes, with a modern triangular Catholic church named in honor of its patron Saint Charles, and a large concrete walkway enhanced by the life-size bronze statue of the founding father Jean-Jacques Dessalines, who had read the Independence Act on New Year's Day, 1804 in that spot.

Suddenly, I felt shadows behind me. Then there was a brusque and violent movement on my shoulder as if it were being pulled from the rest of my body. Viola dropped my hand. I heard running footsteps. I turned around and, for what seemed like a very long time, my gaze was lost in an immense black mass of cloth that enveloped a beast in front of me. Its face was painted with a shiny, motor-oil black paste. It had white dentures the size of lobster tails. The beast held a fat baton and wore black boots trimmed with clunky bottle caps. It lunged at me. I felt my feet leave the ground.

My fear was like a concrete wall between it and me. But it wasn't enough. Incapable of thinking and incapable of running away, I went blank.

"Chaloska!" he shouted. He jumped in my face. The bottle caps clinked and clinked and clinked. Then, he took a step backward.

That's when I saw it was a huge man wearing a Chaloska Mardi Gras costume. This dreadful disguise designed to frighten children represented General Charles Oscar Etienne, who, in 1915, gave the order to massacre 300 prisoners.

I thought he was about to swallow me. A scream from my gut drifted out into the square. I ran and ran and ran. I didn't stop even when I heard Viola's voice calling my name. I forgot who I was and where I was. I simply ran past her, past the cousins, past everyone in the square. I fell. I thought I'd died. But I wasn't dead because I got up and ran even faster.

Then I fell again and Chaloska caught up with me. His bottle caps clinked at me. I saw the shadows of the other children running away, leaving me on the ground. Alone. I felt paralyzed as I faced his huge white teeth and bulging red eyes all alone. I don't know how, but I got braver. I got up and ran. I just kept running.

I made it to the house and collapsed into Papa's lap. It felt good to sit, to find a little peace with Papa. A few seconds later, Viola and the other girls rushed in breathlessly and gathered around. Quivering, I watched Viola tell Papa, "She ran faster than me."

I felt an uprush of pride and delight. I had succeeded at this very small thing: I had run to safety all alone. As Papa gently wiped away the pouring sweat from my face and neck with his white monogrammed handkerchief, I had the momentary illusion that despite my fear of Chaloska, or anything else, I could run away and triumph. I had never felt that way before.

We quickly left Gonaives and returned to Saint-Marc. Once there, Papa drove into the small road to Grosse Roche beach, named after the huge, twenty-feet high boulder that marked it. Behind the natural curtain formed by this immense rock hid an authentic paradise. It must have been designed by the goddess of the sea as a love hideaway. The waves slapped the shore and left a cloud of mist around us. The minuscule bay with its immaculate white sand was our playroom. Viola and I ran back and forth, teasing one another until we finally entered the water. It was so clear we could see colored sea glass and tiny sea shells through it, and so miraculously lukewarm we didn't need to slap it on the back of our necks to get accustomed to its temperature. Papa couldn't teach me how to swim because of his handicapped arm, so I splashed around— eyes closed, arms upstretched to the sky, head turning back and forth— as though the sea were my natural habitat.

The day passed too quickly, the pleasure as fleeting as it was exhilarating. Leaving the beach in late afternoon to go back to the lakou was to fall in a momentary state of grief.

When she heard me recount my miraculous getaway from Chaloska earlier in the day, Tante Yvonne said, "Ala derespektan, ala san wont." I had no idea why she seemed to take it so personally as to call him disrespectful and shameless. I mistakenly understood her reaction as solidarity with my torment. I continued to see Chaloska's eyes, his teeth, his black costume, and hear the rattling of his bottle caps as he ran after me. I couldn't hear the expression Mardi Gras or see images of people in costumes, without feeling a tinge of fear mixed with grace for the singular thing that happened to me.

Later, I would discover the heartache it must have triggered for Tante Yvonne despite her not having stated the obvious; she was just three years old when her Great-uncle Marcel was one of the 300 prisoners massacred by the general who inspired the disguise Chaloska in 1915. Days later, it precipitated the suicide of her father, shattering her childhood. For Tante Yvonne, memory equaled grief.

In a very tangible manner, Tante Yvonne expressed her anger at the aberration of Chaloska attacking me and unquelled an unspeakable mourning. Better, she honored the lives of her dead father and uncle, and those two dead men came alive for me—perhaps their spirit even empowered me to run away from this macabre Chaloska. Tante Yvonne's distant evocation of the incident was as subtle as it was powerful and amounted to her bestowing upon me, just as Papa did with his regular family visits, the legacy of the Saint-Marc men. Although invisible, they weren't only very much alive, they were omnipresent. Somehow, her words gave their wandering souls back to me, even as Chaloska continued to haunt me.

ME, QUEEN?

On Fat Sunday, there I was on the veranda sitting on a high-back chair for several hours as still as I could so perspiration wouldn't ruin my powdered face or wet my costume. For there was no more doleful time than high noon on a Sunday, when the tropical sun sucked out the air, leaving me and other creatures suffocating in the crucifying heat and frustrated with the absolute lassitude it conjured. Even robust trees shut down their leaves in reverence to the mighty sun. The scented breezes that sometimes brought sweet, fleeting music to us abandoned the landscape. Even the ubiquitous card players retired to a cooler location.

Papa was still napping, but I was sitting outside as a matter of honor. I wanted to prove to him, Viola, and the rest of the family that I had the endurance to withstand both the unbearable heat and the upcoming festivities. Preparing for this, I vowed to have fun, and to smile often but also wanted to forget missing Mandedette, which sometimes felt as though I only had one foot on which to walk.

Of course, I also wanted to show off my perfect disguise for the three-day, pre-Lent celebration or bacchanal, after the Greek god Bacchus. It was Papa's favorite time of the year. For my costume, Tante Yvonne had made a frock out of a blue Haitian denim cloth called *carabella*, with multi-color trim on the short sleeves and wide collar. I belted it with a scarf wrapped just below my waist. She had bejeweled me with beaded necklaces of various colors and lengths and oversized hoop earrings that were pulling me to the ground, highlighted my cheeks with red blobs of makeup and painted my small lips scarlet red. A bright satin scarf wrapped my head; on it, she placed a small basket filled with fruits and vegetables that I had to hold. I wrapped the cording of the traditional peasant leather sandals tightly around my ankles.

That costume became my uniform for the next two days and gave me some gravitas. I was no longer the unsmiling schoolgirl. I was no longer the little sister who always dressed like the elder. I was transformed into someone else—a peasant girl with a new, sparkling personality. I was convinced people could see the difference in me, if only because I looked stunning in my new frock. In the photographs of the period, I smiled, my face shining with beauty, and I believed the costume explained the metamorphosis. Although I wasn't sure it gave me any insight into the life or feelings of a peasant, I was happy to have chosen to be one as a testament to their beauty and endurance.

After an interminable wait, Papa's scent, a combination of cigarette and perfume, announced his arrival on the veranda along with Viola. He had a bright Hawaiian-style print shirt on regular pants and a straw hat sideways on his head. Viola was disguised as a Chinese girl with a coolie hat, black pants cropped just below her knees, and a wide smock with a Mao collar. She looked exquisite, and I loved the black eyeliner that made her eyes look slanted like a true Asian.

"Let's go," Papa said. I knew him to be a man in a hurry, so I walked quickly next to Viola to keep up with his long stride.

"Where are we going?" I asked.

"First, let's get beignets," he replied.

He took the wheel of his car with Viola next to him and me in my usual back seat. Papa believed the best beignets in the city were made by Madame Jeune, a local he knew up the hill in the Bel-Air neighborhood. There, the houses were small, the people were middle-class manual laborers and artists, though somewhat poorer than we were, and the view of Port-au-Prince harbor was spectacular. Madame Jeune had her own food stand, always with lines of people waiting. Papa made us stay in the car and when he came back with his large beignet order we feasted on these tiny pancake delicacies made with crushed banana mixed with flour and baking soda topped with sprinkles of sugar, which for centuries have been eaten as part of the abundant feasts that preceded the forty-day fast of Lent.

Then he drove the little Simca a few miles west, passing throngs of people who had taken to the street as if it were their living room. From my back seat, I occasionally waved timidly to no one in particular. It didn't take long to reach City Hall, the official headquarters for the celebrations.

In one ear, I heard the noise of onlookers grouped around the building behind rope barricades; in the other, Papa's voice asking me to follow him. He was like a boxer making his way to the ring. Holding his right hand, I walked straight ahead as we insinuated ourselves into the center of the activities.

When we got to the large ballroom overlooking the bay, I fixed my eyes on the queens, who were visible through the rows of officials and people in costumes. I leaned a bit on Papa, held Viola's hand tightly, and waited breathlessly. I had never seen queens so up close: three tall, lithe, exquisite young women standing on a small pedestal. Each one wore a long and colorful dress that flowed around her. Each had her hair in curls or upturned, and her eyes highlighted by false eyelashes and makeup. All stood erect, with their heads high; their smiles as if painted on. They looked like subjects of a painting from centuries ago.

I was hypnotized. Papa must have known I would have preferred to be on that pedestal. He bent down slightly, grabbed my hand to end my trance, and told me, "One day, I will make you queen of the Mardi Gras." I froze in disbelief.

I saw him whisper to Viola and wondered if he made the same promise to her. I was jealous because I knew she would be queen before me since she was older.

I came out of my stupor, laughed, and said: "Me, queen?"

"Yes, you queen," he said.

It made sense to me that Papa would make me queen. Queens looked ravishing, did what they wanted, and got all the glory. He was simply appropriating and redefining the narrative of what me, his little Black girl, could dream of. Yes, Papa had the ability to make it a reality; such was my trust in his power and love. At that moment, I felt the intense pounding just below my skinny ribcage. I thought of what would happen when I was queen, and my face froze into a smile. Yes, I believed I also belonged there on the pedestal of beauty and power.

I was forced out of my daydream precipitously because Papa ended this official part of Mardi Gras. It was time to go back to the lakou to watch the parade. Viola and I followed him as we passed the huge crowds pushing and shoving around City Hall. Papa didn't like people crowding him, wrinkling his clothes, speaking too close to his ears, and generally entering his private space. He so resented intrusion that several times he threatened to install electric sensors on his car to shock people if they leaned on it. The thought was nauseating to me because everyone could be a victim. Fortunately, he never did.

Back in the lakou, we climbed onto the top of Grand Angele's *boutik,* which had become a makeshift viewing stand. There, we took our front-row seats, joining the happy medley of family and friends joggling to watch the parade. I looked in awe at the floats depicting historical or fantasy events. They came from City Hall up to the National Palace, through the Champ-de-Mars, and then down by the medical school and in front of the lakou. Each one had a magnificent queen blowing kisses left, right, and center as she turned her head and waved her hands like a mechanical doll. Some floats featured a king with a huge stomach, confirming a very different criteria for the choice of the male monarch. Even when the queens were tired when they reached us, I felt they gave us a special treatment by throwing more kisses, since we always reserved huge bravos as well as balloons and candy. I was mesmerized.

Every now and then groups with identical costumes paraded between them. I treasured every moment because some were multi-colored cows with wooden horns, still others strutted down with traditional Taino headdresses made of chicken feathers. Musical groups competed fiercely with decibels and lyrics to keep the loyalty of their followers. Each group stopped to salute Papa and the family. One of the most popular ones was Diabolo, who wore a red shirt and white pants uniforms; Fritz was a fanatic. The other was Deranje with their black and white uniforms; Wilfrid was an ardent member.

By nightfall it made complete sense to me that Papa recognized some purpose in me being a queen. I'd understand much later that he was preparing my mindset so that I could think of myself as a queen against the odds in a universe of possibilities, which is why he had pointed out the ones at City Hall, so I could accept the reality of such an opportunity. And much like when Fritz brought me out of my insecure shell, I went to sleep believing Papa could make his dream happen. It became my dream.

APRIL 26, 1963

Everything started the way it did every morning. Anna served us our breakfast of buttered bread and watered-down coffee sugared to perfection in an enamel cup. Viola took my hand and walked me to school, even though I was ten and she, twelve. In our well-pressed uniforms, we bypassed the medical school, cut across Chavannes and Capois streets, and entered the crimson, wrought-iron gate of our school. We agreed to rendezvous after classes, and then we went to our respective homerooms.

Classes had barely started that Friday when the director, standing on her spike heels and nervously shaking her head back and forth, entered with a commanding presence that matched her great severity.

"School is closed!" she announced and gave us permission to go home.

The scene is still written in my memory with a very dark ink. Amid the noisy confusion of everyone talking at the same time and asking the same question, "What happened?" I rushed out disoriented. Breathless, I found Viola at our habitual spot. Not at all accustomed to early dismissals, we headed for the gate. I saw parents grab their children's hands to walk home and others hustle them into cars idling by the gate. Along the short concrete wall, other students sat crying for no one had yet come to fetch them. Desperation was written on their faces, and I felt the same. The morning sun caressed my visage as if an antidote to the chaos and desolation all around me in the courtyard.

That's when I heard Anna call, "Viola! Monique!" from outside the gate. She motioned for us to join her. My eyes searched her facial features, trying to figure out what had happened. Beads of sweat gleamed on her forehead and fear was in her small eyes.

"*Bonjour, Anna*. What a miracle. Why are you picking us up?" Viola asked.

"Your father ordered me to do so and fast," she responded in her low voice.

When Anna reached for my hand, I grabbed it and felt it trembling. She grasped Viola's and held both our hands tightly as if she wanted to wrap us around her body.

Viola asked, "What happened not only to make school dismiss us early but to cause you to fetch us?"

Anna was determined to stay silent and concentrate on getting us home. After a couple of hesitant steps, we walked briskly down the narrow streets, taking the shortest route. The scorching sun pushed me to keep moving faster, faster. We passed children in school uniforms, some with adults, all hurrying and talking at the same time as if all the birds in one area were sending their call signals together.

"Anna, what happened?" I asked, echoing Viola.

She looked left and right continuously as if some danger were lurking around. I sweated profusely and my legs almost buckled as I tried to match her brisk walk stride for stride. The concrete was hard as a rock and time was slow. She didn't speak during the short ten-minute trip that seemed to last several hours.

I was happy to find Papa waiting for us at home, which was unusual. He explained there had been a car accident, which made the streets unsafe. He thought pedestrians like us would be safer than people in cars. So, he sent Anna to fetch us.

It didn't take long for me to realize something was terribly wrong, despite Papa's calm and reassuring welcome. On the veranda, everyone huddled under the grapevine as if they were obeying an order to assemble. Some changed the topic of their conversation or simply halted their talk as if I were an intruder when I walked hesitantly into the common space.

I heard the radio loudly playing the ghastly song "There Is Fire in the House; Call the Firemen." I couldn't stop my legs from shaking uncontrollably. *What bad news did it herald?* I wondered. Not content with the song, the radio announcer himself repeated the refrain "Dife nan kay la." On and on. Relentlessly. Endlessly.

Hours passed. But then, we would all learn to wait.

I didn't know what to imagine: Was the President dead? Was there a fire at the National Palace? I wondered as I went back and forth between my room upstairs and the veranda. Somehow, we all knew that whatever had happened was linked to the President and must have been catastrophic.

The adults spoke quietly so as not to be overheard by the neighbors, as if words could fly like birds carrying seeds. I heard it all since I was what some called a nosy and naughty child. I just thought I was curious, particularly since the air was transmitting echoes. They speculated in whispers. Someone said there was shooting in the streets. Another said a car had been shot at. It took me little time to understand that the hidden subject of all the gossip was each person's attempt to foresee the immediate future because today was so terrible.

Within a few hours, the veranda grew still and mute, a sign of the increasing fear. Each was scared. I looked around and only saw dark, empty eyes. After a while, Tante Yvonne asked me to go upstairs to my room, multiplying my distress.

How bad was it? How bad could it be? I couldn't keep still. Braving punishment or public shame, I came down under the vines. I heard whispering voices say that men had tried to kidnap or perhaps even assassinate the President's twelve-year-old son, Jean-Claude, and fourteen-year-old daughter, Simone, while they were being dropped off at school in the morning. The assailants shot at the car, killing the driver. I'd never thought of the Duvalier children as such and realized they were only slightly older than Viola and me; I imagine how scared they must have been to have been shot at.

Within hours of the botched assault on his two youngest children, President-for-Life Duvalier rushed to deploy military officers teamed with his Tonton Macoutes to chase down the alleged kidnappers.

The president's men entered Lieutenant Francois Benoit's residence in the Bois-Verna neighborhood just a few miles north from our lakou.

They killed everyone in the house except Benoit's nine-month-old baby Gerald, whom Captain Max Dominique carried out and put in a car; he was never found.

Another group of armed men went to the Edeline house, Benoit's brother-in-law's dwelling. They killed almost everyone except a few family members who managed to escape and went into hiding.

By day's end, Duvalier's henchmen had effectively exterminated the Benoît and Edeline families with guns and machetes; only a couple of brothers survived. They then grouped the bodies in the courtyard and burned them, leaving others in full view in front of their houses.

The terror continued. In Port-au-Prince, they raided a house of alleged opponents. The Vieux family lost four of its members. Other people were killed in the street or while driving their cars. Several dozen others were taken to the Fort-Dimanche prison, referred to by some former prisoners as Haiti's Auschwitz, and were later "disappeared" or executed.

That night, when the killing abated in Port-au-Prince, the armed men travelled to other towns to turn them into killing fields. The total number of victims of this massacre was close to a hundred. Most were from the country's military, social, and intellectual elites and almost perfect strangers to the precipitating incident.

The more time passed, the more desolate and fearful I became. I had night terrors, but I downplayed my emotions. I did what others in my family so often did as when Papa was shot, when Maître Jacques disappeared, when I couldn't see my playmates: retreat into silence. Who would listen to me? And what would I say? I was beset by a sense of exasperating dread.

A name and a story stood out in this carnage, shedding a light on all the others; that of Lieutenant Francois Benoit. Duvalier suspected him and his brother-in-law Edeline of the attempted assassination of his children because both were trained military sharpshooters. Of course, this logic was totally misguided, according to a cousin I overheard on the veranda: "Why would trained military sharpshooters miss such an easy target?"

Still, rather than finding the two men, Duvalier's henchmen indiscriminately hunted down their families, including their children, and their domestics, as well as strangers.

Overnight, I stopped going to school. I missed walking the city's streets. I missed my teachers. I missed learning.

Within days, the gossip on the veranda said that Duvalier had discovered the attempted kidnapping was orchestrated by his close associate and the former head of his intelligence service, Clément Barbot, whose forehead I had kissed at Papa's poker table. But knowing the identity of the would-be kidnapper didn't lessen the fright we lived with every day under the grapevine because he was a fugitive. I was petrified when a cousin said even animals were not safe from the dictator's tyranny. That's because when someone told Duvalier that Barbot had miraculously transformed himself into a black dog during an escape attempt, the President-for-Life ordered all black dogs in the country put to death.

The siege continued. And our summer vacation started early. That's because that Friday, April 26, was the last day I, like all students in Haiti, attended school. Papa forbade us from stepping outside the gate, so the lakou transformed itself into an animated prison. Viola and I idled our days playing cards, marbles, and dominoes. We also binged on the sweetest mangoes and the creamiest avocados, now in season. Still, I missed going to Papa's impromptu restaurant lunches.

Three months after the attempted kidnapping and the ensuing massacre, the radio announced that Barbot had been killed.

Four months after the massacre, the Edeline family members, including Madame Benoit's mother, two sisters, a brother-in-law and a six-month-old baby who had survived April 26th came out of hiding, only to be hunted down and killed.

Six months after the bloodbath, in October, the new school year started. I thought that day wouldn't ever come. But during that half year in which I clung to my family in the physical safety of the lakou and forcibly learned what waiting meant, I had heard of people killed and burnt, of babies disappearing, of black dogs decimated, and of fire in the house—yet not one adult amid all who crowded the site attempted to put any of it in perspective for me. Still, when the time came, I eagerly attended all my classes with the other little brown children. Yet, the quasi-imprisonment and terror I had endured felt like weights on my legs when I walked to and from school.

FIRST LOVE

On an indolent Sunday afternoon, I showed off my brand-new dress to no one in particular by walking back and forth on the veranda while absent-mindedly watching a card game. The players seemed to be dozing off. Their game was passionless, mostly because of the hot sun and the absence of Fritz, conceivably the best player in the house. He had emigrated to New York a few weeks earlier. I missed him, for I knew he would have complimented me. Still I refused to be bored by the feeble energy of the game, so I stepped out on the sidewalk to pass the time until Viola and Papa came downstairs.

I stood languidly on the front steps of the compound.

All I could think about was how to avoid sweating before it was time to go out. The sun's rays sieved the layers of cloud to grill me into a catatonic state. The blazing heat laid a film of sweat over nearly everything and everyone. A few neighborhood children shot marbles on the concrete sidewalk next to a cadaverous dog leaning for support on the wall, too hungry to wag its tail.

"Little girl, you look so very graceful in that dress," a man said softly. I felt as though I were the only other person in the whole world. I glanced up from his polished black shoes to his perfectly pressed black pants to his crisp, light blue shirt over muscular arms. I saw a very tall, honey-brown man twice my height and likely four times my age standing a few inches from me.

"*Merci, Monsieur*," I responded, ten years old but suddenly feeling like an adult. I looked into his dark eyes and saw sparkles in them.

"What's your name, little girl?" he asked in a melodic voice. It sounded like a song I had heard on the radio; it felt like Tante Yvonne's velvet fabrics.

"Monique, Monsieur," I whispered, realizing I had stalled with trembling knees on a doorstep. Worse, I was talking to a stranger without permission. My damp palms were signs of the impending doom of perspiration as my usual spunk evaporated. Somehow, I managed to smile, less by desire than by reflex. Papa couldn't stand it if I didn't smile when introducing myself.

"Monique, you and your yellow dress are magnificent," the stranger said.

I was happy because that's exactly why I wore the cotton pique, daffodil-yellow dress. It was the first time that I had the freedom to choose the fabric, the color, and the design all by myself and persuaded Tante Yvonne to sew it for me. It had a princess-style bodice that ended in a V just below my slim waistline. And it made believe my tiny bosom, with absolutely no breasts, was bigger than it was. As I put it on earlier, I felt so very light on my feet, so much so that I looked in the mirror to see if the gathered skirt spun even a little bit.

The sound of the man's voice sent an electric current through me. I was hypnotized into silence. I was frozen in the middle of everything around me: marbles clinked in the distance, cars passed as fast shadows in the street, and the sun's rays split my head in two. All I could hear was my heart pounding irregularly. I lowered my head as if ashamed of my feelings. I was enraptured, somehow feeling like the woman I would one day become.

Then the man looked me in the eye, smiled, turned away his big brown eyes, and walked down the street. I watched him stroll away, following his blue shirt as it moved up and down through throngs of people. His head turned from side to side every once in a while, until he became invisible in the crowd.

The only certainty in that moment was the soothing cadence of his subtle voice echoing in my ears.

I sweated profusely, as if my body were crying tears of sadness. I was all alone on the front steps. For a fleeting moment I twirled my daffodil-yellow dress around his empty space in slow motion.

I grieved the unknown man. Only men who were family members or Papa's friends told me I was beautiful.

If I hadn't lived it that Sunday afternoon, I would have thought it didn't happen, so ephemeral the encounter. It was important to me that *we*—he and I—existed, even if our history lasted only a couple of minutes. It powered my confidence.

When I regained my composure, I looked through the gate at the lethargic men playing cards and was deceived by the somber décor. I looked at the sky as if I wanted to talk to it. I walked back onto the veranda, hesitantly, lost in my thoughts. In my bubble.

The glow of love had erased my memory.

Moments later, Papa's distinctive perfume and cigarette cough preceded him under the grapevine; he was always prompt, so much so that checking his *Longines* watch had become one of his nervous tics, like the motions he made to strengthen his hand after he had been shot.

Viola and I hurried to join him as he left the lakou with Cousin Madeleine, a thick-boned, light-skinned woman with big greenish eyes and a loud giggle that projected a contagious good humor. She was lucky, for there was stiff competition among the cousins to chaperone us because Papa paid for the tickets and refreshments. Viola's smiling eyes were fixed on me, and her grin was as large as I imagined mine to be —we were going to the theater for the first time.

Papa drove slowly through the late afternoon heat by the empty stadium and the small houses down the street where the neighborhood's poorer people lived. Then we passed by the canal, and I saw the majestic sea framed by the car window. A timid breeze wafted across my face as Papa turned into a large courtyard lined with palm trees. We had arrived at the Theatre de Verdure complex.

He walked fast. Viola, Madeleine, and I trailed behind. My eyes did a quick tour of the place and saw many modestly and well-dressed people, as dark-skinned as we were. Most spoke Creole, not French, with one another. By the ticket kiosk, other children talked and laughed, but I was more interested in the Greek-style theatre than in anything else. It was impressive—with its wide, semi-circular open space, concrete steps that served as seats, a stage at the center, and a bright blue sky as its ceiling.

"Are we going to see Civita dance?" I asked.

"Probably," Papa said.

Our regal and terribly shy next-door neighbor, Civita, was a dancer in the theater's dance company. She fascinated me, and not only because her name, Ci-vi-ta, sounded like a poem. Some of the fascination owed to the way she smiled with her whole, angular face dramatized by her smooth, pulled-back hairstyle, like she meant it. Some of the fascination owed to her having skin the color of a vanilla pod and her back so straight that when she stood her small breasts rose effortlessly to the fore. I knew from the first time I saw her that I wanted to be just like her when I grew up, just like I wanted to be like Grand Angele, like Aniz. Some of the fascination owed to her being so tall and slim, that when she walked her long legs floated on the floor as if she wasn't really touching it. Viola and I tried to imitate her movements with little success. Still, most of the fascination owed to the way she stood and walked so gracefully that I imagined seeing her dance like a gazelle flying across the savannah. Months later, she would win a gold medal at the First Black Arts World Festival of Dakar.

Papa walked us to our seats in the center of the front row and leaned down to say, "I'll be in the cockfighting arena next door." Madeleine was to fetch him at the end of the show.

A circle of colors flew from the side of the stage and twirled effortlessly toward the center. The dancer's arms flapped as if in flight, like a magnificent bird. I grabbed Viola's hand when I saw it was Civita. It was a dance of love called "Congo," performed by the Théâtre Folkorique d'Haiti dance company. Civita's lips were painted vermilion, and her eyes were highlighted, projecting drama and confidence. In her multi-colored costume, she pirouetted on shoeless feet as if she were the only person on the stage.

I sat stunned as she came back in different costumes for different dances with different partners, but always with her body swaying, her bare arms draped in colorful bracelets, her long, muscular legs making movements that appeared impossible. Every muscle in her body and in her face expressed love, joy, sadness, or anger. I was overwhelmed by the discovery of this new language called dance. Her smile was so captivating; not only did I want to look like her, I wanted to be a dancer just like her.

The crowd yelled, *"Bravo! Bravo! Bravo!"* When she bowed and disappeared backstage without looking back, I felt empty, as though part of me had left with her. I remained in Civita's luminous dance; it took days for me to disconnect from her and the language of her body.

Dusk started falling and the sea breeze became crisp, bringing a hint of salt to my lips.

From the wings came a line of men dressed in dark uniforms, first the brass section with each carrying a saxophone, a trumpet, a trombone, or a flute. Other men with conga drums took center stage. This was the Super Jazz des Jeunes, a big band whose sounds coalesced into tumultuous Haitian konpa dance music accompanied by Creole songs that valorized Haiti, love, and our folklore. Some in the horn section pumped so much air to push the notes that their faces ballooned as if they were swallowing golf balls. One percussionist beat his drums so furiously that audience members joyfully jumped up and down. Then Selina, a songbird with a shrill, almost nasal voice, sang her specialty songs inspired by Voodoo as if she was born for that purpose.

Then a man walked slowly from the wings and stood center stage. I became a zombie staring at him. It was he, the stranger who had complimented me and my yellow dress. He was inches from me. I heard the same voice from the front steps of the lakou singing as easily as he had spoken to me, like water flowing out of a mountain spring. He moved with subtle assurance to the right, to the left, then back to center stage. I wanted to believe he was smiling at me. I tapped my feet on the ground and my head swayed with my body, captivated by the tumultuous rhythm. Then Gerard Dupervil continued to sing:

"Ma Brune, Dark Beauty listen to my song, my song filled with love and passion."

I convinced myself this love song was written just for me. With my eyes fixated on him, I was back in my bubble, hopelessly enamored of my first crush.

His voice echoed gently throughout the theater as he sang his well-known hits: *Maman, Fleur de Mai, Chouboulotte*. And then there was the way he so delicately rocked his lean body back as he sang; the musicians were mere props. I lived my love all alone because I was the only one who knew of my feelings for him since I hadn't yet told Viola about the afternoon's unforgettable encounter. I repeated the words "Bravo!" and "Bis," almost mechanically with the audience that obviously adored him. Next to me, Viola and Madeleine were giving him an ovation.

As Dupervil walked off from the stage, I felt sad, abandoned even, for this was the second time he had left me. His melodious, satin voice and his sweet smile filled my heart. But I just giggled to myself.

That Sunday as dusk chased away the sun, a singular thing happened: the open-air theater with its music and dance became a second home for me. The saxophone, trumpets, drums, and Dupervil, alone and with his accordion, introduced me to harmonies I didn't know existed. That day transformed me as I went from a place of silence and fear to a world of rhythms, colors, costumes, words, movement, and stories that the dancers, musicians, and singers expressed with their bodies and sounds. The distance with my culture dissolved leaving no boundaries for me. I learned what I did not yet know. They were written in me. I stammered, I hollered, I laughed, I smiled, I screamed, profoundly.

"Papa, I want to go to the Theatre de Verdure every Sunday of my life," I told him and thanked him, as did Viola. His reaction to us recounting the show was a huge smile. He understood. From then on, practically every Sunday, he asked me to be on the lookout for when Maestro Saint-Aude walked past our house with his saxophone on his shoulder. That would be the signal for him to drive us to the theater.

And each Sunday afternoon at the same time, I stood on the front steps wearing the yellow dress. It was the only way I knew to hold on to the experience.

I wanted to believe I looked as magnificent as Gerard Dupervil, my first love, told me I did.

ANSWERED PRAYERS

In July 1963, Tante Yvonne, Viola, and I followed our vacation ritual and went to Jacmel for a month. Once back in the lakou, as lassitude set in, the sun seemed to be slicing through the roof. Every lazy afternoon, I stayed in the coolest place to be which was upstairs lying on my bed talking to Viola about nothings.

One day Anna came in looking as happy as I had ever seen her, except when she talked about Lucien. She told us Mandedette was on the veranda talking to Tante Yvonne. Instantly, Viola and I rushed downstairs and straight into Mandedette's arms.

"I've just arrived from the airport and came to fetch you," she said, muffling tears.

Twice every day for the two and a half years I lived in Grand Angele's lakou on rue Oswald Durand, I uttered the same prayer: "God, please make my mother come home soon." He must have capitulated from exhaustion because my mother was with me. At last.

I rediscovered her dark brown eyes as she stared back and forth at Viola and me, much as we did at her. In those eyes I saw only tenderness and love. She hugged me tightly, and I felt comforted by her arms but more so by her familiar scent: she was still wearing Shalimar. Mandedette was back.

Her slightly shorter hair and her body lithe, not at all skinny, showed she had lost none of her beauty, in fact, she was luminous. Her flawlessly applied makeup made it clear that perfect grooming remained her trademark. Tante Yvonne ordered us to quickly pack a small bag of clothes so we could leave with Mandedette and promised to inform Papa when he got home.

In the chauffeur-driven car we rode in from the lakou, she sometimes stretched her long arms and peppered her phrases with, "Take it easy," and "Thank you," as if she were still living in New York. Viola and I laughed with delight at this brand-new Mandedette transcending all notions I had of womanhood. Again, I fell under her spell.

RUE BAUSSAN

LET'S TWIST AGAIN

The driver took us to rue Baussan after a short but exciting ten-minute drive from Grand Angele's lakou.

All the tools I needed to reconnect with Mandedette were in her luggage. She had enough props to keep us occupied for weeks. She brought along the African American singer Chubby Checker, or rather his records. And a turntable. We had instant music with "Let's Twist Again..." She played the 45" disc repeatedly.

"Wiggle your legs side to side," Mandedette sang to Viola and me as she danced the Twist. Checker's voice was so musical it didn't need any instruments to accompany it. I couldn't understand him, but the joyous energy he conveyed was contagious. Being immersed in a sound so radically different from what I had known made me lose my reserve. The music was new to my ears, and, at the time, my body only knew how to walk, so I fell flat on my back. But through hearty laughter, I quickly stood up to continue dancing. In the feelings of the moment, the room became *magnetic*—a space of freedom for the movement of our bodies. Decades later, when I came across Chubby Checker's Cadillac at the Smithsonian African American Museum, the excitement in my body came from somewhere deep where the Twist had settled back in rue Baussan.

Mandedette also brought a toy called a hula-hoop made of thin plastic circle in a multitude of colors. I wiggled my torso, moved my thighs side to side, and threw my arms straight up in the air—all to balance the hoop so it wouldn't slide to the ground as it twirled around my neck, my thin limbs, and my waist. Sweat seemingly poured out of every pore of my body. Aside from getting a good workout, Viola and I competed as we tried to see whose hoop would fall more or faster, and particularly who would stand back more quickly.

I was hooked.

Mandedette sang, danced, laughed, and sweated along with us. In that incongruous, sometimes sunny, sometimes dark room, something serious was happening. All three of us were by sheer instinct weaving enough lost bits of time together to bond again. I was rediscovering my mother. Being with her was different; even though she was as quiet as Papa, her energy was as intense as his temperament was subtly cunning.

I was frightened and thrilled at the same time. Frightened Mandedette would disappear as suddenly as she had returned, leaving me buried once more in despair and unhappiness. Yet, I was thrilled to be alone with her and Viola and finally to live all the fantasies I'd had while she was away. I loved that she had planned everything, even ensuring the house was properly furnished before we moved in. She was like a rock, well-grounded and solid like a marble wall.

When it was time to say goodnight, after supper, after the dancing and the hula-hooping, I was ready for Papa to come home. Exhausted and sleepy, I asked Mandedette for him. Her smile, which made her look like a model at the end of a toothpaste commercial, comforted me.

"Il viendra demain," she said. "Tomorrow." Chubby Checker stopped me from sleeping because I was still humming, "Let's Twist Again."

The aroma of coffee and the sounds of the backyard kitchen rushed me out of bed the next morning. But Papa was not home, so I waited for him. Then Mandedette announced she was going to see him in the lakou. But she returned alone. Then she put us in a taxi to go meet him and pick up our bags.

When we got there, Papa told us he hadn't come the night before because he didn't know where we were staying. I realized not only that Mandedette hadn't told Papa she was returning to Haiti but that somehow when she picked us up, she purposely didn't give Tante Yvonne our new address. My mind told me perhaps Mandedette was afraid Papa wouldn't let us go with her. Something was wrong. Whatever it was, made me unhappy. Their bodies, their allure, their words were so different, yet each spoke with the same uneasy smile. Nothing reassured me.

Papa drove us back to our new house, dropped off our bags, and left without entering.

"Why didn't Papa come in?" Viola asked Mandedette.

Pressed to answer, she relented: "Papa is not coming to live with us anymore."

This was how they revealed their secret: Mandedette and Papa had separated. The sun was shining dazzlingly through the windows, but the room was turning dark for me.

What happened next was a scenario I never imagined. Just like that, my family lost a member. I had spent the last two and a half years imagining what life would be like when Mandedette returned. I prophesied the four of us would go to drive-in movies together, take Sunday afternoon walks by the seafront, and go to the theater. I hoped Papa would once again pace the hallway outside their bedroom while she put on her makeup. But sometimes dreams are just dreams, a way to keep oneself from falling apart.

"Why is Papa not living with us?" I asked Mandedette. She gave me the how-dare-you-ask-me-something-like-that-look, which always had the effect of stopping talk. But I was impetuous, and I really wanted to know.

"Why is Papa not living with us?" I asked Viola repeatedly, like a broken record.

"You are always asking me things I don't know," she responded.

I yearned for my parents to be together again. I was relentless, even obsessed about it. I didn't remember ever hearing either one of them ever raise his or her voice at the other, nor at Viola or me. I never heard any argument between them. I couldn't understand why he had to stay in his house by himself, rather than be with Mandedette, Viola, and me, the way it was before she went to New York. I cursed New York which upended my life.

Papa was no help, either. "When are you coming home?" I pressed each time I saw him. His smile was his only response.

"Why?" I asked, even though I should have been used to the sound of silence. No one said the four of us were over, nor did either of them answer questions about it. No story was invented to explain it. No lie was told to mask it. In a way, the reason was left to my imagination. I lived in a world of say nothing and explain nothing, a world of smile through it or stare through it. I looked at the world through the prison of silence. I had already seen there was something terribly debilitating about it. But this was the moment when I confronted silence as the rule of the house. I was almost eleven. That was their model. After all, since my early childhood, my family had practiced a cult of silence. At first, I didn't dare ask questions, but as I grew older, I became bolder. I often breached the code, even if children weren't supposed to ask elders anything. Each of my parents had a physical representation to mean silence: he, the mischievous, omnipresent smile. She, more creative, used two different styles. One was a direct and frontal stare that could pierce you like lightning. The other was the invented, completely meaningless, and utterly frustrating word "Beski" we were brought up with. In a small way, it showed she wasn't oblivious to the discontentment her silent stares caused.

I was apprehensive because I didn't know what Papa's absence would mean. He was the only adult present throughout my whole life, except for the few months he spent in the hospital. It brought back memories of Maître Jacques disappearing when I was younger. I wasn't angry; I felt worthless, as if I didn't exist, like when Mandedette told me at the last minute she was leaving us for New York. I was powerless to change the situation. I didn't cry, nor did I see or hear Viola cry. It just was.

But I never tired of searching for answers.

One habit that did not change: Mandedette still took what seemed like hours to dress and perfume herself to walk a few inches from her bedroom to the veranda. And if I played it right, I could get sprayed with Shalimar. I'd smelled wonderful for days because I solemnly refused to wash any part of my neck touched by perfume. Its scent meant I was connected to her.

With Mandedette and us back together in our new home, the French language re-entered our lives.

THE ROCKY ROAD

Rue Baussan, where we moved with Mandedette, was unpaved and made of gravel in neutral hues of grey and sand. It was a quiet street named after Georges Baussan, a Haitian architect who had designed the neoclassical National Palace, Port-au-Prince's City Hall, and our parish Sacred Heart Church—all three eventually destroyed beyond repair in the 2010 earthquake. I didn't like it at all that each passing car showered me with dust, soiling my shiny black shoes and turning my immaculate white socks a dirty brown. The novelty of living on a gravel road wore off quite quickly.

Rue Baussan was dotted with houses that were larger than the ones on rue Oswald Durand. Although clustered close together, each stood alone in its independent yard, unlike our family lakou. The one-story homes outnumbered the larger two stories and unlike rue 3, the upstairs people in this neighborhood didn't drive fancy Mercedes, Cadillacs, or Buicks.

Mandedette had rented Tante Yolande's small, concrete two-bedroom house. It was furnished, but she moved things around, creating a protective and beautiful environment within its walls. On the veranda, she placed an abundance of large potted plants and by the time she finished, it was converted into a very dramatic living area decorated with colorful Art Deco metal chairs. The green wall of plants created an intimate, heavenly atmosphere, particularly when the early evening breeze blew through its open metal gates, and it also spared us from the curious glares of passers-by. We spent most of the early days after her return there, her sitting in an armchair with Viola and me at her feet.

I never knew Mandedette to be idle. After a couple of weeks spent making the house a home and bonding with us, she took a job as a secretary at the Haitian American Meat Company (HAMCO). Every day, the corporate car transported her to and from its headquarters in La Plaine a few miles north. I knew very little about her job, except that she spoke English with her foreign bosses.

I was lost in the new landscape of rue Baussan. Part of the reason was that I didn't have my large extended family, the one that had filled my senses and challenged my sensibilities. Although my new home was only a few kilometers away from the lakou, it was a world apart socially. Life seemed at a standstill on this road. It lacked the seething ambiance of rue Oswald Durand. Yet the quiet moments, so very different from the noise of the cousins on the lakou's vine-covered veranda, were among the most exhilarating things about my new neighborhood. I had forgotten the comforting feeling of quietness, which was like the solitude of a soldier returning home after war.

And on rue Baussan, people didn't talk in the street. Neighbors grouped around one another's low front gate or around a tree inside the yard. They did so less because of the lack of sidewalks to stand on and more because of social norms that made it unacceptable for them to stand in the street talking; that's how they viewed themselves. But there was also the unspoken: everybody knew it was not safe to be part of a group discussion in the street. A neighbor, a passer-by, anyone could report it. Tyranny was only one indiscretion away because fascism had invaded Haiti, since an innocent conversation could be interpreted as a political conspiracy, putting people's lives in danger. Fear terrorized people into silence and withdrawal to safe places off the streets that had ears.

My new neighbors 'profiles were also different from before. At the Turgeau entrance, where rue Baussan and avenue Marguerite merged, lived a doctor; across from us there was a lawyer; and on both sides there were teachers. These were middle-class professionals, not the working-class laborers near the lakou.

As the newcomer, Mandedette followed tradition when she walked over the rocky road and stopped for a courtesy visit to every neighbor to introduce herself. Sometimes Viola and I tagged along to meet the children our age. Almost always, the adults with daughters launched invitations for us to play with them; girls didn't play with boys then. Having a mother who had just arrived from New York attracted friendships. As the news of Chubby Checker's Twist spread, girls came by spontaneously and we made friends almost instantly. Never did I imagine Viola and I would be so popular! Viola also could quickly turn strangers into friends with her smile.

The neighbors on our left were named Baguidy, one of the rare families, along with the Conde in Haiti, that still carried a name descended directly from a West African royal family of Dahomey/Benin. Their forbearers, like most of mine, were brought to Haiti in slave ships. Baguidy was a big bear of a man who was forever playing with Bobby, his large German shepherd. Bobby roamed the yard with great energy, chasing the bones his master threw him, trampling the grass, and racing back and forth. I had never seen a dog so ridiculously clean, so obviously healthy and so joyously loved. Dogs weren't loved as domestic animals in popular culture in Haiti. They barked for security, nothing else. We were not rich, and as a rule we were forbidden from leaving any portion of food, no matter how small, on our plates. What was served was measured to be just enough to prevent us from going hungry. There was precious little to spare, let alone for us to feed dogs or to waste. The dogs I remembered from rue Oswald Durand were skinny and hopelessly dirty from roaming the streets peeking into neighbors' yards looking for wasted food. One afternoon, as I sat cross-legged on the concrete wall that divided our house from the Baguidy's, Bobby jumped up to rip my left thigh. I escaped while Baguidy yelled, "Stop, Bobby!" I had no time for tears, my shock was too sudden. I never sat on that short wall again and I developed a phobia about dogs.

Bébé, Baguidy's sultry wife, was always dressed in a tight straight skirt with a provocative slit at the back and a blouse that squeezed her breasts, uplifting them perfectly. She wasn't particularly beautiful— her skin was not smooth, her body was not a perfect size—but she was remarkably free of any inhibitions about her body. She simply fascinated me. I wanted to walk like her, gliding alluringly side to side on short spike mules as if they shouldn't touch the ground. I wanted one day to dress like this neighbor who exuded wild charm and brute beauty. I also wanted to speak like her, for she said even her rushed, "Bonjour les enfants," in a breathlessly sexy voice. She was a thread in the tapestry that connected me to strong women, all with such assurance in their bodies, speech, and demeanor.

Bébé, whose real name was Berthe Posy, and who had two adorable little girls, was a pioneer in radio history for having her very own show, "Horoscope en musique." The day's horoscopes intercut with French and American songs were broadcast early in the morning on Radio Haiti, the only station Mandedette listened to during the day.

While Bébé's velvety, sensuous voice reached us at sunrise from downtown Port-au-Prince, a man's decidedly forceful one infiltrated Haiti clandestinely from across the ocean to our house late at night. It was Fidel Castro. In Spanish, he explained the reasons and the vision for the revolution in Cuba. Duvalier had forbidden all things Communist, including radio broadcasts. I would never know if listening to the Spanish broadcast had been an assignment for the language class Mandedette was attending at the Lope de Vega Institute. It was the kind of thing nobody could ever talk about; even listening to it was a huge risk. But she took it. Every night.

It was during an innocent walk going north on rue Baussan that I first saw Claude, a teenager of about seventeen with a perfect command of his block. I would quickly learn he imposed his own territory on the street by erecting a barrier around the perimeter surrounding his house. Short and slim, Claude had a clear, chiseled face that always showed a grin of triumph. Over whom was not clear to me—possibly his sidekick Cadney who smiled constantly in return. They harangued everyone who walked by.

"Look at this undernourished girl," Claude said to Cadney as they both smirked at me during our first encounter. I felt their cold stares on my flat chest and skinny legs, and my knees trembled. He made other derogatory remarks with words Mandedette forbade us to utter or to hear. She was very strict about cursing and other offensive language.

That night, under my cover in the darkness of my room, I heard Claude repeat his injurious words and relived his gaze penetrating me the way water seeped into the earth. I saw him menacingly flailing his arms in the air a few feet away from me.

But fear didn't beat Viola, so Claude couldn't stop her. When the time came to walk in that direction, she devised a strategy.

"Go peek to see if Claude is stationed at his headquarters on the wall, with or without Cadney," she instructed me.

The goal, she said, was to avoid any semblance of confrontation. If he was not posturing there, we would go. Whenever I saw him holding court on his turf, Viola grabbed my hand, and we circled the block to avoid passing him. As a result, we conquered. I never had to confront him again, even though I still called to mind the cold sweat, the goose pimples, and the trembling knees he had caused.

Claude was a nuisance if judged by his behavior. But he had a gift: he was brilliant in mathematics. A few months later, he travelled to France on a university scholarship. That his intelligence was rewarded brought us enormous relief; we could finally walk undisturbed on his part of the street. But I learned one thing then and there from that difficult experience: never to trivialize the crude language and barefaced posture of arrogant men trying to force me into submission or otherwise render me powerless. I needed to always imagine ways and strategies to resist, even if one of them was as simple as detouring around the block as Viola did.

Everything was within walking distance of our house. We walked to school, we walked to friends' homes, we walked fifteen minutes south to the lakou, and we walked a few streets down to church, whose cross looked as if it were hugging a white cloud hung over it. My identity was intimately linked to Port-au-Prince's city streets. They were safe for us little girls, and they were clean. I was a pedestrian; that's who I was and had always been. I walked out of necessity, except on the rare occasion I was allowed to take a taxi or was in Papa's car for an outing. The streets gave me gravitas, owing to my knowledge of the geography of a large part of the capital city from Pacot to rue 3, from Bois-Verna to rue Waag, and from Bicentenaire to rue Oswald Durand. Walking gave me the freedom, the ability, and the confidence to maneuver the city's streets, which is why I was so tremendously beaten down and wandered so aimlessly as a result of the earthquake that destroyed my city's streets.

I knew Port-au-Prince's streets had their own narrative; they told the country's history with names honoring conquering heroes or cultural icons like the poet Carl Brouard or Alfredo. Some days at a corner, I met the authentic Alfredo, a medium-height, lean man who, in impeccable French, recited poetry hailing the virtues of love to the point that he was said to be suffering from the folly of love.

Then, there was the way the sun always marked its territory over our side of rue Baussan. It was as though someone had turned on a light switch. It was a signal for me to jump up and run to look outside to see nightfall. I never tired of that moment.

On October 4, 1963, a few days before school started, Hurricane Flora stormed in. Strangely, in a few hours we went from a sunny, dry, and protected environment into a dark, wet, and totally vulnerable one. Menacing gray clouds descended from the sky and hovered over us. Night fell in the middle of the day. I hid under my bed sheets. All afternoon, all night, I stayed still as if I wanted to disappear. At times, I wanted to pee, but I held it endlessly until it apparently reverted, way inside my body.

When the rampage started, I saw sparks of neon-colored lightning. Thunder abruptly silenced everything. The wind shook the windows and doors so hard that I thought the house would lift off the ground and fly away. I was afraid it would crash against a wall or a tree or slide away towards the river with the rain. The raucous noise of nature rendered me breathless. It never ceased.

It rained for two days. A deluge. Some actually thought it was *the* deluge. It was so disconcerting that I wondered if God's tears were endless.

Finally, the sun shone shyly from behind dark clouds, and I got out of bed. The brunt of Hurricane Flora struck the South and West regions. Water rose. Land slid. Cattle died. Farms were ruined. People were displaced. The diseased and the deceased were in the thousands; more than 5000 people died in our country of four million. Everything was ravaged. Everything gone. Nothingness. Desperation.

When school finally started after Flora, I found myself enamored again with mathematics and geography, my favorite subjects because I liked the precision of numbers and rivers and mountains. I took home first or second place on the monthly report card; being second was the motivation I needed to study even more to attain the position at the head of the class.

Mandedette, not being content with our idleness, enrolled us for dance and music lessons.

Madame Lavinia, as we respectfully called her, was my dance teacher. This ballet mistress was molded in black leotard and tights and had more movement in her body than all of us, hundreds of little bourgeois and middle-class Black swans-in-waiting of her dance school. Lavinia Williams was a star, who had followed other African Americans such as Zora Neale Hurston and Langston Hughes, who visited Haiti in the 40s and 50s. She came with the dancer and anthropologist Katherine Dunham, who invented the well-known Dunham dance technique before becoming a long-time resident of Haiti. *Soignee* in her appearance, Lavinia wore her hair pulled back in a chignon framed by a black bandeau that highlighted her high cheekbones and cat-like eyes. When she talked, she used an English-accented French that projected an aura of another world.

I felt lucky to be near her, for she was so regal in her moves. I tried to do everything I was supposed to. I was content wearing my black leotards, pink tights, and slippers. I loved that my hair was pulled back in a small bun on top of my head. It was kinky, but every hair was greased enough to stay in place. During our weekly dance hour, I straightened my back, tucked in my stomach, and put my feet in the various ballet positions. The goal was for us to learn to tell stories with our bodies, and I started to feel the possibilities of my body and confront its limits. I understood being in that world of dance was a privilege.

On the day of my eleventh birthday, Mandedette handed me a musical instrument and a long wooden stick. I had no idea what they were.

"It's a violin, a present from Tante Yolande," she told me.

I had to admit it was special to have such an unusual instrument. I loved Viola's baby piano, and now I had my own baby violin, all to myself. A few days later I started taking lessons with *Monsieur*, who never smiled. Just one problem: he said the instrument was too large for me because it didn't fit my body, or rather, my body didn't fit it. While waiting for the perfect one to arrive from New York, *Monsieur* let me use a spare one while I fantasized every day about the new one. I was obedient and sincere about learning how to hold it against my chin and shoulders, almost as if I were preparing it to be stroked. Which is where the bow came in. I learned how to use the long stick with what looked like a ribbon by delicately moving it front and back on the strings. When I heard the music that resonated from it I erupted in joy—it felt magical. Something else was happening, though. I felt like I was in the midst of a small miracle: I became one with the violin and I rhapsodized about this emotion to Viola and Mandedette. A few weeks later, when the new violin arrived, it was too small. I continued with the lessons until another one came. It was too large. That was the last time I held a violin. I was calm but still felt a twinge of sadness because I was abandoning something that had started to stir intense feelings in me.

Mandedette wasted no time enrolling me in piano lessons with Madame Cazeau, Viola's teacher. A petite, impeccably dressed woman with short, perfectly coiffed gray hair that sometimes looked blue in the sunlight, she lived a half-block away on Impasse Cazeau, the cul-de-sac named after her and her husband.

I observed Viola's class scrupulously; she was in full possession of the piano as if she lived to play Mozart and Chopin. She moved her upper torso and legs in harmony with her hands as she happily gave life to the notes she read in her book. That talent—but mostly her unambiguous wish to express herself—made her a natural piano player. Madame Cazeau constantly praised my sister's playing. I struggled. Nothing was easy for me, not even the basic Do, re, mi. Madame Cazeau applied her pedagogy in an unusual way by placing pennies on my hands when I performed my scales. If one penny fell, as it often did, she'd ask why I couldn't play as well as Viola.

Penny on, penny off. Because I lacked motivation or simply couldn't play— sometimes both pennies fell at the same time. She punished me by hitting the back of my hands with the wooden ruler she held tightly to her heart. My knuckles hurt from the pain, which is most likely why I didn't like either her or her lessons. They were tedious and unproductive. I felt inadequate. I felt shame. I felt pain. I suffered the piano. It didn't feel right because it wasn't. Thankfully, the piano lessons ended.

Fortunately, our card playing outlasted these artistic pursuits, and they brought Viola and me every afternoon after school to the neighborhood house of five sisters.

Mandedette probably wanted to do more than simply fill our time with so many creative explorations. Perhaps she intended to help us better appreciate the wondrous beauty of the arts like Papa had started to do when he took us to the theater, or create a precocious bond with Occidental culture, and maybe even stimulate the understanding of bourgeois pursuits and the efforts they required. Perhaps Mandedette was fulfilling a dream through us that Grandma couldn't provide for her. Somehow, it always seemed, she was trying to create for us a childhood she didn't have. Or maybe it was how Mandedette measured her success as a mother by her ability to expose us to arts as a preparation to join a higher socio-economic class. I'd like to think Mandedette was satisfied. Even then, I saw her persistent sacrifice as a woman to push us to dream and to learn.

SYLVIE

I did a double-take when I first saw her because it was so unexpected to have a domestic with such coloration. Most of the maids we had before, whether Anna, Marlene, or Viergine, or the ones I saw in other people's houses, had dark chocolate skin tones with brown eyes. A round, curvy woman with a thick mouth, Sylvie had light yellow skin and pale green eyes which made her look like one of the rich upstairs people from rue 3.

Sylvie was totally unusual in that she was raised in the rural southern town of Fond-des-Blancs, which literally meant "white people's base." One of several former Polish strongholds in the country, this small village was populated by white peasants who were *Haitians*. And considered *Blacks*. And most definitely *poor*.

Sylvie was a descendant of a Polish soldier—one of those who stayed behind in Haiti after refusing Napoleon's order to massacre the Blacks who had revolted against the re-establishment of slavery in 1803. When independence was declared a year later, Haiti's Emperor, Jean-Jacques Dessalines, officially rewarded them by making them both *Haitians* and *Blacks*.

I loved that cooking was Sylvie's art form. Whatever meal she created combined nourishing ingredients seasoned with a rich mix of spices, from garlic to chives to cloves. She made thick corn meal with spinach leaves and bits of herring or, if we were lucky, codfish. Sometimes she cooked *diri-ak-pwa,* the Haitian mixture of rice that derived its pinkish color from the red kidney beans. Other times, she crushed the kidney beans into a creamy soup with cut-up plantains and small chunks of lard, which she served when we came home for the midday school break.

"Let me have some extra lard, please," I begged Sylvie.

"Timoun sa a, always wants something extra."

"Give me more plantains, please," I asked again.

I liked Sylvie because she would put as much lard and as many plantains in my bean soup as she could without arousing Viola's suspicion or jealousy. I gave myself a mission to make Sylvie's fiber and protein-filled soup last as long as it could, for it had become my fetish, so worshiped it was for its magical power to revive my tired, hungry body.

Her culinary masterpiece, though, was the rice pudding. When she managed to save a pittance from the daily groceries to purchase a pocket-sized box of raisins, delirium set in. Her rice, overdosed with those small, dried raisins, was almost too good to eat; it was heaven to me.

At night, she presented another self. She was a spinner of tales, a *raconteuse* who told riddles, proverbs, and stories, embellishing them at will. The minutes before we went to sleep were suspenseful, but full of humor and amusement.

"*Tim, tim?*" Sylvie said to challenge us.

"*Bwa chèch,*" Viola and I responded instinctively. It was the traditional indication that we wanted to continue the game.

"Abiye san soti?" "Who gets dressed without going out?" Sylvie said, looking in the sky, attempting to trick us into an erroneous answer.

"*M bwe pwa.*" "I don't know."

"*Ou bwa chèch?*" Sylvie asked if we didn't know.

"*Kabann.*" "Bed." She said triumphantly because in Haiti, dressing or making up one's bed is customarily the first thing one does after waking up.

"Tim, tim: Dlo kanpe?" Water standing up?

"Kann! Sugar cane," Viola said.

"Bravo. Timoun, time for bed," Sylvie interjected.

"No, another, please, Sylvie," Viola and I told her as we grabbed her bosom to hold her in place for more storytelling.

"Ok, let me tell you one proverb as a *degui* before I go to my room." Sometimes, she was tired or didn't have the patience and wasn't keen on telling us long stories like the one about Tezen, the fish in the water, or Bouki and Malice. My favorites included "Pale franse pa di lespri pou sa a." Speaking French doesn't mean you are intelligent or wise. And "Si travay te bon bagay, moun rich ta pran l depi lontan." If work was so good, the rich would have seized it a long time ago. These proverbs owed to the wisdom of our uneducated but oh-so-brilliant folks like Sylvie.

Her stories poked fun at the three different worlds that existed in Haiti: the one with the underclass who didn't know how to read or write, the middle one with families like us struggling to live off meager earnings, and the most affluent upper class, better schooled, and for the most part, disdainful of the other two. She made us laugh at them, or at least smile at their incongruities.

Sometimes, sleep overcame me, and I didn't see Sylvie walk out of our bedroom.

Distance gives perspective. I discriminated against Sylvie without realizing it. Fortunately, she didn't hold it against me. We were acting out the things we had learned. I never knew Sylvie's last name; norms stated that she was a servant, so last names simply weren't important. Even though we weren't rich by any measure, our insignificant backyard was the frontier between the main house where we lived with a modern bathroom, and Sylvie, who lived in servant's quarters with a latrine behind it. While Viola and I spoke French with each other, our parents, and friends, we spoke Creole to Sylvie, who understood some French from hearing it repeatedly.

When I think of Sylvie, I recall her mastery of mixing a bit of this with a bit of that and spicing it up to produce something delectable. I often wondered what would have happened if I hadn't met Sylvie. For it was with her cooking that I killed my boredom, and it was with her storytelling that I continued, after Viergine, to learn how to spin words to tell stories.

LOULOU

Before I realized it, a man began to visit Mandedette. Every day. He always came as the sunlight faded from the city. He parked his black Corvair to block the front of the house as if he were daring the curious to peek inside the veranda.

Loulou and Mandedette had grown up in the South a few towns apart. Mutual friends introduced them when she attended secondary school in Cayes, but each was at a crossroad when moving to Port-au-Princeso they went their separate ways. By the time they found each other years later, each was married to someone else.

But now Papa was out of the way. And maybe it didn't matter to Loulou or Mandedette if he was free from his own marriage. He was her choice, not an imposed one as Papa had been. She seemed to revel in that freedom. One thing was certain: Mandedette wore a permanent smile when Loulou was with her. He looked at her all the time and projected a sort of assurance mixed with humility, as though he knew who he was and the price he had paid to get where he was.

I didn't like anything about Loulou, who I remembered as her client at the Ondine *Salon de beauté* manicure kiosk. He walked with his shoulders hunched; Papa walked with his back straight. His skin color was a dirty creamy beige; Papa's was a warm caramel brown. Loulou had a mustache; Papa's face was clean-shaven. Loulou wore a scent I didn't know; Papa smelled lavender fresh from his usual perfume.

Loulou and Mandedette could have passed for brother and sister, so similar their coloration and their quiet bearing. They sat side by side, so close not even a tree leaf could slide between them. And they whispered and whispered for what seemed like forever. I resented that he sat much too close to her. And I couldn't understand why they spoke only in hushed tones on the dimly lit veranda.

"Loulou is Mandedette's boyfriend," Viola told me one day. I took it in, stoically.

From then on, I thought he wanted to be my Papa. I already had one and didn't want another, which is why I disliked his visits. At first, I hid when he came so I didn't have to greet and acknowledge him.

"Monique, you must say bonsoir Loulou," Mandedette instructed me in her firm teacher tone. Only then did I comply. On the other hand, Viola—who everyone said was nicer than I—always greeted Loulou with her infectious smile and a loud kiss on the forehead.

Eventually, I changed my strategy. When he came, every few minutes I walked to the veranda and said silly nothings just so I could interrupt their conversation. Then, it was never just the two of them because Viola and I always purposefully sat nearby. The rare times Loulou spoke to me, his moustache moved in tandem with his thick lips, and he enunciated every word like a teacher, an actor, or the lawyer that he was with his corporate and personal law firm near the city's docks. He never did go home while I was awake.

Papa also came by in the late afternoon, sometimes unannounced, but he came to take us to eat ice cream or *griyo*. Perhaps he was conscious of his new status as an outsider because, for the first time since I was born, he had to visit Viola and me. We also visited him and the family in the lakou whenever we wanted to. Still, Papa seemed obsessed with Loulou, often asking us if he gave us presents. The answer was always "No." That is, until the day after Christmas.

"Surprise! Loulou brought you gifts. Come see," Mandedette announced, looking at me as if she were a child who had just received her own Christmas gift.

At first, deadpan, I wanted to know, "Why?" But since it was a question of presents, I followed her outside where Viola was already standing by Loulou's car. Through the back window, I saw two wrapped boxes with huge colorful bows on the back seat: a very large one and a much smaller one. Viola carried them to the veranda where Loulou and Mandedette were sitting.

"They are your gifts," Loulou told us with a smile that took over his whole face.

"Bonsoir Loulou," I said, eyeing the boxes, still reluctant to show real interest since I didn't like him, even as a gift bearer.

"Pick the box you want," he said, gently edging my shoulder towards them. I was not the type of girl to be a pushover, but I could see he was eager to become my friend. After all, I was the only perceptible adversary in the house.

"I want the large box," I said, still sulking but positioning myself in the battle I saw coming.

"I want the large box," Viola retorted.

"Viola, let Monique have the larger box because she is younger and you are wiser," Loulou counseled her during a tête-a-tête. She smiled in agreement.

I ripped the wrapping off the big box, which was almost my height. Looking at me with fixed eyes was a small doll with white skin and short, curly black hair. I named her Betty. I was happy, so happy that I thanked Loulou, even if reluctantly. And I meant it.

Viola hurriedly opened her box. She pulled out an equally small doll but with a curvaceous bosom and long blond hair. "Marilyn," Viola said breathlessly, ebullient in this peculiar naming ceremony. I didn't know what to say. I couldn't stand it because I thought Marilyn was so much more beautiful than Betty. Marilyn had long hair; Betty's was short. Marilyn's hair was blond; my doll's was black. Marilyn also had seemingly everything Viola and I did not: a pale face, long blond hair, and a foreign name. The soundtrack I heard was composed of Mandedette's, Loulou's, and Viola's voices laughing as Viola joyfully told Marilyn in her high-pitched voice, "Que tu es belle!"

I stared at Marilyn in silence for what seemed like forever. The raw nerve touched by Marilyn underscored my race shame. Somehow, at my young age, I understood light skin was better than my dark one, through no fault of mine, and was beset by a sense of unworthiness of a staggering magnitude.

With twilight, I heard the buzzing of flies and the humming of mosquitoes.

After Christmas, a certain peace prevailed between Loulou and me so much so that when Mandedette suggested I show him my entry for a contest, I agreed.

One morning, listening to Radio Haiti as we did every morning while at breakfast, the clear baritone voice and perfect pronunciation of Maurice Duviquet spoke to me. A former communist anarchist in the 1930s in his native France, Duviquet became a popular radio host and businessman after moving to Haiti in the 1950s. He invited his listeners to submit a text for a radio commercial contest on his show.

I leapt at the idea. I told myself I could do it. Then, I told myself I couldn't do it. I was afraid to fail. I had never written a commercial nor had I ever participated in a contest. Every day, Mandedette told me to dream it. I could write the text when I wanted to, and she promised to correct it. That's how I came to write a radio commercial. Over several days, whenever I wasn't studying, I tried to find the few words that could tell a story. I had always been greedy for the pleasure of hearing words, whether for Viergine's or Sylvie's storytelling, the oral histories passed down on the veranda, or simply my cousins' talk of werewolves and other demons. Without knowing it, they were initiating me into writing. However, I didn't realize I had to master a new skill of finding the appropriate words, organizing them logically, and crafting them to create a narrative. I was buoyed by Mandedette's energetic support while never questioning my ability to rise to the task. So over and over again, I put the words together in what was to be a dream scenario. Loulou proposed some changes, which I accepted.

A few weeks later, I received the announcement that I won the contest and an invitation to Duviquet's live radio broadcast, which helped seal the détente between Loulou and me. Until this moment in my life, I had just been Viola's little sister or my parents' younger daughter. I had no identity of my own. But now I was not only a writer but a winner of a commercial writing contest for the most important radio station in the country. I wasn't bashful about my joy, for I was in a special light. I had done this. It was a small thing. But it was also a huge thing. Having achieved this goal at eleven gave me some of the confidence I so desperately needed.

THE SUMMER OF TERROR

On April 2, 1964, President Duvalier organized a referendum and forced anyone talking about him to adopt a new terminology: "President for Life." Worst of all, after 150 years of independence, the flag of my country was now different. All my life, I proudly saluted a blue and red flag that had flown above my school and other public buildings. Suddenly, the short dictator with round, black-rimmed glasses and a black hat changed its colors to black and red. He devoured everything, yet no one around me said anything about it, perhaps feeling the confines of the dictatorship. I was totally confused but also totally afraid to ask why. It was as though a new life began for us and the country.

When Saturday, June 27, 1964, arrived, school had just ended with me passing to sixth grade when close to twenty men entered Haiti from the Dominican Republic to take up arms against the dictator and his regime. We started hearing coded messages of visceral dread as the musical score of the dictator played again on the radio. "Dife Nan Kay La." After a time, those four words, "Fire in the House," were so ingrained in me—and I'm sure in all of us—I didn't need to hear the rest of the song to start trembling.

For reasons unknown to most, the army and the Macoutes decided not to fight the insurgents. Rather, they chose to execute arbitrarily people living in some of the southeast towns bordering the Dominican Republic. At least forty-five members of the Madoumbe family and nineteen members of the Fandal family were shot. Then, they killed more than 600 people in the border towns of Thiotte, Belle-Anse, Grand-Gosier, and Mapou not far from Jacmel. These assassinations of peasants so haunted Haitians, they gave them a name: the *Masak Peyizan Thiotte*.

On August 5, thirteen young men calling themselves "Jeune Haiti" arrived in the country with one goal: to provoke an uprising against the dictator. They docked their boat on the country's western peninsula near Jeremie, where most of them were born. That twelve of them were light-skinned and from well-to-do families, and only one was dark-skinned would predict the racist brutality to come. From listening to adult conversations on the veranda, I knew that Duvalier gave the order to target and execute light-skinned people, in priority the family members of "Jeune Haiti" members—which is why many called this massacre a genocide. The cousins said they heard that Army officers like Lt. Jose Borges, and Macoute militiamen like Astrel Benjamin and St. Ange Bontemps, carried out the bloodbath by assassinating twenty-seven members of the Drouin, Villedrouin, and Sansaricq families, including several children under six; a pregnant woman; two elderly, including a handicapped one, most after being tortured. Hundreds of other people died because whoever was thought to have provided assistance to the thirteen men was exterminated.

The invaders fought on, some were killed, some committed suicide so as not to be caught, but two managed to escape into the countryside. The country was put on high alert to find them. The propaganda said that our national house was on fire. And that's why the song "Dife Nan Kay La" played non-stop on the radio. President-for-Life Duvalier wanted to let us know he would set fire to the house—the country, really, burn it down if necessary—if he ever felt it was threatened; and he took it all personally. The song was a cruel, indelible marker that was imprinted on my brain. It put me in stunned silence. To cope, I sometimes covered my ears. It didn't matter because the terror was insidious; the song continued to play in my body even as I went to sleep. Sometimes, I woke up trembling and heard its echo in my head as I saw images of cousins huddling to whisper.

Wherever I went—to other people's houses, to Jacmel—the whispers were endless. When I searched the whisperers' eyes, they looked for the eyes of others, perhaps to exile themselves from the reality, to protect their slippery good conscience, or to silence the executioners' deeds.

Later as an adult, I understood Duvalier's fire as a metaphor for the annihilation of family bloodlines, much like Hitler did the Jews or the Hutus of Rwanda with the Tutsis.

On August 24, rainwater rose higher and higher, flooded the plains, and ripped through plantations with brute force, carrying houses, dogs, pigs, goats, chickens, and cattle out to sea. More than 200 people died in the massive destruction as Hurricane Cleo ravaged the southern countryside region of Haiti like a cleansing gesture.

To end the summer break, Viola and I went to spend the month of September with Grandma. She lived in *Lakou Amelia,* a compound much like Grand Angele's, except it was up the mountain in Petion-ville. It was named after Grann Amelia who had migrated from Kenscoff to settle closer to the city on that particular piece of land. It was her new homestead, and there she had her children, and they had theirs.

I was in the midst of shifting realities from one of the schools and games on rue Baussan to *Lakou Amelia,* a totally different, tiny universe that became my world during my stay. As I walked around the cluster of small houses in the lakou, I could look through the lace-decorated windows and see my neighbors face to face. In this semi-rural neighborhood, goats and chickens of all sizes ran in all directions, from the tiny hens to the mature ones ready to become our Sunday meal. At least two roosters, each with its particular distinctive crowing, announced dawn. Mornings were wet from the dew, so I drew animal shapes with the water specks on the ground by Grandma's wooden front door. When night fell, temperatures went down so much that I needed to put on a sweater and socks to warm my cold toes. Still, I preferred Kenscoff's air because it was imbued with the scent of the pine and eucalyptus trees.

The place was permeated by the charm of those who lived there. One of the main characters was Grann Amelia's oldest daughter, Miracia, a tall, dark-brown woman with thick lips who smiled at us all the time. She navigated between her minute two-room house and Grandma's, where she came to clean and cook. Miracia wore an intense look on her face as if she carried an equal measure of joy and despair in her body. She was so skinny that the bones in her chest, front and back, protruded, likely a result of not having enough to eat.

Miracia had several children, but it was her youngest girl who became Viola's and my live doll. Tita was her nickname, but she was named Antoinette in honor of Grandma, her godmother who pledged at her baptism to shepherd her into the French-speaking world, so utterly different from the one she lived in. At five years old, Tita was round and pretty and went barefoot all the time. Viola and I played with her constantly. I combed her hair, put ribbons and barrettes in her braids, and dressed her several times a day. One sign of the affection I had for her was that I gave her my all-time favorite dress: the pink one with cut-out blackbirds. It nearly broke my heart to give it away even when I outgrew it, but seeing how pretty she looked in it consoled me. The colors brilliantly contrasted with her charcoal skin.

One particular day, Grandma served *kalalou* that Miracia cooked with beef meat served with white rice. Also called okra, it was undeniably sticky and green and healthful. I eyed the full plate placed in front of me on the card table with the lace tablecloth and saw that its gluey sauce didn't look appetizing. I glanced at Viola, who stared blankly back at me as she started eating.

"Grandma, I don't want to eat the *kalalou*," I told her.

"Fine. Someday you'll eat it," she told me quietly with not a trace of anger in her unusually low voice. She removed my plate. It wasn't the type of house where snacks were kept, so I couldn't forage for food. I pretended to ignore the growling in my stomach as I waited anxiously for the sun to set and supper to be served.

Hours later, Grandma served Viola a supper of hot chocolate and bread buttered with guava jelly. I got the plate of okra I had rejected at lunch. At first, I thought she was teasing, even though she wasn't the teasing type, but I quickly realized she was not happy with my independent stance.

"May I have some supper, please, Grandma?"

"No. You were disrespectful to me earlier when you said you wouldn't eat *kalalou*," she told me. So, I went to sleep hungry with a stomach that felt like it was burning.

The second day, normalcy returned, or so I thought when I ate breakfast with Viola. But at lunch, okra was placed prominently on my plate again, this time cooked with chicken neck and feet. Grandma knew I loved chicken, but she insisted I eat the okra and the white rice first. I refused even though I was starving. Viola ate voraciously. The stance I took isolated me, but I hated *kalalou*.

"Fine. I'll wait, then," Grandma said, and removed my plate from the table. I had less and less energy as the day went on, but my resolve not to eat the slimy green vegetable didn't waver. I didn't go to bed starving that night because I was served supper. If this was an attempt at empathy on Grandma's part, my anger only increased because of the lesson I was being forced to learn.

On the third day, Grandma had Miracia prepare okra with chicken again, this time adding *djondjon*, the tiny, dry, and extremely tasty Haitian black mushrooms. They tinted the okra black, but it was still very slimy. By then, I was frightened. I was embarrassed. And I was too hungry to protest. I capitulated to her ferocious counterattack and ate it all. Viola gave me a smile of relief. Grandma acted like I was invisible just as Tante Yvonne had when I asked about Olga taking Serge's soul, or Papa when I asked about Jacques.

Grandma tested me several other times by cooking kalalou again. I dutifully ate it, if only to avoid going hungry. The paradox was that Grandma, an intransigent figure of authority, had a simple philosophy: "You must eat the food you are given because you may not have any the next day." Yet, she had food stocks for several days; she had money to send Miracia to the market. Perhaps it was rooted in her precarious life growing up or raising Mandedette when food was often scarce. To like or not like okra was not the point, which I finally understood.

She probably thought here she was feeding me, and here I was breaking tradition by telling her I wasn't eating. I wasn't accorded that kind of freedom as a child, so my decision took on even more meaning than intended because it insulted her, and the food cooked in her home.

Grandma's system of power and domination didn't allow my voice. But I had the disposition to resist. I failed. I resisted. I failed again. By the end of that summer, I spoke often, claiming a small space of resistance to survive.

FLAGBEARER WITNESS

In October 1964, when the new academic year began exactly a month shy of my twelfth birthday, I was a senior in elementary school and Viola entered an elite, mixed, private secondary college, after passing the standardized state tests.

We walked together for the first leg of the fifteen-minute trek. Following a quick goodbye in front of her school, I continued alone for the few blocks to mine. I kept my eyes wide open and alert as I passed the small kiosks or baskets tended by men and women selling peanuts, ice frescoes with flavorful syrups, and candies, which wrappers littered the sidewalk. On the way back home for our lunch break, I walked up to Viola and we continued home together. For the afternoon sessions, we repeated the same steps. It was useless to say it was hot, as some days the unforgiving noon sun seemed to pound my head like it was the skin of a drum. The walk wasn't tedious, it was just depleting. It was our destiny. Viola and I talked on the way up and down, and we laughed about little things, but most times, we repeated our lessons to each other.

While each morning at 8:00, all of the students, teachers, and staff lined up in the central school courtyard to follow the ritual of singing the national anthem, I always thought of when I would become one of the flagbearers.

I had imagined myself one for a very long time. I'd carefully observed the other students who carried out these duties: they all had perfectly pleated skirts, immaculate white blouses, every hair in place, and brilliantly shined flat black shoes. I liked the image of impeccable cleanliness while in service to the flag and I was prepared to follow their leadership model.

But it was so much deeper than that. I was really attached to the values of the flag as I learned from my history class. I was extremely proud of my heroic ancestors, who, by ripping the white color away and leaving only the blue and red, made the flag a huge symbol of Haiti's independence from colonial France. They had a vision and an ideal of a country where everyone was a *moun*, an important person with rights to be respected. I understood the flag to unite one Haitian with the other to fight for freedom and for justice. Those concepts of country and flag filtered into me ever so gently.

Now that I was a senior, I could finally volunteer for the job of flagbearer. I felt so proud of myself for being chosen to be part of the elite group of girls, two on duty each month. I was separate from Viola, from Papa, from Mandedette. This was me learning how to hold the rope on one side with another girl at the other to string the flag. Then both of us tied the rope in position on the metal rod on the ground. Our job was to maneuver the thin cord as the flag rose and rose and rose to the top of the pole. One thing was beyond clear: we had to raise the new black and red flag of the President-for-life Duvalier since the penalty for not doing so could even be death. While I performed this task, I sang along with the other girls: "For the country, dying is great. For the flag, dying is great." You had to time it right, so the colorful emblem reached the top as the singing of the hymn ended. The flag floated and caught the morning sun. I was thrilled.

Something about singing and raising the flag made me feel I was a small part of the heroes' circle. I truly believed that to honor protect and serve Haiti was a noble act. I performed a protected ritual—a love session with Haiti. I knew what it meant, and I adhered to that completely.

On November 12th, 1964, a month after school started, and three months after the massacre in Jeremie, Duvalier ordered all Port-au-Prince schools and universities to take their students to the main cemetery area. Civil servants and private sector employees were also summoned.

It was so all of us could witness the execution of two men: the last of the thirteen "Jeune Haiti" men who had invaded the country during the summer.

Louis Drouin, Jr. and Marcel Numa were caught after a three-month manhunt. They had put up a valiant resistance, with numerous human lives lost on both sides. But the opposing forces had won. Their eleven companions were assassinated; now, it was their turn to pay the price of challenging the rule of Duvalier.

Why would this short man with a high-pitched nasal voice order us schoolchildren, or anybody for that matter, to watch a killing? I swallowed my question. Had I asked Mandedette or Papa, they could have been assassinated like the Benoit and Edeline families or disappeared like Maître Jacques. Fear had infiltrated our intimacy.

Mandedette forbade Viola and me to go to school that day. Like most parents, she was most likely afraid of the confusion and anguish we might suffer from witnessing two executions. To pass the time, I wandered in the backyard and in Sylvie's kitchen, and Viola and I played our favorite game: *besigue*. We ate lunch, and then played bones and some more cards. That evening, I glimpsed images of the men with the rifles and the crowd around them on television with Mandedette, who quickly shut down the set, calling it off-limits. I did not know that I had briefly seen some of the worst that men who are sick with hate did to feel powerful.

The following morning at school, I overheard that some of the thousands of schoolchildren who witnessed the ghastly scene had fainted.

That afternoon when we visited Papa in the lakou, I heard whispers on the veranda about the huge crowd, about a man's head not turned properly, about the white priest. Some talked of the twelve crazy young men who thought they could fight Duvalier but now faced the consequences of their stupidity and arrogance. No one said these young men were resisting the barbaric oppression of the president-for-life; the option of speaking freely didn't exist on the veranda or anywhere else. One cousin called Duvalier a genius. I could feel everyone's anguish in my bones. I shut it away and never asked any questions, so fearful was I that the killers might come for me or my family. Terror was my constant companion.

The news managed to filter through, despite Mandedette's best efforts. It was broadcast over and over and over again for several days, just in case one had missed the live event. One day, out of curiosity, I watched the black and white video.

They put them on display like slaves, but the two men stood stoic and dignified with their backs to the cemetery wall. They also roped them; someone tied their upper arms and hands to a wooden pole with white cord. A priest in a white cassock and holding a black Bible walked briskly toward thirty-one-year-old Louis Drouin, Jr., the mulatto with the thin moustache and wire glasses. Drouin responded by turning his head toward Marcel Numa, only twenty-one. The priest then strode to the taller, darker Numa, who moved his head up and down, as if acquiescing. Seemingly by instinct, the priest made a furtive sign of the cross, giving Numa his last rites before walking back to Drouin to do the same. He walked away, leaving the men alone to face the platoon of army officers in beige uniforms and metal helmets positioning their long rifles. The firing squad offered no mercy: gunshots tore the silence. They hit the men in the chest.

Both collapsed to the ground almost kneeling, their arms held back by the ropes. Their limp, disarticulated bodies intersected the wooden poles as if they were upside-down crosses. Numa's head looked up. A lone man in camouflage quickly walked to him, pointed the weapon with his right hand, and shot him in the head. Now, both heads looked to the ground as if praying.

I saw that after attending this macabre theater, throngs of people filled the streets, some in school uniforms, others in the denim blue of the Tontons Macoutes, still others in army uniforms, soon scattering as though they were symbolic pallbearers.

Tears filled my eyes. A new desperation took hold of me, and my body tried to shake off the abject deed. Every single thing in me rejected the president and his accomplices. I sat dazed as I watched everything over and over again. I stared at the screen, trying to understand how the Army, the Tonton Macoutes, and the others could follow Duvalier in such barbarous actions. I understood nothing.

GONE AGAIN

Two months after the public execution, Mandedette left Haiti on a planned trip to Washington, D.C. By then, she had become a legal resident of the United States. Better yet, she had a spectacular opportunity waiting for her as an executive secretary at the embassy of a newly independent African country. That's why, in a rare moment of openness right before flying away, she told Viola and me of her threefold plan: to send money to take care of us, to set up a home for us in the United States, and to save money to send for us.

She completely assumed the role of breadwinner, having freed herself of the confines of her marital expectations. Having just celebrated her fortieth birthday and with the political situation getting more repressive, she'd come to realize the hopelessness of her plans and dreams of making a productive life in Haiti. The dream of living with her children had been a moving target for her and most of the women in her family for a long time. Now, she was betting everything she had to give her two poor, little Black girls a better life. She decided this time would be different; she wouldn't leave her children behind again. At least not for long.

She promised we would be together within months.

There was one big problem: I didn't believe her.

Why? I shook my head because when she had gone away before, it had taken her years to return. I couldn't believe her promise. Besides, this was the first time she talked about Viola and my leaving Haiti. And I didn't want to leave Papa. And I didn't want to leave Haiti.

Still, what I most feared had finally happened: she was gone again. She left Viola. She left me. She left Loulou. She left our home. She left Haiti.

She had last taken off in January 1961. At times back then, I was disdainful of her whereabouts. Other times, I felt revengeful because she had abandoned me. Now that I was older, I took some measure of comfort in the time we had spent together. Yet, I seemed to dwell more on her absences than her presences, even though when she was with me, I was in sheer bliss.

THE NEIGHBOR

Very quickly Lieutenant Edouard Guilloux, our new neighbor, controlled everything on our street. He had moved next door a few months after us. Children stopped playing when they saw him, cars slowed down when his was spotted, and his young wife stayed indoors when he was home.

When I woke up that morning, Sylvie was telling Grandma a thief had broken into a house up the street during the night. He had stolen a few kitchen utensils and some rags from the backyard before he tripped over a bucket, making enough noise for someone to yell, "Volè, bare volè!" "Catch the thief!"

For the Lieutenant, it was personal. A thief had the audacity to rob a house on his street, while he slept soundly with his wife.

Lieutenant Guilloux's wife was a ravishing beauty barely over eighteen, who spoke with the exotic sing-song accent of people of Cap-Haitian. She had a caramel complexion and long, dark hair that brought to mind pre-Colombian royalty, namely Anacaona or Golden Flower, the Taino tribal queen who ruled over part of what was called Ayiti before Christopher Columbus's arrival. In my history class, I learned that *Cacica* Anacaona's period of time was rather extraordinary because she ruled her kingdom as a powerful political leader with the same level of autonomy and equality as the men who governed other parts of the island. The iconographic images I was studying showed her either sitting regally on a straw bed carried on the shoulders of her subjects or composing poetry and songs while resting in her hammock. Another one was of her in chains just before being hanged at twenty-nine years old for refusing the clemency offered by the Spanish invaders, which was to accept to be one of their concubines. I grasped just enough of the meaning to understand that she said no to being a sexual slave. She was my new heroine.

The Lieutenant's wife was constantly baking cakes and other desserts, as if to assuage the pain from her husband's beatings. "Arrêtes, Edouard," I sometimes heard her yell. It was hard for me to imagine how a man could beat a woman. I had never seen that in my life. I also thought a woman who was so beautiful and also baked such deliciously sweet things was a treasure to be protected. She was also a generous soul; she'd call Viola and me from above the short concrete wall that separated our houses to share her desserts with us. We rushed over and exchanged small talk with her, her little girl, her sisters, and her mother.

But the thief was truly Lieutenant Guilloux's business. As an officer of the Criminal Investigation Unit, he had the job of catching thieves and other lawbreakers. Lieutenant Guilloux was of medium height and had an olive complexion, muscular arms, and not an ounce of fat showing. He was quite handsome, but maybe the uniform made him look so good, or my childhood eyes, or even the value system of the time that revered men in uniform. When he got out of his car, he walked briskly into his house in his starched, light khaki army uniform holding his Colt 45 gun and holster, as if he could shoot it in an instant. Every time I saw him, I hid behind the tall plants on the porch. I never saw the Lieutenant's eyes, for he wore his military cap very low on his forehead and his dark-green sunglasses and well-trimmed moustache hid everything else.

Until that day.

It was somewhat after eleven o'clock.

It was desert hot.

I had just come home from school for my lunch break when the commotion started outside. I ran to the street following Viola, Grandma, and Sylvie, and saw neighbors standing on their porches and in their yards with hesitant looks on their faces. Perhaps it was the first time they had seen a thief; I know it was the first time for me. He was a bald man, naked except for his torn underwear. He was all white, as if he had rolled in powder. I watched Lieutenant Guilloux brutally push the emaciated man toward us.

"Spit on him," the Lieutenant yelled. Some neighbors came out of their houses and yards ever so timidly to the street. The thief's hands and feet were tied with rope, and he moved in spurts as if he were jumping. Two men in army uniforms held both ends of the rope while the Lieutenant hit the thief, and neighbors spat on him.

"Hit him with stones, so he knows never to come back to this neighborhood," the Lieutenant ordered the assembling crowd. My neighbors bent down in the stifling heat to pick among the pebbles and rocks that littered the unpaved road. The circumstances forced me to watch them throw stones and insults at the thief. That was his punishment. It was supposed to make him confess.

His confession mattered because, although everyone believed he was the thief, unless he admitted his guilt, doubts would remain. It was necessary for us to demystify him, almost as a way to desacralize the power he had over us. In the final analysis, I, just like my neighbors, couldn't understand why a thief might want to steal on the street where Lieutenant Guilloux lived.

Nobody asked mercy for the thief. Fear had consumed all of us in spinelessness. I knew that because every part of my body understood what a coward was, even though I couldn't articulate it at the time.

The man, whose shabby underwear barely held on, had a smooth, white oily paste all over his bald head and body, almost like a second skin acting like a repellent to the obscene cowardice of the Lieutenant. His chafed knees bent a few times, but he never fell. His skin bruised and tore in a few places and bled in others, like an offering to the scorched street. I remember the white mask of suffering on the man's face. No movement came from him except when his scrawny body rebounded each time he was struck. I jerked every time a rock hit him.

That high noon on rue Baussan, I walked the few feet back home sweating profusely. I hid behind the veranda plants, terrified by what I had just seen.

It was obvious to all of us that Lieutenant Guilloux's action was deliberate. After all, he drove the prisoner back to our street after his arrest, parked the car in front of his own house, and pushed the man on us as prey, leaving him no place to run.

As a child, although I'd already seen a lifetime of brutal violence, I wondered what drove Lieutenant Guilloux to ask the crowd to help him do his dirty job.

Later, as an adult, I questioned why they allowed us children to watch a public beating. Lieutenant Guilloux—like his kind in khaki uniforms—not only didn't provide us any human shield, he silenced us. I thought that's what they wanted, and quite insidiously we became accomplices to their brutality. We lived in a world where absolute self-repression was key to survival.

My twelve-year-old eyes witnessed the Lieutenant picking up the disheveled man and hurling him onto the back seat of his car. The Lieutenant circled the car. His hands were covered with blood. He slammed the door shut. My eyes hurt as the windows reflected light on the man's expressionless, white-masked face. I stood condemned to silence as the car moved slowly at first, rocking a little bit over the stones, before it picked up speed until I didn't see the Lieutenant anymore.

I remember praying the Lieutenant didn't kill the thief after they left our street.

Then, I ate lunch and walked back down to school.

At supper that night I asked Sylvie, "Why did the thief have on a white glue?"

She tried to explain the thief's white body mask, saying it meant whatever one interpreted it to mean. It made him unrecognizable. It enabled him to slide away if someone tried to hold him because the paste was slimy. It prevented sleep because the paste was made of special herbs; this way, the thief could steal uninterrupted for hours while others slept. By the time she finished her story, I chose to believe the real reason for the paste was to scare us.

Afterwards, silence took the place of everything. Nobody talked about my neighbors' own spitting or stone-throwing assaults on the thief. Nobody. Those who would dare knew they could face dire consequences.

The thief and his red eyes protruding from his whitened face, terrified by the lack of humanity shown him, still crowded my mind.

THE PREY

For Grandma to act as my surrogate mother and take charge of our house, she had to have enormous power over me, the unyielding and unpredictable one. At sixty-three, it had been a long time since she was scared of anything or anyone, let alone little me. Built like a tank, she was full of frenetic energy that allowed her to do almost everything she wanted. With her silver hair and commanding brown eyes, Grandma showed a fiery determination to make me bend to her will. That was surely her plan when she took possession of Mandedette's bedroom, wielding her power in unimaginable ways, particularly since Papa didn't live with us anymore.

Grandma had set simple rules designed to tame me: no back talk, no profanity, no complaints from me about anything, and no complaints about me. And if I didn't behave according to them, she spoke to me in the only language she knew well: violence.

Grandma was not the affectionate type, and I don't remember her ever gathering me in her arms or beckoning me with a smile. True, she fed us and made sure we went to school. Yet she never told us stories at night. Maybe she thought they were for the countryside and not for us city girls who were always encouraged to speak French. I so loved the nighttime ritual of storytelling that I reached out more and more to Sylvie for her tales before going to sleep. But Grandma was still a praying woman and continued preparing for church at dawn every day.

She was close to Sylvie, and they talked nonstop. On one particular day, I discreetly listened to her tell Sylvie her satisfaction at having only one grandchild when Viola was born. I thought maybe her statement meant she wanted a grandson, or perhaps I was the bad seed. Regardless, her words were like a dagger thrust into my heart. Sylvie, nonetheless, offered some wisdom: "Madan Laroche, even when you're poor and can't afford to take care of many children, one child is never enough."

Soon after, I was playing *bezigue* across the street, when a girl called me a cheat. Without a thought, I uttered a profanity and told her, "Funny, I always thought you were *the* cheat."

Seconds later, her mother, looking very upset, rushed out of their house crying: *"C'est fini!* The game is over." I thought my arm was being torn from my body as Madame yanked me from the chair to drag me violently across the street back home. It took a moment for me to straighten myself.

"This child curses and cheats. Her behavior is unacceptable," she complained.

Grandma didn't ask me what happened. I spoke up to explain but she shut me up with a raised hand. I knew I was in trouble because I had broken three of her rules—I uttered a profanity, I talked back, and now

Madame had complained about me. Grandma wasn't about to tolerate my unruly behavior. I had to accept the consequences.

She yelled at me in front of Madame, loud enough for the world to hear: "You are a cursed child. You are a disgrace to the family." Madame walked away with a smile, fully satisfied with her success: the protection of her daughter's honor.

Grandma raised her flabby arm to grab the belt from its hook. She spanked me in silence with the full force of her body, across my entire back. She repeated her gesture. I grunted from the pain. Regardless, whatever lesson Grandma was trying to teach me was a resounding failure. I was stoic, emboldened from knowing I was right; Madame's daughter *was* a cheat. Afterward, I went into my room and cried myself to sleep.

In the following weeks, I was extremely prudent. My mouth, or rather the irreverent things that spilled out of it, was what got me in trouble most times. I would call a cheat a cheat. I would say a curse-word when unnecessarily bothered or when I imagined myself an adult. Therefore, I avoided speaking unless I was spoken to. I didn't play cards with the girls. I learned my school lessons to perfection. I did my best not to provoke any other assault from Grandma.

But some days, I forgot. Other days, I purposely ignored the rules. I was the opposite of Viola: I was rebellious against orders and bold in expressing my opinions. Once in a while, my school sent notes about my behavior to my family. These posed a problem for me because Grandma would reprimand me.

One afternoon as I walked from my mathematics class down the U-shaped hallway, I heard Mademoiselle Etienne summon me. She was the assistant director, a slim, elegant woman, who never smiled and held the real power in my school. Her gray hair perfectly coiffed and in a pageboy-style, shone like blue and purple rain. Her strict attitude forbade any misbehavior; she could punish harshly the student responsible for it. At her advanced age—the late 40s—she was officially recognized as a spinster. In the hallways, I heard the girls say her unsmiling face and severe demeanor were the reasons no man wanted to marry her. People considered unmarried status such a shame at the time. It didn't occur to them, nor to me, that she could've been a single lady by choice.

I wasn't so much surprised as terrified to see Grandma standing next to her by her office. I saw their tense, almost cold faces. I knew my cursing a girl the day before had come to roost.

I watched Grandma transfer her power to Mademoiselle Etienne in a clear, strong voice: "You have my permission."

I stood still as Mademoiselle Etienne reached for the school's twisted cowhide whip lying on her desk. She made me count each time it came down. One, two…five. After that, I stopped counting. The blows continued. The brunt of her force fell on my shoulders, on my arms, on my back, and perhaps most of all on my pride. I mustered all my might not to cry, but the balance between overwhelming pain and powerful shame tipped. Teachers, staff, and students stopped in their tracks to watch the sordid spectacle. Some jested, some laughed when the belt came down on my skin. I gasped for air. Everything in my stomach was about to come back up.

No one said, "Stop!" I could not understand why not a single adult at the school said, "Enough," to this severe and gratuitous violence. Not one, either out of complicity or of acquiescence.

My sobs subsided, but I didn't run. I didn't scream. I took my punishment. I showed fortitude in the face of injustice. No submission, I decided.

When it was over, my mind was blank. That Mademoiselle Etienne, and not Grandma, had lacerated me caught me off guard. And when Grandma thanked her with a handshake, it confirmed their odious pact. I looked deeply into Grandma's eyes; with insolence in mine, I saw cruelty and hatred in hers. My defiance towards her was limitless. She knew this. Then she walked down the stairs and left swiftly.

I stood there by myself looking down at the patterned mosaic floor. I couldn't look up because I believed, and rightly so, that everyone was watching me. The aches on my shoulders and back were extreme. The pain of my unseen bruises would collect for a very long time, more like a lifetime.

As I trotted home after school, I cursed Grandma silently. Repeatedly. I wished for her to disappear from my life. I was taciturn when I reached Viola at our meeting place. She didn't know how good it felt when she grabbed my hand, and we walked home.

After we arrived, I calmly put my school bag down on the dining table. Then I stepped out of the door to the street, not looking back.

I took the first taxi that stopped. I ran away to Papa's house. Papa wasn't at home, so Tante Yvonne paid the taxi. The smell of coffee perfumed the veranda as I walked in crying. My feet remained firmly planted on the ground, but I felt elsewhere as if I were levitating. I kissed Tante Yvonne who stopped sewing to console me. "What's wrong?" she asked, pulling me down to sit on her lap.

I whispered as if the revelation might annihilate me: "Grandma had me spanked in front of my whole school."

"It's over now," she said. "Papa will straighten it out." Her voice and her arms comforted me. She asked Anna to prepare verbena tea to calm my nerves.

The first sip was bliss. As the aroma rose through my nostrils, my tear ducts started to dry. The hot liquid warmed my veins. At last, I just fell into my body. My sight was blurry. Anna took control and walked me upstairs to rest in Papa's huge bed. Quiet slowly invaded me. Then, sleep took over my body and my mind.

Hours later, Papa woke me up with a kiss on the forehead and a soft touch to the shoulder that hurt enough for me to scream. He listened attentively as I recounted the incident. I told him whatever crime Grandma believed I had committed certainly did not merit such a savage punishment. He looked me in the eye, smiled the way I loved him to, and told me, "Let me take you home." I sat up for a moment to ponder for there was something about the word "home" that disturbed me. At home, Grandma watched me all the time as if she were a spy. My laughter was no longer welcomed, and even talking was controlled, mirroring the country's political situation. I had to restrain my energy, my enthusiasm. I lived with dread; in reality, I felt like a prisoner at home whereas all my life, my home had always been a safe place, protecting me from danger. I didn't want to go "home," but I had no choice.

Pink and orange specks colored the sky as night started to fall. A cool breeze flowed across my face through the window as Papa's car went up the street to take me back to what was home in name only. On the way, he stopped at a street kiosk to buy *griyo* and fried plantains covered with *pikliz*, served in a small paper cone. That was comfort food, if ever it existed. I savored mouthfuls all the way home, resisting the temptation to eat the portion intended for Viola.

As the car drew closer to rue Baussan, sweat beaded on my face, and my legs trembled. But I trusted that Papa had enormous power, much more than Grandma could ever have. He kept her on the veranda for several minutes of conversation. I overheard him tell her to stop berating and beating me. I buried my fears, convinced that she'd heard reason. I retreated to our small bedroom without saying anything.

I had my own mind, and I was forgetful. So the truce didn't last long, because some weeks later, I did it again. I cursed at something, and Grandma heard me.

It's almost as if I smelled the danger.

Now, I was the prey.

I was scared and didn't want to be spanked. So, I took a risk. I walked out the back door and down the corridor. Grandma followed me. She barked: *"Ou se yon dyab, ou gen madichon."* I cringed from hearing that I was a devil, that I was a curse; it was torture to my young ears.

After I slithered down the narrow corridor, I felt secure enough to scream back at her, "Why do you hate me?"

I felt her hate. Grandma was the only person who didn't talk to me, the only one who scolded me, the only one who beat me. Even worse, I knew she was capable of love. She showed it to Viola, who she believed was flawless. To her credit, Viola really was perfect, but this only partly explained Grandma's violent treatment of me, so visceral, almost epidermic. Although Viola and I were as close as any sisters,

I bore a different burden because I was several shades darker than she, Mandedette, and Grandma. The narrative had been constructed carefully to differentiate, to denigrate. I believed Grandma didn't love me mostly because of that.

Once on the street. I turned to face Grandma. Our eyes met. I could tell she was waiting for me to make a move, but I also knew any move could spur an attack. She was a predator hunting for prey.

I saw neighbors in their yards or sitting on their porches, slyly pretending not to see or hear us. No one came to my defense. Perhaps I was seen as a troublemaker and Grandma's assault a mere item for gossip. But I was as vulnerable as a street dog. It was also clear to me that if I waited for their help, I'd be dead from their complacency.

I had to get out of her way, so I walked quickly over the dark, ashen stones, looking back to watch her movement. The next thing I knew, she squatted to grab a large gray rock on the side of the street. She ran towards me. I instinctively knew the rock would kill me if I didn't get away. I ran faster, faster. Her eyes were spitting fury as she threw the rock at me.

Just then, I heard the brakes of a taxi pulling to the curb. I threw myself into it. I had just enough strength to give Papa's address. As I folded my waiflike body into the small car, I shook like a bird drying its feathers. The taxi sped away. The cab driver commented on how mean that old woman looked in the middle of the street. I held my head with trembling hands to reassure myself it hadn't been cracked open. Grandma meant to kill me; I was convinced.

The instant the taxi stopped by the gate of the lakou, I could hear Papa's smoker's cough as he came down the front steps to pay the driver. I was short of breath. I wanted to say something, but words wouldn't come. He planted an affectionate kiss on my forehead.

For the rest of the day, Anna brought me cup after cup of verbena tea to soothe my emotions, noticeably raw. I sipped the infusion and rocked my body gently back and forth as the unfathomable pain and shame seeped out of it. Cocooned under a soft cotton sheet in Papa's bed, I wondered if the hatred I had for Grandma would ever diminish.

That first evening Papa did what he could to console me. He took me to the restaurant where I ate my favorite *griyo*. He let me sleep in his big bed while he went out into the night.

The next day, he moved me into my old bedroom. In the dark of the night, I woke up sweating from nightmares of Grandma running after me in a tunnel. Whenever Papa was present, I clung to him as if I had retreated into babyhood.

In the days after I ran away, Papa drove me to school every morning and had me picked up every afternoon as if, perhaps he, too, was afraid Grandma would make good on her threats. As the days passed, my body and mind unmuted themselves progressively. In the safety and intimacy of his car, little by little, I recounted what had happened.

In Grand Angele's lakou—for the first time without Viola—not only did I feel protected, but I started to determine my own worth. My consciousness had also emerged from Papa's love, Anna's care, and Tante Yvonne's attention. I refuted Grandma's belief that I was bereft of goodness and blessings. I refused to be devalued. I freed myself even though underneath this freedom, I felt excruciating physical and emotional pain. Grandma could take everything from me but not *that*. But now, more than ever, I knew I had value. And this was what it meant to no longer be a victim because I had willfully escaped her violence. This was what it meant to be a survivor. This was what it meant not to surrender. And I did not.

Being a man of few words with a face that rarely showed any emotion—Papa must have noticed my defiant stance and my distant attitude. They must have spoken to him. He knew, as I did, that I would never be the same again.

But I was still only twelve years old. I did not know why adults felt the need to beat up others who were younger or appeared more vulnerable than them. I did not know I would continue to encounter grown-ups with such needs in my lifetime. I knew that with Grandma in charge, my life wouldn't get better. I had escaped, but I needed a safe haven, even if it meant being away from Viola. That's why one morning I went to Papa's room and asked to move back permanently with him. As I massaged his feet, dead skin fell to cover the bed as if it were raining sand. This moment brought back the days when I was little and living with him and Mandedette and feeling safe.

"You can stay here for a while," Papa responded. The "a while" wasn't a complete win for me, but I didn't lose hope.

"Why doesn't Grandma love me?" I raged.

"She loves you but doesn't know how to show it," Papa said. He then promised me I'd never be assaulted again.

Days later, I saw his poker face crack a bit with a smirk when he recounted his visit with Grandma and her promise never to brutalize me again. The interlude had lasted two weeks. It was twilight when Papa drove me back to rue Baussan after this conversation with Grandma. Viola told me how happy she was to have me back. I smiled, near tears.

Returning home from Papa's house marked the start of my new life. My internal voice repeatedly shouted silently to me, "If you're ever hit again, resist. Forcefully." Still, home was no longer my refuge. I lived uneasily with a feeling of constant vulnerability. Little did I know my disillusionment would continue almost in direct proportion to my transformation from a victim to a resister.

Grandma never hit me again. Silence became her new language; that was her strategy of erasure of me.

Years later, on African safaris, I understood that conforming, sticking with the herd, and not venturing far from the safety of the group were crucial for safety, for not becoming prey. I thought about when I was little and recognized that I wasn't a conformist; I wasn't that kind of child. What I was, was raucous; I talked. I laughed. I played dominoes and cards for money from when I was eight years old; I won, too. Grandma saw me as uncontrollable, and maybe I was. The truth was that I was just normal. And I was simply a child. But my normal wasn't to my grandmother's liking.

So many dramas and traumas of my childhood were born of her refrain: "This child is a devil. This child is cursed. This child is a disgrace to the family." I heard her voice like a mantra. It marked me forever as if it were a tribal scarification.

RAIN SHOWERS

They usually came in late afternoon, when time seemed suspended between the slow descent of the sun into the horizon and nightfall. They were the rainstorms of the tropics with this particular feature: they had their own schedule. They fell the hardest on the city's dusty streets, forcing people to find refuge by huddling together under storefront canopies, in the shade of verandas, under large trees, by the facades of houses or churches, inside storefronts or gas stations.

"Se yon lapli m ap pare," people said while waiting for the rain to pass. This collective metaphor actually meant, "My problem is temporary and will end when my hardship ceases." On rue Baussan, after Mandedette left, I often felt as if I, too, were waiting for my hardship to end. Perhaps that's why the rain held a special magic for me.

Timid and colorless, my rain always brought a moment of sweet indecision. It drew us in as if we had to be patient before savoring the pleasure that awaited us. First, we watched it slowly, almost afraid to feel it. Its sound held something mysterious, a mixture of everything from quiet hesitation to mighty force.

Then Viola's voice called, "Come with me." Her warm hand grabbed mine. I followed her, always, because the only time we were allowed to play on the rocky road was when it rained. We rushed down the corridor with Sylvie, who stayed on the veranda to keep track of our movements. I was hit with the fresh scent emerging from the soil quenching its thirst with the first soaking rains.

We walked to the center of the street. Fortunately, we found ourselves all alone on the deserted road as everyone stayed inside on rue Baussan, allowing us to live the limitless possibilities of the mood of the heavens. Viola laughed, took off her dress. I let go of mine also. Then we galloped back and forth on the gravel in our panties. Rain felt like divine, blessed water falling from the sky. The torrents released the day's suffocating heat. Time stopped for me. I abandoned my body to its senses. I shut my eyes and let the rain shower my body. Each drop danced slowly on my face, then on my bony back. It glided down my flat torso in strokes that massaged and caressed my skin to a transparent sheen, much like the bright patina of the pebbles and rocks smoothed over time by waterfalls. Rain left my hair totally wet, my face luminous from the healing mask of the douse.

Raindrops fell onto my tongue and their bland tastelessness surprised me, for they were delicious. I tried to hold the rain in my hands. Sometimes I succeeded, but then the few drops collected fell to the ground as if to reclaim their freedom.

It blurred everything, but Viola was close by. She was my intimate accomplice.

"*Je serai la plus belle…*," she sang French singer Sylvie's hit song, her voice synchronized with the falling water. I repeated after her. We sang and jumped up and down as disjointed bodies enthralled with the pure joy of playing in the rain.

Sometimes, the sun shone brilliantly through the rain. Sylvie commented, "Folks back home say that happens only when the devil is beating his wife." I knew they had it wrong, those folks back home. Even then, I saw the rain as an invisible spirit with great intelligence, magical beauty, and benevolent powers too.

You had to have taken a shower in the rain almost naked in the middle of an empty street to appreciate the abandonment of your body to its senses, the intensity of the water splashing the body before slithering into the gravel, and the drops on your tongue to know that you have tasted luxury. I did that. Again and again.

The rain showers of my childhood were nourishing salves. They couldn't shelter me from the external tremors, but those moments tempered the feeling of worthlessness I felt around Grandma because they soothed the wounds from her continuous assaults and muted her harangues. Little by little, the rain eased my anxiety about Mandedette's absence. The rain totally captivated me, for it was also a much-too-brief musical interlude—its sound momentarily silencing human voices, muffling our disquieting neighbors. The rain showers also released the heat, and I believed, healed the pain of that scorched street. At night, I slept easily as if the showers had washed away the day's tiredness.

I felt joy—by any monumental metric—from those rain showers.

ON MY OWN

If the neighborhood was a playground, Viola was the manager, and I was a low-level assistant. I followed her wherever she went, like a little dog with her mistress. She was effervescent. She was irrepressible. On school day afternoons and weekends, she, a genius of logistics, organized our lives. She chose where we went, how long we stayed, and what games we played. We often visited the neighbors. They had bigger yards than we did; besides, we couldn't play in ours even if we wanted to because Sylvie used it as an outdoor kitchen and laundry space.

We went to see Viola's friend, Jessie, who lived diagonally across the street. She was spoiled by all the women she lived with: a white-haired aunt who was perhaps her great-aunt; a grey-haired mother whom some of the girls whispered was really her grandmother; and a black-haired sister they said was really her mother. Jessie had books strewn on her table, her bed, her floor. Viola began borrowing them from her and read ferociously, rushing to return them and to get new ones after a few days. I saw mostly books by French author Delly, but when I asked if I could read them, Viola refused: "They aren't for children your age." Probably, but because I wanted to be with her, I didn't complain.

Jessie often had other visitors, two girlfriends from her Catholic high school, both light-skinned. One had long blond hair, green eyes, and a funny, German-sounding name. It was the closest I had ever been to someone with those features. One day I got the courage to ask her, "Can I touch your hair?" She wore her beauty with a nonchalance that made me feel insignificant.

Viola and her new friends sat on Jessie's bed while I stood demurely by the door observing every detail. Those girls talked and talked and talked. I had never before heard girls close to my age talk to each other, so I listened assiduously to everything. On the way home I bombarded Viola with questions in a futile attempt to make sense of what I'd heard. Rarely did I get a straightforward response, as if keeping me in the dark gave her some older-sister power over me. Later at night when I was in bed, my head was filled with their stories about boys, books, and even kissing.

Five teenage girls lived directly across from us. I never went inside their house but sat nearly every afternoon around a small square card table in their front yard. Viola and I played *bezigue* with the two youngest. I gambled paltry sums, equivalent to less than a quarter because up until then, I had bet only with Viola and other family members. Now I didn't hesitate to gamble with strangers, so sure was I of winning. But was it wise to bet when I played with people whose styles and temperaments I hardly knew? I would learn soon enough.

Whenever I think about rue Baussan I remember that card game, played in the afternoon heat that hit me like a double smack in the face. I was propped up at Viola's back, watching her play *bézigue* with three girls. Each held a set of cards and alternated between putting them down on the table and grabbing them in conquest when they won the hand. Viola beamed as she talked to the girl next to her. I noticed she held her back straight as if to wall me out.

There had never been any Monique without Viola. Ever since I could remember I was her shadow. Everywhere she went, my little sister, cigarette-thin body crowned with a head of nappy braids trailed behind her. Self-possessed, relaxed, Viola was effortlessly engaging. Her beauty came from her charming everyone with her soft and curious gaze, and overall sweet disposition. I felt no sibling rivalry, even when the cousins and others called her nice and me aggressive and nasty for speaking my mind. All my life, she'd been not only my best friend but my only friend. Since moving to rue Baussan, making other friends her own age, going to secondary school, and celebrating her fourteenth birthday, she had relegated me to the sidelines, yet never indicated she didn't want me around her all the time. I watched her bond with girls older than I was and felt left out, but I had no other options.

That day at the card table she was wearing light capri pants and a loose shirt over her tiny burgeoning breasts. Her friends were all dressed in the same manner, as if they had agreed on this uniform ahead of time. I still remember what I was wearing that day; a striped dress.

Viola, like Papa, was passionate and focused about playing cards. I knew this. But I was also that way, which is why I wanted so much to play. So, I bent down to whisper in her ear, "When you finish this game, please let me take your place."

She turned sideways to look at me over her shoulder. Below the stylish bandeau that crowned her head of braids, her lips were pursed. Her smile had vanished. Her skinny hands pulled her cards close to her body to prevent me from seeing them. As the game continued, she kept talking to the other girls, pretending I didn't exist. Did she resent me for something? I couldn't comprehend her new attitude, for through the years we always had a codependent relationship in which we spoke a similar language.

No breeze blew through the almond tree leaves to lift away the hot, suffocating air; only a tropical rain could do that, and one wasn't on the horizon. Standing under the sweltering heat, I felt steam rising from my body, sweat running down my forehead, and moisture on my hands.

Viola won the game and laughed loudly. I was happy for her, partly because her victory would make ceding me her place so much easier. But then she began to shuffle the cards with her friends.

"Can I take your place?" I asked, this time with a strong voice to camouflage my trepidation. I was still hopeful I could play the new round.

She backed up her chair and stood up. As I moved to take her seat, she raised her voice and said to my face, "Why don't you get your own friends? Leave me alone."

I stood in silent disbelief.

None made a sound. Viola wasn't the yelling type but now had done the unthinkable. I saw the stunned faces of our girlfriends, whom she had just claimed exclusively as hers. She had always made friends more easily than I, being the more alluring soul, and I benefited from this. I had taken for granted that all the girls were *our* friends. They were in fact *her* friends. The truth was that I had no friends of my own. I simply didn't see that she was becoming her own older self, with her own friends, in her own separate world.

She had her back to me, so she couldn't see my hunched shoulders as I walked away. I left the girls, the table, and the yard, with my eyes staring at the pebbled ground. The sun blinded me as I tried to look back to watch her pick up her cards from the deck just as I reached the gate. I carefully crossed the street and went home alone with my bony self. In spite of my eyes raining lightly on my cheeks and the sun lighting a fire in my head, I saw that she hadn't looked back. It buried me.

I was unable to explain to myself what had happened. I felt as if my umbilical cord had been cut in the middle of an open square. Viola's public rejection of me triggered memories of my school beating. In real-time, not only was *ViolaetMonique* irretrievably broken, and I was no longer part of a "whole," but I was also being shunned by my "other half."

When Viola came home, she apologized. "I'm sorry to have hurt your feelings," she said as she tried to console me.

But I was so humiliated that I wanted to disappear like dust blown away by wind. I stayed by myself most of the time in the tiny bedroom we shared and went to bed early so as not to face her. Sleep did not come easily. I felt as though I was drowning. Every time the card table scene repeated itself in my mind, my eyes filled with tears.

I was entering an entirely different world, a world without Viola. I had known our separation as conjoined twins was inevitable, but I wasn't prepared for it to happen either that soon or that abruptly. My whole existence derived from being her little sister. I trusted her as she led and protected me through Port-au-Prince's streets with generosity, tenderness, and love. They were ridiculously insignificant gestures, yet to me seminal, formative, transformative, and loving.

But now, I was on my own.

Moving on after this rejection meant confronting the reality that my fairy-tale sisterhood was over.

Yet, we were still inseparably locked in the lives we lived side by side. On some days, she felt it was still her big-sister duty to invite me to visit Jessie and it was part of why I followed her even if I longed to be elsewhere. I was miserable so I stayed in a corner, never spoke and simply watched her girlfriends talk about the romance novels they were reading or the latest French hit songs. I accepted my place in the margins of her life, glad I still belonged close to her persona, somewhere in her space.

My nerves were raw when I started wondering why Viola would push me off a cliff. I wasn't blind to the fact that she had nurtured me and sustained the sisterhood since my birth, so why did she do it? Was it because, as my big sister she knew I would rise to the occasion, navigate the troubled waters, to stand on my own?

Granted, by this time, even if I didn't see it, I had also started to feel my own individuality. When I visited the lakou, I continued to face all the names and narratives constructed to disempower me, sometimes *"frekan" "tilanding"* "snotty," other times, *"tèt fòl"* "crazy." But after adapting to Mandedette's absence; after two brutal public humiliations; after running away from home; after getting Papa's unflinching support; and after deciding to resist Grandma's abuse, I started to own those insults like homegrown battle scars and survivor's instincts. They made me stronger. To me, those words indicated a certain respect, so I took them as compliments, the result of being forced to assert myself. I didn't fit the mold. I was disruptive, sometimes transgressive and it made the cousins and others uncomfortable. They were all threads that lingered in the new me.

Yet on rue Baussan, I was still an achingly solitary and isolated twelve-year-old girl, yet stronger than ever before.

THE DEPARTURE

At dawn that summer day not a breeze blew through the open windows of our small two-bedroom house. When the soft morning light entered on that June 27, 1965, the ballet of people preparing our departure started. Speaker of impeccable French and grammar teacher in several high schools, my sixty-year-old maternal great-uncle, Gesner Laroche arrived with the airline tickets. The perfect image of the elegant gentleman dressed in his Sunday-best gabardine suit and white Panama hat, he was the only man I knew from Mandedette's side of the family. He removed his hat, as men did when they entered a house, before folding his tall, bony body in the chair around the small dining room table. There, the man who was relentless in correcting my spelling and punctuation sat silently sipping a Haitian espresso that perfumed everything. Grandma sat across from him with her lips pursed and gazed impatiently at her brother as if time couldn't pass fast enough.

Uncle Gesner managed our travel plans, which is why he came so early. It is also why, a few days earlier, Viola and I had accompanied him for the taxi ride downtown to the cable company where he picked up the money sent by Mandedette, and then to the Pan American office to purchase our one-way tickets to New York. There, I heard him make arrangements for a stewardess to take care of us since we were too young to travel alone, and it would be our very first plane trip.

A little later that Sunday morning the hairdresser arrived. She placed a couple of chairs face-to-face with a charcoal stove, and like magic, a makeshift hair salon was set up in our minuscule backyard. She straightened Viola's hair with a hot comb, then did mine, burning my scalp a few times in the process. I was thrilled when she agreed to Viola's suggestion to comb our hair in the bowl-hat style worn by our idol, the hugely successful French pop singer Sheila.

Outside, the city was calm, almost noiseless. After a light breakfast of bread and butter with watered-down coffee, we got ready. Viola and I dressed in identical, starchy-pressed, teal blue two-piece skirt suits, sewn for us by Tante Yvonne. It wasn't lost on me that, in a way, wearing a skirt suit was a nod to our new life since we'd previously only worn dresses. As I waited for Papa to pick us up for the drive to the airport, I had to admit I felt excitement at the unknown; at the prospect of getting on an airplane; of going to another country; of seeing Mandedette again. I looked forward to the adventure that awaited me. At moments I wanted the trip to be a vacation because then I would have the best of both worlds. I would travel and see a new land and meet different people and spend time with Mandedette. I didn't have to look further than her to know the benefits of travelling, since the last time she returned from her trip abroad she looked prettier and came back with diplomas from several schools. After the vacation, I would come back to my life in Haiti and to Papa. In fact, I couldn't understand why Mandedette wasn't the one moving back to Haiti. Why did I have to go? Sadly, I knew I was leaving my country and everything I had known for what seemed to be forever.

It felt as though my childhood was ending. After all, I was old enough to travel, to a foreign country no less, and with no adult protection. At twelve, I had just finished primary school. My life revolved around playing cards and dominoes and talking to Viola while waiting for the day when she would deem me mature enough to share her books with me. If my Grandma was sad we were leaving, she didn't show it. What was certain was that I wouldn't miss her at all.

As Papa drove us to the airport in his small beige car that June morning, I looked with melancholy at the streets of my city, Port-au-Prince. The sun almost blinded me as I tried to capture the vivid colors worn by street sellers. The rich pastels of the small houses. Adults and children dressed for Sunday mass. The ubiquitous marchandes walking city roads with huge vegetable baskets on their heads as if they were balancing the world. The cacophony coming through open windows. I hadn't left, yet I already profoundly missed Haiti.

As the car arrived at the newly inaugurated Francois Duvalier International Airport, Tante Yvonne and our neighbor, Bébé, waved furiously from the sidewalk. Both were in tears when they greeted us, and quickly said their goodbyes. I thought they simply didn't want to be part of the sad scene.

We followed Papa and Uncle Gesner to the airline counter, and rapidly our luggage went beyond my view. "This lady is responsible for you," Uncle Gesner said to us as he grinned at a slim, smiling white lady who wore a blue hat and uniform that made her look like an army officer in a skirt. She was the stewardess. Perhaps she smiled because she wanted a pleasant image to stay with us, for she knew it was the last time we would see her. "Your mother will be at the foot of the plane to greet you," he added. In the midst of my sadness, that news brought some comfort.

Viola reached out to Papa first, said goodbye, and walked away crying profusely. For the first time in my life I saw him wipe away a tear. Then, it was my turn. I held on to him and he to me, not our habitual stance; a brief kiss and a wide smile were his most common signs of affection. Our bodies didn't want to separate. "I'll come to see you two soon," he murmured.

"I'll wait for you," I whispered.

Ripping myself from his arms was brutal. Through my tears, I saw his red eyes and his face trembling as his inalterable poker face failed him.

Papa was the constant figure of my first twelve years on earth. He had been father and mother to Viola and me during the two and a half years Mother was away studying. He had been my anchor these last few turbulent years, and more importantly for me, my safe haven when Grandma was abusive. It made me love Papa even more. I felt broken leaving him behind. Saying goodbye to him now on the tarmac, I felt pain in my stomach, as if he were being pulled from me at an unthinkable velocity. I had never been apart from him, except for a few weeks during summer vacations and the months when he was in the hospital. And now we were separating. For how long? I didn't know.

It was around nine in the morning when I walked toward the plane as if a thick fog enveloped me. Even the hot tropical sun could not dissipate that sensation. Papa didn't call to us, but I knew he was suffering. I felt like I was losing him. Climbing the steps felt like a funeral march. I turned at the door to wave as I had seen Mandedette do the last time she traveled. It was as if a powerful wind was uprooting me violently from my land.

In the plane, the light was pale, the temperature was cold, but the seats were comfortable. The window was a magical accomplice as I immediately took to it to wave furiously to Papa and to Haiti. Papa became smaller until he disappeared, and then Haiti started to erase itself from my view.

That Sunday afternoon, I was closer to the sun than I had ever been. Bright white clouds floated above the azure sky like oversize cotton balls. I was gazing through the side window of a very large airplane thousands of miles above Haiti, the only home I had ever known. Viola held my hand, but tears soaked our cheeks despite the turns we each took consoling the other.. I was crying because I didn't want to be on the plane. I didn't want to fly away from my home, my family, my country—everything I knew and loved.

As the plane flew higher into the white cotton clouds, dreams crowded my mind. Dreams of what I wanted to do with my life in Haiti. I dreamt of getting older so I could dress in long, fancy ball gowns like my cousins when they danced to the popular big band Nemours Jean-Baptiste at Cabane Choucoune nightclub. I dreamt of being queen of the Mardi Gras as Papa promised, blowing kisses to people in the streets from the throne of a Carnival float. What was I to do with my dreams? They might have been quixotic, but they were mine, and I was crushed to put them off. That's why, years later, I became enamored of Langston Hughes after reading "What happens to a dream deferred?" in his poem *Harlem.* Sleep momentarily stopped my sadness.

Four hours went by.

I thought I wouldn't have enough tears to last that long.

I did.

As the plane landed at JFK International Airport in New York, Viola and I squeezed our heads together into the window glass to see the scene below. It was early afternoon and a bright light shone on the city. I was mesmerized by the horizon. Tall buildings. Many very tall buildings. They were of different heights, but everything I saw was colossal. The plane flew over them like a bird flying from tree to tree.

Everything should have been fine at our arrival, but in a few minutes our joy turned to worry as nothing happened as planned. We still didn't see the stewardess who had so kindly told Uncle Gesner she would take care of us until she delivered us to Mandedette. This was the first time we had dealt with a white person. She did look human just like us, except for her light skin and her straight hair, which reminded me of the diplomat neighbors we once had. I couldn't recognize her because all the other whites looked the same to me, although I remembered her uniform and her wide grin that showed bright-white teeth. We waited for her. Viola wondered out loud why she didn't remember us. But she didn't and either hid or disappeared, leaving us, her two small Black charges, all alone.

Then, Viola stood. She decided to move forward with the last passengers. I followed her as usual, even if this time she didn't hold my hand. Surprisingly, no one stopped us at the door. As I slowly descended the stairs so I could avoid the embarrassment of falling on my face, I was blindsided by the panorama of massive buildings and grounded large airplanes. We walked military-style behind the people in front of us, and I trusted we would find Mandedette when we reached the terminal. But she wasn't there. I was very disappointed not to see that she wasn't the first person to greet the plane, as Uncle Gesner had promised. We looked all around us, and she wasn't there. I wondered where she was. I was fearful we would never see her again, but I didn't show or tell Viola anything.

We sat down in a row of seats bolted to the floor near a Pan Am service desk. I stuck close to my chair and to Viola, with our backs against a wall. Across from us were gigantic glass windows from which I could see the tarmac and several planes. I held tightly to my doll, Betty, and to my small purse, and Viola to hers as we waited patiently for the stewardess or Mandedette to arrive.

As if I were on a reviewing stand, I watched families with children, couples, and women and men of all ages walking the hallway of the terminal. Some slowly, as if on a stroll, others lugging their suitcases, still others almost running. During long minutes that became hours, I saw white faces and bodies of all different shapes. I don't remember anyone smiling at me. And I don't remember seeing a Black face. All my life, I had been surrounded by Black people with a rainbow of skin colors, ranging from high yellow to blue-black. How come there were none here? I learned immediately that I was in a strange country, which was also a very white country.

Still, I didn't see Mandedette. Where was she? I had travelled from far, very far, to see her and couldn't understand why she wasn't there. Besides, I was sleepy.

Daylight started to fade away. Every once in a while, I glanced anxiously at Viola. I was hungry. I was thirsty. I needed to pee, but I sat quietly with my heart beating fast. I imagined I must have looked like a lost puppy who wanted some sign of affection.

In preparation for the trip, Viola, who had studied English at school, taught me the word *help*. Very softly, and to no one in particular, I said, "Help." There, I said it, perhaps too quietly to be heard. Nobody responded.

I repeated it to myself several times, as I used to do when reciting a history lesson or a multiplication table. Then Viola, to pass the time, read out loud every sign posted on the wall close by. Then she timidly raised the volume of her voice to utter the word *help*. Still, no one heard, or rather no one responded with either a word or a gesture. No one. I felt totally invisible just as I had so many times when I was at home in Haiti. I was overwhelmed by a feeling of helplessness.

Still, Mandedette didn't come. I was impatient, but we had no plan other than to wait. Where could she be? She knew we were coming, so why wasn't she there to greet us?

I thought of the last time I saw her. It had only been six months since she left Haiti. Then she had told Viola and me she would send for us. She kept her promise. Yet, I questioned why she preferred we join her rather than her returning to Haiti. And here we were in New York, and she wasn't even there to pick us up. I was sad. I remembered her outrageous belief in promptness and attendance. She said the first day of school was the most important and each day afterward was the second most important. I don't remember Viola or me ever being sick enough to stay home. To have us travel at the end of our school year was Mandedette acting like the school teacher she was. This way, we wouldn't miss any classes. Her discipline was like a second skin for her, which is why her lateness was so puzzling.

As I looked through the airport glass, after what seemed an interminable time, I noticed the horizon had darkened. But then, as far as I was concerned, a bright light had gone off my universe the minute I boarded the plane to leave Haiti. Towering lights that appeared to scrape the sky illuminated the runway. This worried me because it was past our curfew. Wherever we were, unless accompanied by an adult, Viola and I had to be home by the time streetlights were turned on. If we ever did otherwise, we faced punishment.

I sobbed quietly, for reality had set in: we were in New York, all alone, in the dark, past our curfew and forgotten by both the stewardess and Mandedette. I was paralyzed with the fear of what would happen if Mandedette didn't come get us. But I was never quite able to express my fear of abandonment to Viola. Stoic, strong, and caring, she was the last person I wanted to disturb with negativity. Worse, I was exhausted. I was hungry. I was thirsty. I was angry.

I faced another complication. My bladder was so full I feared it would empty itself right there in the JFK hallway if I didn't immediately go to the toilet. I didn't dare tell Viola before because I was afraid Mandedette wouldn't find us if we left our seats. Besides, I was petrified of the immensity of the airport, which seemed as big as Port-au-Prince.

"I can't hold it any longer, I have to pee," I finally confessed to Viola.

"Me too. Let's look for a toilet," she said. From where we sat, none was visible, nor was a sign indicating where one might be.

"Look!" Viola exclaimed, pointing at the people gliding smoothly up a stairway. It was incredible. For the first time ever I watched in awe as people a few feet away from me went from one floor to another without ever moving. Their feet didn't budge, but miraculously, they went upstairs. As we stared, the stairs opened like a fan. Viola and I looked at each other with delight and smiled at the marvelous discovery we had just made.

"Let's go upstairs the same way; we'll find a toilet," Viola told me. We took baby steps until we reached the escalator. With great hesitation, we both stood on the first step. She had the good sense to grab my hand to avoid an accident like me falling. The escalator moved us. We smiled at each other as I held her hand more tightly because I was afraid after seeing the stairs in front of me disappear into the upper floor. Then, a miracle occurred: the escalator stopped moving, and we were standing upstairs. This time, we both laughed with joy. It seemed to me, and I was sure to Viola, that it was a victory, albeit a small one. For not only had we made it upstairs, but we weren't hurt. All because of Viola's decisive leap and sharp eye.

Immediately after we got off the escalator, a second miracle took place. We came face-to-face with an overweight, fifty-something Black woman with a delicious smile, standing incongruously in the hallway. It was as if I'd entered a fairy tale when she greeted us in French with a soothing, "*Bonsoir les enfants.*"

"*Bonsoir, madame,*" Viola responded quietly, forgetting we were forbidden to speak to strangers. We laughed with abandon, and I remember the moment as one of exultation.

"Are you related to Yolande Pierre-Paul," she asked Viola as she scrutinized my face.

"*Oui, oui,*" I yelled, thankful, at least for the moment, for being recognized and for finally being able to release my overwhelming fear.

"Tante Yolande is our mother's cousin," Viola replied. She now lived amongst Haitians in Brooklyn but often came to Haiti with bags full of gifts for us. It felt like Christmas whenever she visited, and I loved her.

The heavy-set lady told us Tante Yolande was her friend, which is why she saw a family resemblance in our faces. "You, little one," she said, looking at me, "you look like Tante Yolande's daughter."

For a moment, I felt like I was back home in Haiti, where anyone felt compelled to tell me about a family resemblance—it was just how it was. Her name was Madame Jean. At last, I felt safe. It felt like a substantial weight had been lifted from my frail shoulders and back.

Viola told her everything; the plane ride, the disappearance of the stewardess, Mandedette's no-show, our interminable wait. Madame Jean took our hands in hers, in a gesture aimed at comforting us. As she walked us to the toilet, she calculated that we had sat waiting for close to eight hours. Afterward, all three of us went to the Pan Am counter. For years, I wondered how Madame Jean, a total stranger, managed to see us on top of the stairs when the white stewardess didn't see us at the door of the plane, particularly since she should have been looking for us. Perhaps, it was racism.

The white man Madame Jean spoke to was in a blue uniform exactly like the one worn by the stewardess in the morning, except hers had a skirt. He listened to her attentively for some long minutes. Afterward, in a calm voice and precise language, she explained to Viola and me what she had told the Pan Am agent. I heard Viola utter Mandedette's name and saw her give the man the travel documents she guarded so preciously in her purse during our trip. Madame Jean assured us that even though he didn't speak French, the airline agent would make the arrangements necessary to get us to Mandedette.

She was quick. All of it took just a few minutes, but her words have since assumed such importance in my life for their air of familiarity, but more important, for their generosity. In her own way, Madame Jean negated the indifference of the stewardess and all the other people who saw us but didn't say anything. I had never been so aware of white people, and to this day I question why we, two little black girls who appeared hopelessly lost, spent so many hours alone in an airport full of people without attracting some question, some concern, some attention. Was it because we were Black? Was it because we didn't ask for help? Or was it because American culture was too busy to see others in need?

Whatever the reason, this most vulnerable moment caused fright and despair when what Viola and I needed most was hope. I hadn't imagined such a dramatic entry into the United States. Madame Jean, like an angel, kissed us goodbye and in great haste moved her large frame away as if she were flying elsewhere. She filled me with gratitude, jubilation, and hope. Her image has accompanied me ever since.

I had lived enough on that day, despite my meager years, to feel overwhelmed by life. But with Madame Jean, I felt as if the most dangerous part of the journey was behind me.

The Pan Am agent talked ceaselessly on the telephone as he wrote on papers in front of him. Viola and I whispered to each other that he was unusual. First, he was white, then he made us sit on a bench close to him, and then he dialed the telephone tirelessly again, again and again. While talking, he looked at us with a mixture of concern, as if he didn't want us to disappear, and satisfaction and his constant smile confirmed to us, and to him, that he was indeed making progress.

"*A qui parle-t-il?*" I asked Viola. "Who is he talking to?"

"*Aucune idee.*" No idea, she responded.

It was a lot to deal with. The interminable wait, the unrelenting procession of travelers walking back and forth, the physical exhaustion, the agent's incessant conversations. I thought it would never end. Finally, after spending what seemed like several hours on the telephone, the agent tracked down Mandedette. It was near midnight.

He handed Viola the telephone, and she gently pulled me close to her to hear Mandedette on the other end. Tears of joyful relief flowed abundantly. In her soft voice, Mandedette explained we had traveled to the wrong town. We had taken a plane to New York City, but she lived in Washington, D.C., about an hour away by air. An unimaginable thing had occurred: Viola and I had arrived in New York quite by accident. Despite Mandedette's having told Uncle Gesner that she now resided in Washington, D.C., in his mind, as in everyone else's in Haiti, New York was synonymous with the United States. To make matters even worse, she wasn't even aware we were traveling that day because he hadn't called or cabled her our flight details. While we were lost and terribly afraid in New York, Mandedette was out with friends in Washington, believing we were home, and when we traveled, she would pick us up at a different airport.

Throughout most of the ordeal, Viola was my guardian angel. I had often been in situations where she held my hand, like when we walked to school; but this time the gesture took on an extraordinary importance. We were both fully conscious of how afraid the other was and holding hands created a wall against our worst fears. Our bodies expressed what words couldn't.

Then the nice white man walked us through a large door behind his counter. Like the children we were, we followed him, but this time our walk was as brisk as his was purposeful. He led us to a passage that ended with a majestic black stretch Cadillac limousine. I thought it was a house; it was just that huge to my Haitian eyes. The car had a fabulous shine that seemed to illuminate the dark night of that cool evening. The nice white man shook our hands and showed us the open back door of the limousine. I remember his last effusive smile. When he said, "Goodbye. Have a nice flight," I understood him, even though I didn't know any English.

Viola and I sat in the back of the limousine, still the largest car I've ever been in. Another white man, this time in a black uniform and black cap, sat behind the steering wheel. He said, "Hello," and then drove us, never uttering another word. We didn't know it then, but we were on our way to Newark Airport to take a flight to Washington, all arranged by the Pan Am agent. That day everything took such a very long time to happen, or so it seemed, including the limousine ride.

"Look at all the lights. Look at the bridge—it looks like it's touching the sky. Look at the lights," I said, completely captivated by the New York skyline.

Then, I just sank into the back seat, which seemed like a king-size bed. We watched the lights in silence. They were everywhere—front, back, sides. And when we passed several high bridges, we saw even more above the limousine to the left and right. It was spectacular. A soft breeze came through a slightly open window as we drove over a very long bridge to cross what, years later, I would learn was the East River. Going through that city that night was testimony to the fact that I had definitely left the perpetual blackouts and the smelly kerosene lamps of Port-au-Prince evenings. I was sleepy but could not sleep because I didn't want to miss out on anything.

After what felt like a very long time, the car stopped. Through the window, I couldn't see anything but emptiness around us. When the driver opened the door, Viola said, "Thank you." I saw a plane on the tarmac, much smaller than the one we had taken that morning. She held my hand as we stepped onto the plane; we were the only two passengers. I fell asleep seconds after I sat.

Viola's voice woke me up with these words: "We have to get off the plane, we're in Washington."

This time, fortune smiled on us. At the bottom of the stairs, Mandedette stood with her eyes gleaming as she watched us descend the steps. We both ran into her open arms. We all wept. My godmother, Tyanne, whom I hadn't seen in over five years, was with her. Drunk with relief and joy at finding each other, we left the airport in a waiting taxi. We all talked at the same time, but I remember Mandedette calming us with a: "Shuuuuu. It's two in the morning." It was the first time that I was awake at that hour, another of the many firsts experienced during this momentous voyage.

We walked up the stairs to a row house on Hobart Street in Mount Pleasant— known to me from the return address on Mandedette's letters. She unlocked the door of her second-floor apartment. From the small vestibule, she led us to our bedroom, decorated with two twin beds much like the ones in Haiti, except this one had matching bedspreads and curtains. She kissed and held each of us tightly for long seconds, then Mandedette said, "Goodnight" and closed the door behind her.

I was fully conscious that I had entered a vastly different world called the United States.

THE RECKONING

Yet, my Haitian girlhood was not really over. How was I to deal with the consequences of all the secrets, ghosts, and violence accumulated in those years?

After my departure from Haiti at age twelve in 1965, I lived in Washington, D.C. with Mandedette and Viola for over ten years, during which time I attended Howard University. Then, I received a master's in journalism from the Medill School of Journalism of Northwestern University. I then lived in New York City before moving back home to Haiti in 1983.

Mandedette, too, happily abandoned Washington, D.C. after her retirement as an administrative assistant at the International Monetary Fund to return to Haiti in 1985.

On February 7, 1986, I, along with Mandedette and millions of others, witnessed the overthrow of the dynastic Duvalier dictatorship which had brutally ruled the country for twenty-eight years, and the re-adoption of our original blue and red flag.

On January 12, 2010, the seismic shift occurred in Haiti, transforming its story, and that of millions of others, as well as mine. I somehow died that day. How to continue living? The earthquake forced me to revisit that girlhood and realize that inconvenient truths could no longer be avoided to epilogue that story.

Now was the moment of reckoning. And reparations.

THE BEARER OF THE SCAR REMEMBERS

In 1991, barely five years after the fall of the Duvalier dictatorship, Mandedette insisted I accompany her to an exhibit named after the Haitian proverb "*Bay kou bliye, pote mak sonje,* The torturer forgets; the bearer of the scars remembers." It was organized by Port-au-Prince Mayor Evans Paul as a memorial for the victims of the twenty-eight-year dictatorship presided over by the two bloodthirsty autocrats, Duvalier father and son. In a way, the exhibit in the pristine white City Hall was a reckoning for the landscape of interminable terror we had experienced.

I welcomed going downtown to the stunning seafront *Bicentenaire* area where, as a little girl, I strolled with Papa, Mandedette, and Viola on blissful Sunday afternoons. I loved this magical location where I'd watched the infinite deep-blue waters of the Gulf of Gonave.

That afternoon the heat was cruel. I was dressed in white mourning clothes to publicly show respect for the dead. But wearing the color white was also a metaphor for the protest movements against the dictatorship and solidarity towards its victims to which I adhered. Mandedette was very elegant in her starched white attire, which set off her short grey Afro hairstyle.

As I left the harsh sunlight of the street-floor entrance, I immediately focused on the sepia-toned headshot pictures of the victims, some quite fancily framed, lining the walls. All uncertainties about the horrors of those years fell by the wayside in the presence of these faces, from the very young to the very old. My knees shook as I climbed the majestic stairwell of the historic building. By the time I reached the grandiose second-floor reception hall, I saw hundreds of photographs hung side by side on the walls. It was enough to suffocate us. Still, Mandedette and I mingled among the hundred or so other visitors. There was something comforting in my understanding that it was surely best to be in the company of others, even strangers, for such a macabre viewing.

"He was a friend," Mandedette told me as she stopped quite abruptly in front of a man's photograph. She smiled faintly at him. A few steps later, she moved her head up and down like a robot when she noticed another man she had known. She murmured the names of the faces she recognized as if she were doing her school teacher's morning rollcall. I listened. She understood, almost instinctively as she walked through the space, why it was necessary to remove these people from their anonymity by saying their names. It was a call of what had been lost. I discerned that.

Then she paused and asked solemnly, "Where is so and so? Where is so and so?" to no one in particular. She shocked me because she was calling out the absent ones, the ones she knew had been tortured to death. Or had wasted away in prisons. Or had been coldly assassinated.

Or had simply disappeared. They were the ones whose pictures were not on those walls. Perhaps still many others were missing for lack of information or had just been forgotten. Worse, perhaps some remaining family members still had lingering fears of declaring their dead or disappeared, years after the brutes were chased away.

By then, we were surrounded by thousands of photographs of men, women, and children killed or disappeared by the intelligence, security or militia services. Some were hazy, some were unremarkable, some were passport-size, others were big. But this was a partial record of the massive killing fields. Mandedette was right: the exhibit was incomplete. I was overwhelmed.

"I don't see so and so," she whispered again and again, with the haunting force and poignancy of one who had lived through it all. I reached out for her hand. She caressed mine. I felt somewhat protected by her show of affection. But I was furious that those paid to protect us had turned into totalitarians to sap our freedoms and destroy us.

We moved with the slow pace of those taking their last walk. Each photograph, each name became more and more burdensome. City Hall became a place of abject horror. We paused by a wall to catch our breath.

I felt lost in the forest of photographs, but I couldn't take my eyes off the faces. A few times I managed to hide my own face in my hands in a futile attempt to make those images of state-sponsored terror go away. I was less intrigued by the photographs, which in themselves were harmless, than devastated by the gratuitous cruelty, the indignity and the scale of the violence. Confronting it was as unbearable as it was inevitable, yet there was no way to escape the staggering sense of loss.

"Study their names," Mandedette told me. "Never forget them, because they also died for your freedom."

I quickly realized that she had reverted into a teacher. It was most likely because she was afraid that a new enemy, called collective amnesia, could be on the horizon. I understood Mandedette's lesson even though she had never told me that before. I did as told; I centered the faces in those voiceless photographs in my mind. And I told myself, *"Here they are. Look at them; it's no time to retreat or hide. This memorial is a reckoning to disrupt the barbaric echo chamber of fear, torture, dictatorship. But it's also an opportunity to create a different echo chamber: one of resistance, of renewal, of hope, of freedom. Be part of it."*

My lips quivered. My eyes teared up.

After a few more steps, Mandedette's refrain, "I don't see so and so," became a faint whisper. Still, it resonated loudly in my ears.

There was something about the pictures of Lieutenant Francois Benoit's family that made both of us recoil in shock, something I hadn't yet seen. It was a photograph of a baby; of Benoit's nine-month-old boy. He had been kidnapped by Captain Max Dominique on April 23, 1963. Benoit and his wife searched for twenty-four years for their baby, Madame Benoit said in a testimony. It dawned on me at that instant that sometimes courage was just willpower, emerging from infinite longing, profound humility, and deep convictions. I felt Mandedette tightening her grip on my hand. My mouth tasted the acridness of death. I felt the grief. I felt the fury. I felt the humiliation. I felt the exhaustion.

Again, we paused. Mandedette just stood there in the middle of the room; I was next to her. There was no air left to breathe.

"But I don't see Maître Jacques, Ginette's father," Mandedette said in a hushed, slightly trembling voice. She turned towards me with a bewildered expression. I, too, was dismayed, so much so that I heard the pounding of my heart. The pain was searing from not seeing our next-door neighbor, who had disappeared half a lifetime ago when I was six. I wondered if Aniz and Ginette were aware of the exhibit; perhaps they didn't want to get involved. Still, his absence gnawed at me.

This annihilation of so many of our own by our very own was as systematic as it was senseless. It also begged the question of how many dead bodies were needed to satisfy the appetite of human hyenas like the Duvaliers. And the exhibit couldn't nullify the darkness and the injustice. I had a disconcerting feeling of helplessness. I still felt fear. While looking at the photographs, it was as though I could smell the deprivation of those criminals on my skin. It felt like the barbaric past was climbing out of a very shallow mass grave. The three decades of Duvalier terror still overwhelmed me. Though I had buried them deep inside, my scars held a legacy of fear that couldn't be invalidated, they were like an ingrained toenail.

Fear was the whispers, the hushed tones since nobody spoke loudly anymore. The volume of each person's voice could be measured by his or her angst.

Fear was the end of friendly camaraderie, when neighbors stopped visiting, as if the other was a dangerous enemy.

Fear was the paranoia about the spy who could be among us, illustrated daily as the adults stopped talking whenever a domestic was present.

Fear was the silence around Maître Jacques' disappearance because no one ever even mentioned his name again.

Fear was wondering if Papa would come home at night or if they would take him away forever as they did Maître Jacques.

Fear was not trusting nighttime.

Walking the exhibit brought all my childhood fears back to the surface. I felt a searing pain in my head. My feet floated above the floor.

"Maître Jacques was not there," Mandedette whispered again and again as we stepped outside in the heat of the blazing sun and the deafening noise of my city.

I heard her.

That day, I decided it was time to disrupt the plaintive narrative about my disappeared neighbor. It was time to stop the silence. It was time to transform the disappearance of Maître Jacques into a rallying cry. It was time for me to somehow use my voice to keep alive the memory of Maître Jacques' disappearance. It was a small commitment, somewhat like a duty.

I quickly slipped into Mandedette's sheltering arms. Then, moments later, we walked arm in arm so neither faltered, wiping away our tears.

THE CONVERSATION

After the 2010 earthquake, I retreated to New York to my fifth-floor apartment near the 59th Street Bridge. I was surrounded by a collection of paintings from Haiti and artifacts from my African travels. The large windows dominated the dining area just off the living room, bathing the space with natural light. Yet I spent most of my off-work hours in my small bedroom with its large wall of family pictures, hoping that the earth tones and sheer orange curtains that used to provide me with infinite serenity before the earthquake would help me overcome my new posture of anxiety. I continued to infuse the space with my favorite citronella incense to evoke calming childhood memories of Kenscoff. But my mind told me the problem was not the apartment; it was me.

I talked, I read, I listened, I questioned, I analyzed anything I could get my hands on about the earthquake. I explored every feeling, no matter its importance, to try to heal from the trauma. I wrote an essay, "Blue Haiti," about it for *The New York Times*, and it helped me publicly express some of the pain. The overwhelmingly positive reaction it garnered brought me enormous comfort. Yet as time passed and I slowly regained some normalcy, I realized I was brimming with more questions than answers. I desperately needed to understand why my childhood had been disrupted by so many separations and such violence. I had lived a peripatetic existence, as though I were a bird with no nest. I knew what waiting cost; I had done so for over five decades and had accumulated relentless pain, devastating heartaches, and endless trauma.

As a girl, I learned it was sometimes better not to know things, for the burden of knowledge was often too heavy to bear; now fifty years had passed since our family breakup, and close to forty since Papa's death of a heart attack. I knew I could no longer wait for answers to come to me, I had to look for them. I needed to fully own my story, the one with the truths of my mother and father, whatever they were.

While living in New York, I'd invite Mandedette, who'd moved back to the United States from Haiti in 2003 to visit me. I'd get her great tickets to the opera and Broadway shows, and she was delighted to attend them. She was nearing ninety, and although she was in good health, I felt increasing pressure of age—even an urgency—creeping on our remaining time together. The conversation about my childhood took place during one of her visits.

It was a rainy day in autumn. Every now and then the wind blew through cracks in the windowsills. Against that backdrop, I sat next to her on the beige leather sofa in the living room with "The Nearness of You" playing low and Sarah Vaughn's voice tremulous at times over a saxophone. I wanted the jazz sounds to create a live sound barrier, even an anchor, against all the extra stress I anticipated in the vast, dense, and perhaps somber unknown world I was about to enter with Mandedette.

"Why did you and Papa separate?" I asked her with some urgency.

She had a far-away, almost disappointed, look in her eyes as if she too were measuring what had been lost. She seemed overcome by the question, or perhaps the answer she was about to give me. Maybe that's why she stalled. Maybe she felt my hesitation. Maybe she remembered the last time I took up the subject as a teenager. It was in a roundabout way, and she folded into herself, retreating into muteness.

As a teenager I often tried, with little success, to look through her closet and dresser to negotiate stylish hand-me-downs from her considerable wardrobe. Mandedette wore fine cotton, linen or silk dresses or tailored pant and skirt suits that flattered her slim figure, always with the finishing touch of her timeless Shalimar. I wanted to dress fashionably like she did. But she didn't allow Viola and me even to sit on her perfectly made bed, much less go into her closet. On one rare, lucky day, I scored a small victory when she let me rummage through a dresser. In the middle-top drawer I found a small, rectangular, ebony jewelry box lavishly decorated with silver inlays. Inside its far corner was an embossed gold ring among what seemed to be seldom worn or discarded jewels. I'd never seen it, much less her wearing it. When I held it closer, I saw *OC et MC 18.9.48* engraved on the inside. They were Mandedette's and Papa's initials next to the date that matched the one printed on their wedding photograph that I so admired.

While I had reluctantly accepted that Mandedette and Papa would never be together again, I was jolted by the discovery of her wedding ring. It showed in my face that I was still angry with her about how she escaped that relationship. All along I had placed considerable blame on her for the breakup of our family because she was the one who left Papa—twice—each time creating insurmountable distance between us by migrating to another country. In turn, her absences had given me a certain power over her because I could make her feel guilty for having hurt me, for having deserted me. Actually, I resented her for relegating the ring to a back drawer.

"Could I have the ring?" I asked her.

Not a sound. I looked past her eyes and through her. This exchange crystallized something for me: I distrusted her, and this distrust poisoned my attitudes and my choices. I decided that instead of confronting her, I'd quietly ask, "Can I borrow your wedding ring, please?" I let on that I not only grasped its importance, but that it would be a loan and not an outright gift.

"Yes, you can," Mandedette responded.

I was thrilled about my new acquisition. The me of then, still entrenched in my misery about their separation, kept it in a futile effort to hold on to some small part of their union. The ring, while a stunning adornment, brought me few, if any, answers about the decomposition and loss of what was most precious to me—my family. She never once asked to get it back—but then Mandedette wasn't the sort of woman to want a reminder of something as obsolete as her marriage to Papa, let alone a thin gold band that had perhaps never brought her happiness. By then, she had already closed that chapter of her life. I hadn't and needed to.

Rain splattered my windows. Somehow, instead of talking to me—instead of responding—Mandedette walked out after I asked her that question, why she and Papa had separated, and she went into the other room. I was disappointed but didn't complain. Her nonagenarian body could surely use some rest. I'd spent my early morning reflecting on how much I wanted to know, how much I wanted to say. Time had done its work, muting some of the pain. My little body had felt so much sorrow when I was a child, and a lot still remained. It was an intimate disaster, never totally erased.

I saw wet pigeons cooing on the windowsill. I sprinkled Kosher salt and olive oil on two avocado halves, hoping she'd eat them when she woke up. I put on Thelonious Monk, easy and low, and almost immediately, his subtle magic on the piano in "Round Midnight" transported me.

And I waited.

When she came back to the living room, she propped herself up against two large pillows on the sofa with her back to the drizzly skyline. I still didn't have the courage to question her directly. Rather, I spoke to myself again and again, as if I were practicing for a theatrical performance, *Why did you leave Viola and me? Why did you wait until the last night to tell us you were traveling? Why?* I felt eight years old all over again.

Then, I saw her wide eyes gazing at me. We were now face to face. I grasped for air as the words finally spilled out of my mouth after more than fifty years: "Mandedette, why did you leave Viola and me?"

It was done. I had said it. I stared at her because I wanted her to see how determined I was to know the truth.

In a low monotone, her voice echoed her storytelling: she divorced Papa when we lived on rue Baussan. She had tried to make it work, first by opening the beauty salon. "It was exhausting and humiliating. I hated having to borrow money from friends and never knowing how the bills would be paid, despite the fact we lived a simple, no-frills life." Her sad eyes and slumped shoulders expressed the hurt, still raw despite all these decades.

She said, like most women of her generation, she had a vision of what a marriage should be, and it included the belief that the husband bore the primary responsibility for taking care of his family. I remember her repeatedly cautioning Viola and I when we started dating, "Remember, the man has got to wear the pants." Despite her upbringing, she'd even try to wear them when her husband didn't, when her illusions were sufficiently deceived by the increasingly burdensome and haphazard husband Papa had become.

"I realized Papa and I had different temperaments and belonged in different worlds," she said. "Luck was his permanent solution. It took me decades after leaving him to understand gambling was a disease," she explained. In his quest for money, Papa sold huge stretches of land bequeathed to the family in the Saint-Marc area. "He threw away his family's fortune; such a waste!" she commented laconically.

I understood Papa was simply the wrong man for her ambitions. She had buried her dreams long enough. Finally, to ensure the bright future she dreamed for us, she left him. I was fascinated by the incredible energy she mustered to make our precarious lives livable. This is what we expect from our mothers, that they pretend everything is fine even when the reality is vastly different.

I slid by her side on the sofa and my bare feet touched hers. We were close physically, yet the space between us felt as wide as it was suffocating.

If I seemed disappointed, it's because I felt there had to be much more than financial issues. I reminded her of what she often told Viola and me: "A woman never leaves a good man." I pressed, trying empathy to get her to open up, "I know Papa was probably not as good a husband as he was a father to Serge, Viola and me."

"Do you remember the summer when we went to Damien?" she asked. I did. Her stare pierced my calmness as Stanley Turentine surrounded us with his "Salt Song." My mother's dark brown eyes had always been her most efficient communication tool, so I anticipated pain. "You must listen to what happened to me" was what I understood from them.

"We went to Damien after I endured a particularly brutal incident with Papa. I decided it was the last time. So I packed some bags, grabbed Viola and you, and left Papa. It had happened much too often during our marriage," she recalled in a voice that subtly trembled. "Your father didn't know how to talk to people. Any comment I made or little thing I did that he didn't appreciate or understand was a reason for him to slap, shove, or beat me. He wanted us to come back home from Damien, but I wouldn't."

I gasped. My heart drummed through the faint sounds of saxophone riffs. In the seconds that followed, I felt Mandedette's intense pain in my own body, as if I were the one beaten by Papa. Her calmness while telling me this horror story brought me to absolute silence. Still, she looked anguished, perhaps more for my feelings than hers. She had pleading eyes. I sat there and wept.

Then she recounted our return home from Damien: "The morning after, I walked into the Police headquarters across from the National Palace. I asked to see Colonel Marcaisse Prosper," she said. "He was the Chief of Police and the most powerful man in the country after President Magloire. I lodged a formal complaint against your father for domestic violence. I also asked the Chief of Police to stop him from ever beating me again."

Jazz music filled the apartment. I saw a faint smile on her face as she straightened her back in what was clearly a gesture of her determination and elegance. She continued: "Colonel Prosper was also known as the most elegant man in Haiti. He always looked suave, as if he had just taken a shower. He smelled good and was an impeccable dresser, with his clothing pressed to starchy perfection. It was an immense pleasure to see such handsome men. Although they were criminals, they were like jewels of the masculine sex."

"Did you know him?" I whispered, surprised at Mandedette's admiration for a man she called a criminal but afraid I could be heard, even though she and I were alone in the apartment along with Miles Davis trumpeting "Kinda Blue."

She had met him a few times because he was a friend of Tante Yolande. She winked at me as she said, "I believe they were lovers." I laughed for nervous relief because here was my mother telling me about her abuse by my father, and yet she was amused by the affair of the heart of her married cousin with the equally married chief of police.

"How did Colonel Prosper respond to your complaint?" I questioned.

"He summoned Max to a meeting the next day. Your father was very surprised to be called to the police station," Mandedette said in a measured tone, not at all triumphant.

"Why?" I asked nervously.

"Colonel Prosper symbolized power. He and the others in such positions inspired fear. Military men at the time had prestige, but more importantly for me, they had lots of power. Even their mistresses had power."

"What did he say to Papa?"

"He ordered your father never to lay a hand on me again. And Max never did," Mandedette said.

That was it. Just like that, Papa stopped beating Mandedette.

The irony was not lost on me: the man who put an end to my father's violence towards my mother was known for giving orders to President Magloire's henchmen.

"Did Colonel Prosper commit atrocities?" I asked bluntly.

"He was too aristocratic to be a henchman himself," Mandedette concluded.

That a military leader in a period of military rule would be the one to tell a powerful man like Papa to stop his violence towards his wife was exceptional. When the Chief of Police of the country issued the order to Papa to stop beating his wife—for make no mistake, it was an order—Mandedette was probably the only other person in Haiti, besides Colonel Prosper, who made Papa, at the time on the security team of President Magloire, shake with fear.

There was no confusion in my mind, or in my heart, about the revulsion I felt over Papa's abominable behavior. Mandedette had unknowingly entered a war zone. Her marriage had become a battlefield with her husband as the aggressor while I, like Viola, lived peacefully in that combat area in total oblivion, without ever seeing, hearing, feeling, or knowing anything.

I was terribly ashamed that the father I knew as affectionate and attentive was also a serially abusive husband. I apologized to Mandedette. My words seemed to lessen her solitude; I had the impression I'd touched her heart. My hand slid ever so delicately back and forth on her legs so she would know I was there for her.

I took a long pause to collect myself. I made verbena tea to calm my nerves and warm my blood.

All my life, I had remembered the delightful weeks spent at the Damien farm as a taste of paradise. For Mandedette, perhaps it was a kind of breakthrough; the point that made her resolve to stop Papa's violent behavior. And maybe to confirm her own path without him.

Even for women of her generation who, in the 1950s, had professional careers as teachers, nurses, business owners, or doctors, Mandedette's complaint to the colonel was audacious. It was heroic, even revolutionary. Something in her personality made her rise up after a decade of brutality and leave her sacred union to Papa. I tried to imagine what it took for her to perform that act of resistance. There must have been something beyond her public face, that of a woman of few words, never raising her voice and savoring solitude. There must have been something in the make-up of her personality to give her that type of doggedness, that unabated persistence, for her act was also a testament to her intelligence. She had the clairvoyance to understand that only Colonel Prosper had the power to stop Papa, even if it squarely transgressed all the taboos erected by Haitian society. In the Haiti of that time, resistance to any kind of domestic or personal violence perpetrated by family members virtually never occurred.

This much I knew; it also took a certain grace to run away from such a situation, first to Damien, and then to the police station—the Chief of police no less—to seek salvation, even redemption. I discovered I had truly not known Mandedette. After she confessed her deep and terribly cumbersome secret to me five decades after the fact, I realized we can never entirely know our mothers and fathers.

Rain blurred the windows. It was around then that I remembered another conversation I had with Mandedette about thirty years before this one. It happened after my husband of eleven months beat me savagely. A few days later, when I was finally able to put my bruised, disheveled, and shamed self-sufficiently together to use the telephone, I called her. She listened while I relived what occurred in the middle of that night when I woke up to my husband pummeling me. She bore witness as I bared my pain of a marriage destroyed in a few drunken minutes, defying my dreams of a happily ever after. She was discreet and didn't ask any questions but was bold in her advice: "You must not let it happen a second time. When you accept the abuse once, it continues. He will be emboldened. Leave now." She added: "Don't tell him or anyone. Wait until he is out of the house and run. When you are safely away, call him to say you'll never return." A month after that phone call, after I paid the deposit and first month's rent on a new apartment, I followed the road map she laid out for me. It was the best advice ever given to me.

Mandedette knew what I had lived.

Only now, on this wet New York day did I learn she carried skin-deep knowledge of what not leaving after the first beating meant: it translated into ten years of abuse by Papa. When she finally left him, she didn't tell anyone until she was safely tucked away—in her case, in New York.

At last, the whole truth was finally revealed to me: that was the reason she couldn't tell Viola and me about her trips to New York ahead of time. It was too big a risk.

Now, I knew what Mandedette had lived.

The aroma of citronella had settled in the living room. Dinah Washington's voice wept on "This Bitter Earth" before she transitioned to "What a Difference a Day Makes." Mandedette's face was solemn but still showed a shy smile. It was as if both her and me had agreed to take a respite from the melancholy. The jazz diva's clear soprano transported us as we sat side by side on the sofa, my head nesting on her shoulder.

Then, we listened intently to Nina Simone's pain-filled bluesy voice belting out "Sinnerman, Where You Gonna Run to?" Mandedette looked steadily at me for what seemed like a very long time. I listened to the words in her eyes, as they appeared to be talking to me.

Then in a moment of sudden transformation like no other, she started to sing: Sinnerman! Sinnermen! You know who they are? It was as if a spirit had gotten into her. "Those sinner men were far, and they were close; they were everywhere," She lowered her voice to tell me, "Some were in army uniforms. Some had names like *cagoulards* or *macoutes.* Some were even in our bedrooms. They were all like hungry hyenas looking for prey."

She got up and disappeared into the bedroom.

I listened to Nina Simone. I watched and heard the rain like I used to on rue Baussan. Then I stayed motionless for a very long time.

I still had unfinished business with her.

When she came back to the living room, I leaned on her to better hear other truths I had been waiting my whole life to hear. Her confession about Papa's violence had finally opened a door that I was not quick to close.

"Why did you leave me to suffer abuse from Grandma?" I boldly asked her.

"My life has not been easy," she said in a voice that was suppressing tears she was perhaps not ready to shed. "And my mother's life was not easy, either." As if she were smiling and crying at the same time, she told me about Grandma abandoning her with her father during four years: "That was the end of my childhood. There was pain. I did suffer, in a certain manner. Just not intellectually. But then, that's what saved me. My papa was a relentless and ambitious man who transmitted his passion for *Excelsior,* the Latin equivalent of excellence, and justice to me. Because of him, I've also known moments of intense satisfaction from completing my education and getting rewarding work. That was more than enough. My life is a strong denial of what is said and assumed about children living without their mothers."

She stared at the floor as if to better hear the sound of John Coltrane's saxophone reverberating under our feet. "I'd been very unhappy with my life with Papa in Haiti. I had to make a choice. I did. I called on Grandma, although I knew it wasn't the ideal solution. Leaving Papa cost me dearly, and mostly in time spent without Viola and you. But at the time, Grandma as my surrogate was the best I could do to preserve my sanity and my two precious girls," Mandedette said.

"Is that why you wanted me to forgive her?" I asked remembering a few years earlier, when ninety-seven-year-old Grandma was on her deathbed. Mandedette had whispered to me that I was the only thing preventing Grandma from dying peacefully: "Please release her from her sins." The irrefutable accuracy of her request caught me off guard. I thought long and hard about those six words. They meant that *power* had shifted from Grandma to me. For now, I had both a burden and a choice—that of punishing her or of showing her grace.

For years, I had purposely chosen silence. The pain was embedded in my gut, the memory never far away. Once, I saw a woman with a twig in her hand chasing a little girl of about seven. The girl kept running in circles, her friends around her, some laughing, some serious, perhaps worried about what would happen when the woman caught her. I knew better than most what would happen. That little girl was me. I was triggered; my knees buckled, and I began to sweat. The difference was that now I was empowered. I made a choice: I went to the woman and asked for mercy for the girl. I wasn't *them*—the cowardly neighbors and teachers who saw and heard me be berated and beaten and did nothing to help save me.

I had always regarded Grandma the way a prisoner might think of his jailer: as much libation as poison. With her approaching death, I told myself it was time to let go.

I even allowed myself to love one thing about her; her idiosyncrasies. With her mercurial moods, one month she was fanatical about zucchini, then she hated it, preferring cornbread. Once she bragged about how beautiful she was at eighteen years old, so beautiful that no good man could resist her. I was sorry not to have known her then.

Mandedette's plea for me to release her from her sins resounded in my mind.

I tiptoed to Grandma's room. I leaned towards her deathbed. Her eyes were closed but I thought I heard her breathing. I whispered in her ear, "Grandma, I forgive you." I thought I saw a very faint smile on her face. I hoped the last thing she felt was grace.

"I was glad you forgave her," Mandedette told me. In a stream of consciousness, she continued: "I realize I should have communicated more and better with Viola and you about leaving Haiti for New York. But at the time, parents didn't talk much to their children about life decisions. There was also the risk for my personal safety. And by temperament, I'm not one to speak much. I'm so very sorry I didn't do this, because I know the torment I inflicted on you and your sister. I've known moments of deep loneliness being away from you children and from Haiti, moments of excruciating distress and utter shame from having to babysit the children of others when I couldn't take care of my own."

Mandedette didn't express any bitterness, not even a hint of regret. Complaining was not part of her life, nor was self-pity. Her values were rather different; she chose stoicism to prevent the overflow of sorrows.

But that day, I resuscitated a thought I had in the weeks and months after she left Haiti, because even then at eight years old, I was already determined to emancipate myself from the "mother-abandons-child" model that had molded Mandedette's character and life. I confessed to her quietly, "I vowed never to leave my children behind no matter what the circumstances." I didn't want my mother's story to be mine.

I saw the tight line of her mouth when she told me, "I had also made the same vow when I had you children, and it nearly destroyed me to have to break it."

"I understand," I whispered. She was gentle and beautiful, and she seemed relieved.

But I lied. My reality was the disconnect between my head, which fully comprehended what she said, and my heart, which would never understand or accept it.

The silence between us had finally ended. When she spoke her truth about her insecurities, hardships and choices and with such eloquence, a dam had burst and released the many emotions I had carried so desperately in my person since childhood. All I wanted in the world was to bare the excruciating pain written in me and lay claim to the joys and beauties hidden under the heartbreak.

I had made Mandedette the villain in my story. I was wrong.

I had made Papa the saint, the savior, the hero of my story. I was wrong.

I could no longer blur the lines that I now knew were myths. I had constructed them in my childhood to bridge the silences in the absence of any real information. Now, I had to bury them. To repair myself.

The new me accepted that.

Raindrops hit the condenser unit of the air conditioner hard, like plaintive notes of a blues harmonica.

I felt Mandedette's arms embracing my shoulders. We watched the sky cry in a holy silence.

BONES

It was a blazing afternoon in Miami. Inspired by the desire to weave a family bond during Gladys's vacation, Viola invited her, her family and me for lunch. It was now fifty years after we had first met on the veranda in the lakou, close to forty after Papa's death, four years after the New York conversation with Mandedette, and months after her courageous exit from the living to join her tribe of robust women. We made an unlikely sisterhood, and the occasion became, quite unexpectedly, an awakening to Papa's past, which turned into a reckoning.

A few years after my departure from Haiti, Gladys migrated to New Jersey as did Tante Yvonne and most of the cousins. Even though we lived in different cities, I visited them during major family gatherings. At first, Gladys and I exchanged telephone numbers; then we started talking regularly. Warmth infused the relationship, though nothing was ever said about sisterhood. Over time, as life happened, I grew to think of her as my sister, and she reciprocated. The bond held. And because family is a construct that is built, given shape, and nourished over shared experiences, Gladys and I became family.

At the lunch, Gladys arrived with her husband, daughter, son-in-law, and grandson. Her face was weathered yet soft, and her wide body wobbled as she sat cushioned and tucked in the wheelchair she had used since suffering a stroke a few years earlier. Viola wore her elegance with a generous smile, and her house, whose walls were filled with Haitian paintings, was as meticulously decorated as it was welcoming. I was wearing white, my skin dark against the cotton lace.

We clicked instantly and made small talk about Miami and Haiti. We devoured a supremely delicious main course of ham and turkey with Haitian rice and beans around the large, oval dining table. Then, Gladys's razor-thin husband wheeled her to the living room. He placed her near a vase of long-stemmed pink roses by the black piano, where she followed our table conversation with detached attention. He stayed by her side, holding in one hand a glass of water just in case she needed something, and in another a whisky-on-ice from which he sipped with obvious pleasure.

"*Viola, Monique*," Gladys said to grab our attention. Fearless as a wild child, quick as a cut, she stared at those of us still sitting at the table. Then, she wagged her index finger for emphasis and said softly, in an unmodulated voice, "I am your sister because your Papa raped my mother, and she got pregnant with me."

In that moment, I heard her words "I am your sister." At last, I had the naked truth as confirmation that she was my sister. It was an end to so many lies.

I sat transfixed in the sifted light coming through the ecru silk drapes. Heat entered the room and my brain at the same time, creating havoc even though the air conditioner was spitting the coldest of air.

"Dessert is coming," Viola announced in a shrill voice. She gasped for air as she quickly left for the kitchen, less for the mango gelato and more to regain her composure.

"This family has so many secrets. I can't take it anymore," said Gladys's very pretty daughter. I heard everyone's small, nervous laugh.

That's when Gladys's words, "your Papa raped my mother," began to lodge in my body. Something shifted inside of me. A distant memory flashed: The image of Papa driving me to school as I told him of the suffering I endured when Grandma whipped me. His words of consolation came to my mind as did his comforting, protective gestures. For a few quick seconds, I relived these ordinary memories of my loving Papa. Now, I juxtaposed them with the extraordinarily violent memory evoked by Gladys. Now I was the daughter of a rapist, a child rapist, no less. I was overwhelmed with despair. I understood there were no words to describe suffering.

It was the beginning of another type of immense pain.

There is a common belief in my family that the cousins on the veranda in the lakou never really lied, that there was always some truth in their gossip. And in many ways, some of those half-truths lingered and others festered. And so it was that it was from the cousins' hearsay that Gladys had learned the violent story of her origin and her father's identity.

Her life was a fatherless one, even though Papa was often present during her visits to the lakou, and she undoubtedly witnessed him being the doting father to Serge, Viola, and me—assuredly an impenetrable frontier for her. The absence of a father could've become a sort of swallowing black hole. Maybe she felt it becoming one. That's perhaps why one day she asked her mother, "Where is my father?"

That's also perhaps why her mother answered by telling her, "*Dlo Rivyè Bwa-d-Chenn pote l ale nan lanmè,*" that flood waters of the Bois-de-Chène River had swept him away into the cobalt blue waters of the Caribbean Sea. Perhaps her mother wanted to correct the dearth of his presence by creating an imaginary father for her who was rapidly annihilated.

I surmised that both truths, the lakou's and her mother's, were probably imprinted in her, as real as the sun shining in the day and the moon at night. A weaker child could lose her mind living in two such alternate and equally agonizing realities. When I discovered the way she handled this situation, I respected that Gladys's form of courage emerged from the groundswell of off-handed, narrow-minded, and gossipy half-truths.

But the absence of a father was also silence, an all-encompassing silence. Maybe there were dreams of hearing something, anything from him. There could have been dreams of words, of a voice, of a presence, even a promise, a reason to hope. But there was only silence. And that's the silence she broke that day at Viola's house during the time we hoped to seal a family bond; however tenuous. Her calm was as remarkable as it was excruciating to witness, as she spoke in a clear, low voice that commanded us to listen to her origin story as if she were the only one in the room.

She had a single narrative, her own. I imagine she had waited this *forever* to tell us her truth and must have spent days, perhaps years— maybe she had waited her whole life—for this moment.

On the surface, when Gladys told us, "Max Clesca is my father," in the defiant way such obscure things are meant to be revealed, she claimed his name. But, I thought, not to claim it as hers. Rather, I believed, she cited his full name not only to accentuate and maybe even ironize his formerly powerful status but even more so because she wanted to distance herself from him while making him fully responsible for his actions. By virtue of her demeanor, her controlled voice, and her words spoken with such an abundance of confidence, she told us that she had liberated herself from the lifelong denial of her paternity. I took it as a declaration of independence: she was no longer a victim of gossip or of Papa. She was this free woman with enormous respectability. Her eyes appeared relieved and focused. I was in awe of her.

She broke that bridge that existed for so long between our two worlds, and in fact, did create a bond based on her deepest truth. There was no complaint, no challenge. She didn't cast shadows, rather she brought relief, solace, and light. She became the light as we all sat in the stillness that followed. It was so difficult to envision a scene so subtle yet so fierce in its truthfulness, let alone to live it. I stared at her. I didn't know what to say. I had nothing to say. It was her time. Her hands shook slightly as if they were small leaves blown off the ground by a whiff of wind.

Everyone started to fidget in their chairs as they took their last spoonful of gelato. "Could I eat the rose petal?" one asked.

"Yes! It's a flavorful, fully edible, antioxidant loaded with vitamins," I said about the petals I had added as a gourmet touch to the dessert.

After a few long, soundless minutes, Gladys prepared to leave. I saw her face and body tremble as she slid out of her wheelchair into the car seat. I bent down to kiss her. The air was soft, the light was pale as the sun was setting. I heard the rustle of leaves and a minor symphony of frogs croaking and crickets chirping near Viola's large patch of bromeliads.

When they had gone, I sat quietly in the somber light of Viola's dining room. The joyful memories and wonderful images of Papa were battered by the force of Gladys's revelation. It made me see Papa as another man, an extremely violent and even hateful one. It's as if horror had an imagination that greatly surpassed my worst nightmare.

I glanced at Viola across the table as I stroked the linen tablecloth, smoothing out the creases and picking up the crumbs as if that could bring back some sense of order in my life. She sat across from me and gathered the dessert plates. Our hands and eyes did the talking; it was loud enough for both to hear.

As I got up to say goodbye, Viola, always avoiding conflict while trying to round out sharp edges, intuitively knew what I was thinking. Trying to protect me from unforeseen trouble much as she had long ago, she warned me: "Papa is dead now. Don't go searching for things. Leave it alone. If you pursue this, 'wa jwen ak zo grann ou '" She used a common Haitian colloquial expression: "You'll find your grandmother's bones." Metaphorically, it meant, "You might find what you don't want to while unearthing the truth." It sounded to me like a prediction.

Papa had been dead four decades, but he was tormenting my mind and breaking my heart. I felt as if the sky were being ripped apart.

For this was also my story just as it was Gladys's, Papa's and my family's. But overnight, Gladys's revelation set me back by disrupting the progress I was making in my post-earthquake reconstruction. By then I had made peace with Mandedette, yet I paused feeling a crushing disappointment. But I was not deterred. I knew fear couldn't beat me, and I couldn't be stopped.

So haunted was I by Gladys's disclosure, I started to live in two worlds: grieving the Papa I knew while lamenting the one I had just discovered. I pondered if I could ever reconcile with him. Since the lakou was one of my schools of life, why didn't I hear of this story? I recalled the cousins endlessly talking about everything, often reframing events or offering perspectives according to the folktales, superstitions, and the oral history of Charlier, Grand Angele's village. The whispers ran through the lakou like the Bois-de-Chène river flooding into the sea as we passed every story to each other in the day, in the afternoon, in the night under the grapevine. Since the lakou was also my village, which preserved so many memories of the family, I wondered why I'd never heard about this rape and how this particular secret remained so for so long. Was there a family conspiracy? Were there other bloody heirlooms?

Despite my concerns about what I might find, I became obsessed with unearthing those potential "bones."

It paid to have remained close with the cousins; after all, we were kin. I called the one I thought would be the most perfect source of information; slightly older than Gladys, she always seemed to know everything. I was younger but I remembered she had a reputation as a straight talker, a trait rare among the others, who privileged innuendos. Cousin was an unending source of fascination for me because she was energetic and full of dry humor, and she'd always showed great respect and affection for Papa.

"Tell me about the rape Papa committed on Gladys's mother," I said.

She seemed surprised I knew. After her initial hesitation, she told me her storytelling would be inspired by her need to set the record straight. Her familiar voice was faint but controlled. Although I missed seeing her, I was glad we weren't face to face, hoping the distance provided by the telephone would help me be brave enough to face the truth about Papa's true identity.

"It all came to light one day in 1948 when Grand Angele announced she'd heard Papa had a girl child whom she hadn't met. She asked that her granddaughter be presented to her," Cousin recalled. "That's how little three-year-old Gladys, with her long, dark curls, was brought into the lakou to meet Grand Angele."

"Where had she been hiding?" I asked, conscious of the importance of details to the story.

"She lived a few blocks away in a boarding house with her fourteen-year-old mother," Cousin said. "Before that, her mother lived in the lakou."

"Papa raped a fourteen-year-old girl?" I murmured, my voice stifled with tears, to confirm what my whole person was rejecting.

"Yes, he did. She was a young cousin who did various household chores in exchange for room, board, and school. When she was considered old enough to be sent on small errands, she was tasked with carrying Papa's lunch basket to his office," Cousin explained.

"Is that where the rape took place?" I asked.

"Yes," she whispered as if the horror of what happened was still raw. *"Ti Chérie,* are you there?" she asked.

"Yes. In shock. I need some verbena tea to calm my nerves," my voice quivered as my stomach turned. Something fundamental broke in me. I felt my heart's palpitations like drumbeats on my skin.

After being confronted about her bulging stomach, the adolescent girl confessed to the assault that got her pregnant, Cousin explained. Tante Yvonne worked out the details following the discovery of the rape. She concocted an ultra-secret plan. The girl was rapidly removed from the lakou to a safe room nearby as if she were being exfiltrated like a spy who had been outed. Papa and Tante Yvonne were not the sort of people to let something like this tarnish their veneer of respectability. Ignominy had to be avoided at all costs. Like a demon.

"Why didn't they give the child Papa's last name?" I asked Cousin.

She spelled it out for me; "Papa was an authority in the country. He had relationships with high-level politicians up to the presidential level. Recognizing a child who was born in such circumstances would have been a scandal. It was extremely important that this child, and particularly the rape, be hidden."

"Did Papa know about Tante Yvonne's secret plan?" I asked.

"Ti Chérie, your father and his sister were one and the same. They functioned in symbiosis, almost like twins," Cousin commented. She didn't say it with righteous anger or judgment, but rather as a statement of fact. I thought, here was one more woman—Tante Yvonne—complicit in hiding a man's depravity.

"Is this why Tante Yvonne became Gladys's godmother?" I asked.

"Yes. And she got her own son, Fritz, to be godfather," she added.

I wondered, did they really think that Papa's rape of a child would be absolved by his sister and nephew becoming the child's godparents?

In the Haiti of the 1940s and 1950s, a tacit, if not official, entry into a family was perhaps the most that could be done to hide the impropriety of a family connection, simply create another one. Better to have your aunt as your godmother and your cousin as your godfather than your father as your father. They, in effect, dispossessed her while they protected Papa and the family from public shame. This was the Papa I unearthed, and it felt almost as if the entire thing was conjured out of thin air. I *hated* his arrogant gutlessness.

"By the time Gladys was introduced to Grand Angele," Cousin said in a firm, compassionate tone, "Papa was married to Mandedette, so the secret was guarded even more preciously," I questioned if Mandedette knew about the child or the rape, but Cousin said she couldn't be positive. "I always observed a certain coldness, even mistrust between Tante Yvonne and your mother, who rarely ever came to the lakou. You get what I mean?" she asked, without really expecting me to answer.

Cousin concluded her spoken words with the authority of one who had always known the secret: "I'm telling you this, so you know the truth and understand what happened." I treasured her and her remarkable effort against erasure. I also immediately understood she had given me the key to a family deed.

Twilight had descended by the time I hung up the telephone. I made verbena tea, and its vapors perfumed the room. I settled into the ritual of taking small sips. A couple of birds chirped out back. Clouds gathered in my head like battleships lined up for an assault as I sat listless on the soft leather sofa, holding Papa's photograph on my lap. I was almost afraid to bring it closer to look him in the eyes. I was facing a master poker player and his greatest gamble, which paid off for almost seventy-five years. I was dizzy from feeling captive to these family demons in disguise.

In my world of human rights advocates, it didn't matter that Papa's rape of a fourteen-year-old child had occurred three years before his marriage to Mandedette, seven years before I was born, and close to sixty before I learned of it. Rape was rape. The statute of limitations might have been off the table, but there were no limitations on ethical and emotional grounds. I knew better than anyone that the fight for justice was clearly between Papa and me.

For weeks, I obsessed about Papa—with his fully-appropriated imperiousness and omnipresent gun. I knew from my work with survivors of violence that rapists aim to dehumanize their victims and render them weak and powerless. I also knew that rape was never about sex, but about domination. I knew rape was an act of war against a woman's body and soul. That's why I couldn't avoid reflecting on what inner thoughts Papa and the surviving girl might have had.

Papa gambled; that's what he knew best. He probably saw her as easy prey, with her short, skinny body and humble provincial demeanor. He probably thought she was his possession, not only because she was a child, but she was also his family's employee, despite also being his little cousin. He was not a nobody; she, like everybody else, knew he was the patriarch of the family. She probably smiled at him naively when she reached his workplace after walking fast through the city's teeming streets with his lunch. Maybe he thought such a young girl wouldn't have a voice to express herself. He probably even believed the whole vile thing would be over when he finished raping her. He miscalculated. Not only did he rob her of her childhood, he forced her into womanhood with the pregnancy.

Like many poor girl-children in such situations, she bore her burden. I can imagine the dread and the shame she felt when she learned that his abominable waste had fertilized her, when the small womb of her fourteen-year-old body struggled as it could barely hold the baby, and when she had to hide out alone. Perhaps that's when she determined she wouldn't be broken, that she had to develop a will of steel to survive the desecration of her young, innocent body. She never acknowledged Papa as the father, yet she went a step further by symbolically killing him. I wanted to believe that her narrative of him being washed away by a flood reflected the fact that the river carried away the city's sewage. Even though she was only fourteen, she must have realized thieves and rapists were just that—trash.

I was ashamed to the tip of my toes for her suffering. Her pain and humiliation reached the recesses of my mind; they were taxing and oppressive. That's why I so appreciated that even back then, in the late 1940s, she stood tall with grace and not an ounce of fragility against the patriarch who had declared war on her.

What solidified this ignominy was immensely significant: Papa had broken a family tradition. Which is what Grand Angele's demand to meet Papa's child so as to claim her granddaughter as family was all about. *That* was Grand Angele. She was not the sort of person to indulge in denial or disrespect of family, for this was rooted in her African value system, which sacralized family. It would have been inconceivable to her as an African-rooted matriarch to have family she didn't know, much less the child of her child. That he, along with Tante Yvonne, spent so much energy and engaged in such cunning to avoid claiming his child showed the depth of his dishonor of his mother and her traditions. This was why they hid the child from Grand

Angele. Viola was right; I had found my grandmother's bones. *And* my father's bones.

But how and where did I, child of a rapist, stand among those bones?

I struggled with the force of devastation that was Papa. I buried myself in shame and anger even as I tried to find some semblance of bravery or at least equilibrium after I became this child of two different fathers. The chasm between the Papa I loved and the one I hated had considerably widened as I learned the appalling details of the secret. Bridging this chasm was the only way to reconcile both, but doing that made me feel as if I were pushing thorns into my skin, almost begging it to bleed.

I still wasn't brave enough for the reckoning over Papa. I felt tired from the pilgrimage across the yawning rift that divided him and me. A thin thread held me up. My nerves needed soothing. I daydreamed. At night, my mind roamed around our lives. It was hard not to want him back because his charisma was so undeniable. I imagined talking to him. I saw the smile I knew him for and which carried years of my childhood inside of it, along with his firm voice and honest laughter resonating in the hallways of my mind. I had many questions for him, but none could ever be answered since he was dead. There really was no way to neatly tie this story with a bow.

But I knew, without a trace of malice, that there was no atonement possible for him. I also knew I could not hide the truth to protect him and his one-sided legacy. Like Gladys, I had to say, "This happened."

But I had to first make peace with myself by going through the merciless process of exhuming him from muddy waters and contaminated earth.

I knew it was my biggest challenge—since losing myself again was no longer an option—or at least the biggest since the conversation with and the subsequent death of Mandedette, which was the biggest since the earthquake, which was the biggest since the Duvalier political landscape, the generational trauma, the beatings, the belittling and other intimate fault lines, and since the last one, and the one before that.

I turned inward.

Many months later, it dawned on me that Papa was like a gift in a box I never totally opened. When I finally did, I found a much lesser man with a sordid past underneath the poker face and behind the ubiquitous smile. After discovering the many monstrous acts he committed, I accepted that he was a mere human with major moral flaws. At last, I unburdened myself of this extraordinary betrayal of my trust and could finally mourn the death of an identity: the Papa that I idolized as a hero and thought of as a saint.

I let go of the past.

I recognized most of what was inside the box was truly a gift, like the nighttime rituals he had invented to make me laugh while he gently tickled me to sleep, or the remarkable thoughtfulness and unfailing love with which he protected me. Now, I, much like a grave digger searching Papa's secret bones, exhumed a new Papa that I still loved.

POSTWORD

One day, I understood and I was once again grounded.

It was a few years after the earthquake. I was sitting on my leather sofa. The living room was quiet and reflected the faint orange hues of the sunset. The air smelled of citronella incense. That's when something told me with astounding clarity that the extensive parenthesis of time I'd lived, from the near-total destruction brought about by the earthquake to the reckoning, was over. I'd resolved and transcended those pieces of the puzzle that had heartbreakingly engulfed me.

I felt an authentic interconnectedness between my city, my country, my environment, and my people. I beheld the lost souls of my family encountered during that difficult time. I understood the sacredness of Grand Angele's words to Tante Yvonne about her spirits: "They are my mysteries. I must celebrate them." I knew it was all legacy: the spirits, the ancestors, Grand Angele, Grandma, Papa, Mandedette, and even the large black butterfly that visited me every once in a while.

I also got a sense that I, too, was being beheld, and it fostered my confidence. I embraced it all because I had finally achieved a sense of place at the end of my long story and arduous journey of healing. Although never complete, it had brought a positive change in my life.

I felt a profound transformation in my person. It all came from accepting, and also honoring, that all of it—each single, vivid, rich, and nebulous piece of the puzzling patchwork of mysteries—was my life. Despite the obvious and insidious violence endured during my girlhood, it was not all tragic. It had magic, wonder, and beauty. I lived enormous and intense joy. And now joy, another legacy of my childhood, was back in my life.

Grace penetrated this new me with a calm intensity as if I were a bird after the season's molting.

Some of my mutation also owed to being raised by role models, which against all odds, and sometimes ever so quietly, throughout my girlhood surrounded me with a belief system that taught me that everything was possible for me. Some of the transformation owed to their strong narrative about pride, elegance, fearlessness, grace, identity, history, *noirisme*—Blackness—and by unflinchingly clear examples of irrepressible resistance.

Now, with the pale evening light filtering through the windows, I realized my state of plenitude was delicate but not to ever be confused as weak.

Silence and Resistance

ACKNOWLEDGEMENTS

M*y clan*: I am so grateful for the constant love and encouragement of my children, Aissatou and Karim-Daniel, the source of my inspiration and my biggest cheerleaders. Special thanks to Viola, and her children for their love and support. Thanks to my sister Gladys, who passed before the world could know her story of courage. To my cousin Mildred for her unwavering support and the shining example of her own memoir "The Gladioli are Invisible." To the cousins and other personalities of the *lakou* who fascinated me with their stories on the veranda. Big thanks to my mother, who traversed to the other world before I could finish this book that she encouraged me to write.

My writing community: Special thanks to Edwidge Danticat, who never stopped asking, "How is the writing coming along?" I truly appreciate her sisterhood full of advice and encouragement. Huge thank you to Gina Frangello, my no-nonsense editor for whom the expression "tough love" is an understatement! Thank you to the amazing Laura Smith Head, who did meticulous copy and line editing for me at a moment that I needed it most, and Dan Chernin, both of my Skidmore writing community; they encourage and nurture. I'd like to especially thank the writer Douglas Wood for being my amazing "cheerleader"; his loving support and sensitive and brilliant feedback helped me write a particularly difficult part of the book. I am grateful for the friendship of Lynn Faught, for accepting to pick up her red pen one more time; little did we know that being in the BCC Pom-Pom team would take us down this road.

The writing workshops: I'd like to thank the writer Candy Schulman of The New School, for her encouragement and for introducing me to my first nurturing, writing community. I am especially grateful to Phillip Lopate, the "guru of non-fiction" for his blunt sense of humor and constant encouragement during his workshops at the Skidmore Writer's Institute. I've been blessed with Tom Yenks in my life for his workshop, "The Art of the Story" which transformed my writing. Special thanks to Jean-Marie Laclavetine, writer and long-time editor at Gallimard, the venerable French editing house for his tremendous help during the workshop "La Fabrique du récit." Thanks to Dinty Moore, editor of Brevity Magazine, Allison Williams, editor of Brevity Blog; and the Tuscany Retreat community of writers. Big thanks to coach Amy Goldmacher!

The publishers: Excerpts from this memoir were published by editors who believed in me, and I wish to thank them. Special thanks and endearing love to the poet Quincy Troupe, the former editor of NYU's literary magazine *Black Renaissance Noire* for publishing "The Voodoo Priestess" and his stunning wife Margaret Porter Troupe for her flawless copy-editing; thanks to Tom Yenks for publishing "The Departure" in *Narrative* literary magazine and the editors of La Prensa for publishing "The Neighbor."

To my mesmerizing agent and publisher, Yona Deshommes of Riverchild Media, who believed in me from the beginning, and the indomitable Kiev Martinez for their support.

To my friends for their constant encouragement. To you, the reader!

ABOUT THE AUTHOR

Monique Clesca has led two incredibly fulfilling lives. First, as an activist, and second, as a Journalist. As an advocate, she worked in the field of international development, advocating for children's and women's rights, and has participated in high-level policy issues linked to Haiti and Africa. She has been a long-time volunteer of a women-led organization that provides holistic support to girls and women who have suffered domestic and sexual violence. The President of Niger awarded her the country's highest honor, Commander in the Niger Order of Merit, in 2016 for having spearheaded a country-wide movement for the elimination of child marriage.

Since her retirement from the United Nations in 2016, she has worked as an international consultant. Also a leading voice as a feminist, pro-democracy, and pro-social justice activist in Haiti, she has been a speaker at the Yale Law School, Harvard Law School, Georgetown Law School, the Parliament of Canada, and a guest on Democracy Now, NPR, CNN, MSNBC, NBC News, and Black News. Her articles and essays center around Haiti and themes of displacement, family bonds, gender, politics, and identity issues, and have appeared in the *New York Times*, *Narrative*, the *Miami Herald*, *Foreign Affairs*, *Foreign Policy*, *Le Nouvelliste,* and NYU's *Black Renaissance Noire Magazine*, among others.

Monique earned her master's degree in journalism from the Medill School of Journalism at Northwestern University in Illinois and her B.A. in Philosophy from Howard University in Washington, D.C. She is the author of two previous books, her novel, *La Confession*, a portrait of a woman asserting herself after love, grief, and loss in a patriarchal society and *Mosaiques*, a collection of essays about women affected by human rights issues. She is the mother of two adult children and the grandmother of two boys and two girls. A national of Haiti, she lives in Haiti and Miami.

www.ingramcontent.com/pod-product-compliance
Lightning Source LLC
Jackson TN
JSHW080031080725
87176JS00004B/8/J